CURRY

Also by Lizzie Collingham

Imperial Bodies:
The Physical Experience of the Raj, c. 1800–1947

Curry
A Tale of Cooks and Conquerors

Lizzie Collingham

OXFORD
UNIVERSITY PRESS
2006

OXFORD
UNIVERSITY PRESS

Oxford University Press, Inc., publishes works that further
Oxford University's objective of excellence
in research, scholarship, and education.

Oxford New York
Auckland Cape Town Dar es Salaam Hong Kong Karachi
Kuala Lumpur Madrid Melbourne Mexico City Nairobi
New Delhi Shanghai Taipei Toronto

With offices in
Argentina Austria Brazil Chile Czech Republic France Greece
Guatemala Hungary Italy Japan Poland Portugal Singapore
South Korea Switzerland Thailand Turkey Ukraine Vietnam

Copyright © 2006 by Lizzie Collingham

Published by Oxford University Press, Inc.
198 Madison Avenue, New York, NY 10016
www.oup.com

Oxford is a registered trademark of Oxford University Press

Library of Congress Cataloging-in-Publication Data

Collingham, E. M. (Elizabeth M.)
Curry: a tale of cooks and conquerors/Lizzie Collingham.
p. cm.
Includes bibliographical references and index.
ISBN-13: 978-0-19-517241-6
ISBN-10: 0-19-517241-8
1. Food habits—India—History.
2. India—Civilization.
I. Title.
GT 2853. I5C65 2006
394.1′2′0954—dc22 2005016641

3 5 7 9 8 6 4 2
Printed in the United States of America
on acid-free paper

For Rebecca Earle

Contents

Illustrations

Illustrations

11. *The interior of the governor-general's traveling kitchen tent with numerous uniformed cooks engaged in cooking a meal* (1820–1821), Oriental and India Office Collections, Add.Or.4921. Reproduced by permission of the British Library

12. *A servant setting out a meal in camp* (1930s). Reproduced courtesy of Jana Howlett

13. *Grinding curry stuff* (Bangalore, 1901–1904), Higginbothams, Oriental and India Office Collections, Photo 494/(37). Reproduced by permission of the British Library

14. *Kitchen servants* (ca. 1880), W. W. Hooper, Oriental and India Office Collections, Photo 447/3(56). Reproduced by permission of the British Library

15. *The breakfast*, in William Tayler, *Sketches Illustrating the Manners and Customs of the Indians and Anglo-Indians* (London, 1842), Oriental and India Office Collections, X42. Reproduced by permission of the British Library

16. *Delivering tiffin boxes in Bombay* (1996), Catherine Karnow/CORBIS

17. *A dabba-wallah in New Delhi* (1990s). Reproduced courtesy of Thomas Seidel

18. *Packing tea for export* (1901), Robert Arthur Ellis, Oriental and India Office Collections, Photo 304/53. Reproduced by permission of the British Library

19. *Madras tea shop*, Edward Hilder Colebrook (1940), Oriental and India Office Collections, Photo 469/5 (44). Reproduced by permission of the British Library

20. *Sadhu drinking tea in Pushkar* (1990s). Reproduced courtesy of Thomas Seidel

21. *Lovers' picnic* (1970s), private collection

22. *Anglo-Indian picnic* (1930s). Reproduced courtesy of Jana Howlett

23. *Indian picnic* (1980s). Reproduced courtesy of Olivier Mettery

24. *Vegetable market in Pushkar* (1990s). Reproduced courtesy of Olivier Mettery

25. *Chicken seller in northern India* (1980s). Reproduced courtesy of Olivier Mettery

26. *A village store selling curry powder and corned beef on the island of Savai'i, Samoa* (2001). Reproduced courtesy of Thomas Seidel

Maps

Maps drawn by Reginald Piggott

Recipes

Recipes

A note on the recipes
The recipes that readers might like to try are to be found at the end of each chapter. These are recipes that I use myself. I hope they will produce tasty results in your kitchen. Indians cooking in their own homes adjust the quantities of spices to suit their own tastes: some cooks use as many as 20 chillies when making a vindaloo, others just three or four. You should feel free to adjust the quantities to suit your preferences.

An Indian friend from South Africa once gave me a helpful tip that has improved my Indian cookery: when frying onions, garlic, ginger, or spices always wait until the raw smell of the foods has disappeared before going on to the next stage of the cooking process.

I have also included some historical recipes in the body of the text to give a sense of what these recipes were like. Some of them might be interesting to cook, although I do not suggest experimenting with roast black rat.

L. C.

Preface

In 1994 I drank my first lassi at Dipti's Pure Drinks in the Colaba area of Bombay. Its thick, velvety sweetness was seductive. During my stay in the city I kept on returning for more. I also ate my first vegetarian thali in a workingman's eatery, and wondered about the state of the kitchens when a rat sat on my foot. At the home of John and Susan Gnanasundaram in Madras I discovered the delights of Indian home cooking: spongy idlis with freshly made, bright green, sharp, coriander chutney for breakfast and rich chicken curries for dinner. None of it tasted like the Indian food I was used to in British Indian restaurants.

A few months later I became very ill with cholera. While I was recovering I could only manage to eat tea and toast. I also discovered that tourist hotels still served the food of the Raj and recuperated on a diet of yellow omelettes. Once recovered, I sampled mulligatawny soup at an expensive Delhi hotel restaurant, surrounded by the leftover trappings of the Raj—cane chairs and potted palms. The soup was sour and hot and I thought it was horrible. But my interest in Indian food and the British relationship with it was established.

I returned to Britain and wrote my first book about the British body in India. It traced the changing way in which the British managed, disciplined, and displayed their bodies as their position in India moved from commerce to control and imperialism. Part of this process was their rejection of Indian curries in favor of tinned salmon and bullety bottled peas.

Preface

The British relationship to Indian food continued to capture my imagination and while researching this book I was surprised to discover that tea was probably the most important item of food or drink that the British bequeathed to India, hence the chapter on chai. Most of the book, however, is an exploration of the histories of many of the Indian dishes familiar to habitués of Indian restaurants. I trace their culinary roots, their discovery, or invention, by Europeans and the various ways in which they traveled back to Britain, and around the rest of the world. It is a biography of the curries of the Indian subcontinent, as defined now by the nations of Pakistan, India, Sri Lanka, and Bangladesh (not of Malaysian or Thai curries that carry with them a different history).

Lizzie Collingham,
Montolieu, France 2005

Acknowledgments

I began research for this book while I was a Research Fellow at Jesus College, Cambridge. I would like to thank the master and fellows for providing me with an environment conducive to research and writing. I would also like to thank them for the warm welcome I receive whenever I return.

I also spent a few months as a visiting fellow at the Research School of Social Sciences at the Australian National University, Canberra. I am grateful to my colleagues there (especially Barry Higman and Tim Rowse) for making my stay such a pleasurable and productive one.

Many people (too numerous to mention by name) have taken the time to speak to me about Indian food or their lives in India: Natasha Eaton, Martin Jones, Peter Garnsey, Riho Isaka, Partha Mitter, Vijay Naidu, Ryoko Nakano, Kathy Prior, Michael Shapiro, Jo Sharma, and Emma Spary provided me with useful references and information and Mike O'Brien read the manuscript with great patience and scrupulous care. I am extremely grateful to them all.

I would like to thank the staff of the Centre for South Asian Studies, Cambridge; the Oriental and India Office at the British Library; Cambridge University Library; the National Library of Australia, Canberra; the Mass Observation Archive, Sussex University Library, and the Imperial War Museum, London.

I would also like to thank John Cornwell and my agent Clare Alexander who both encouraged me to write this book; Penny Hoare,

Acknowledgments

my editor; my sister, Sarah, for her enthusiastic enjoyment of my curries; the Gnanasundaram and Sivasubramanian families for introducing me to delicious Indian home cooking and Namita Panjabi for a helpful conversation and a delectable lunch at Veeraswamy's.

My absurdly itinerant lifestyle while researching and writing this book has put me in the debt of a great many generous friends: Fiona, Andrew, Alistair, and Sarah Blake, Clair and Keith Brewster, Jan, Frank, and Jack Collins, Vic and Pam Gatrell, Sophie Gilmartin, Geoff and Joan Harcourt, Francine and Jacky Imbert, Mike and Tricia O'Brien, Megan and Jeff Thompson, Jeremy Riley, Lionel and Deidre Ward, and my late mum, Mary.

Rebecca Earle collected tidbits of information for me and provided constructive criticism each of the many times she read the manuscript; she, David, Gabriel, and Isaac Mond have provided me with a home whenever I needed one. I cannot thank them enough. Thomas Seidel, as usual, instigated many adventures in the name of research and kept my spirits up while writing.

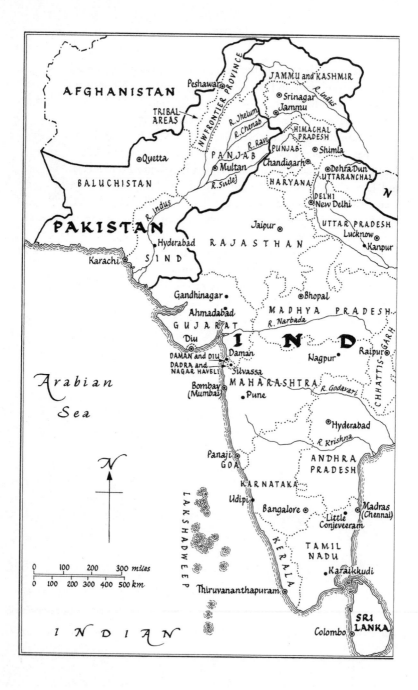

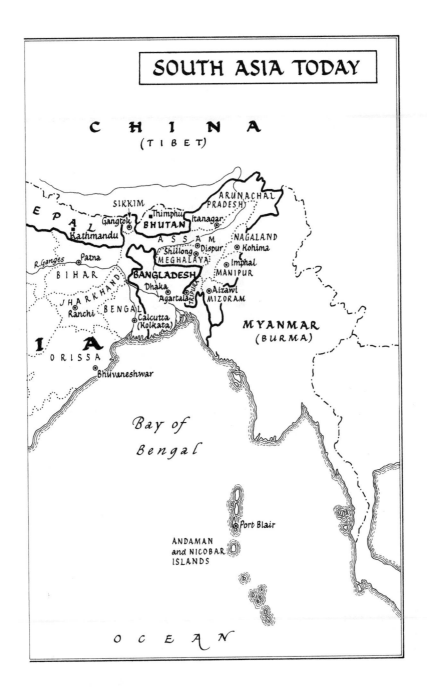

SOUTH ASIA TODAY

C H I N A
(TIBET)

E P A L

SIKKIM
Gangtok⊙ Thimphu⊙ ARUNACHAL PRADESH
Kathmandu BHUTAN Itanagar⊙

A S S A M NAGALAND
Shillong⊙ ⊙Dispur ⊙Kohima
MEGHALAYA

R.Ganges ⊙Patna
B I H A R BANGLADESH ⊙Imphal MANIPUR
Dhaka⊙
J H A R K H A N D Agartala ⊙Aizawl
Ranchi⊙ B E N G A L MIZORAM

I A Calcutta⊙ (Kolkata) MYANMAR
(BURMA)
O R I S S A

Bhuvaneshwar⊙

Bay of
Bengal

⊙Port Blair

ANDAMAN
and NICOBAR
ISLANDS

O C E A N

Chicken Tikka Masala:
The Quest for an Authentic Indian Meal

Tʜᴇ ᴀʀᴇᴀ ɪɴ Manhattan where 1st Avenue intersects with East 6th
Street is so overcrowded with Indian restaurants that it is known
as "Curry Row." Here you can order a lamb vindaloo, a seafood
biryani, a sweet yellow dhansak, or a mild and creamy beef korma with
side dishes of aloo gobi and nan bread. This catalogue of dishes conjures
up the aroma of fried onions; windows adorned with bright red fairy
lights, white tablecloths, patchy service, Indian music humming in the
background, and a two-course meal for under $20.

Further uptown at Utsav on 6th Avenue the cheerful but utilitarian
atmosphere of gaudy lights and bright colors have been exchanged for pale
peach walls and plush carpeting. Utsav is an example of a new breed of
Indian restaurant. The fountain in the entrance gives the place a touch of
class; high ceilings, large airy windows, and comfortable banquettes add
a luxurious feel to the dining room. The menu too, is different from the
standard Indian restaurant. The choice of any familiar curry with chicken,
lamb, or beef has been replaced by more specialized regional dishes, ranging
from Kashmiri-style shrimp curry to Goan chicken xacutti and Konkan
coconut-flavored fish. Utsav places great emphasis on authenticity of
flavor and the higher prices match this attention to detail and quality.[1]

Utsav is an example of one of the many new-style Indian restaurants
that have begun opening in both America and Britain. In London

restaurants such as Veeraswamy's and Zaika are examples of this new trend, the result of a new breed of Indian chefs making a bid to elevate Indian food from its status as cheap nosh to an elegant cuisine, every bit as sophisticated as French cookery. On both sides of the Atlantic, these high-class restaurants place great value on the authenticity of their food. The chefs are often specially trained in India and cook only dishes from their home region. Even the more traditional restaurants are beginning to follow this trend and advertise their dishes as "authentic." Supermarkets, too, offer an "authentic" Indian experience with every ready-prepared Indian meal. But what does authenticity really mean? And is authenticity really the right yardstick by which to judge an Indian meal?

In Britain this debate was brought to a head in 2001 when the then foreign minister Robin Cook announced chicken tikka masala as the new national dish of Great Britain. Food critics immediately responded by condemning it as a British invention. Chicken tikka masala, they sneered, was not a shining example of British multiculturalism but a demonstration of the British facility for reducing all foreign foods to their most unappetizing and inedible form.[2] Rather than the inspired invention of an enterprising Indian chef, this offensive dish was dismissed as the result of an ignorant customer's complaint that his chicken tikka was too dry. When the chef whipped together a can of Campbell's tomato soup, some cream, and a few spices to provide a gravy for the offending chicken, he produced a mongrel dish of which, to their shame, Britons now eat at least 18 tons a week. Chicken tikka masala's most heinous crime, according to its critics, is not so much that it tastes horrid but that it is not authentic.[3] In fact, journalists in Britain and America report with glee that none of the curries we eat in old-style curry houses are authentic, not to mention the fact that the "Indian" food they serve is cooked by Bangladeshis.[4]

The majority of Indian restaurant owners in Britain, and most of the proprietors of New York's East 6th Street establishments, do indeed come from Bangladesh. However, for much of the period that this book covers, Bangladesh, like Pakistan and Sri Lanka, belonged to a broader food world that can be termed Indian. It was not until 1947 that Pakistan became a nation. Sri Lanka followed in 1948. And Bangladesh split from Pakistan in 1971. Food on the Indian subcontinent does not divide into different culinary styles and dishes along these relatively new national boundaries so much as along much older regional boundaries. The food of Bangladesh belongs to the culinary world of Bengal. Punjabis share a food culture although their region was split in two with the creation of Pakistan. These are just two of the many culinary regions on the Indian subcontinent.

In fact, the food of people from one region of India is sometimes unrecognizable as Indian food to someone from another. Satya, a villager from the Punjab, arrived in Delhi in the 1950s. She had never traveled outside the Punjab before and she found the customs of the other people living in her apartment building strange and fascinating. She noted with astonishment that the Madrassi family "preferred rice with their food, not chapatties like our Punjabi folk. Whatever vegetables they prepare— lentils, aubergines, tomatoes—they must have rice to go with them. Then they scrape it all up in balls with their fingers so that the juice runs down their forearms, not neatly with a piece of chapatti or a spoon. So one day I said . . . 'Look, why don't you eat like we do? After all, you are people of good family. Surely where you come from people don't eat like that?'" The neighbor "was very offended and abused me roundly, when I had only meant to tell her nicely that we didn't like to watch such messy eating."[5] The outraged Madrassi might well have retorted that while her food might be sloppy and messy to eat, at least it wasn't heavy and greasy like the Punjabi food Satya and her family ate. If the women ever recovered their friendship, they might well have united in condemning their Gujarati neighbors for their penchant for sickly sweet food, their Bengali neighbors for filling the place with the reek of mustard oil, and their Telugu neighbors for producing meals that were unbearably hot.[6]

The differences in regional tastes are so pronounced that they translate into foods from other culinary cultures. In Bombay, a Maratha Hindu street vendor serves "Chinese" lunches to office workers on Narima Point. But before preparing the food he assesses the regional origin of his customer and adjusts the flavor accordingly. For Gujaratis he adds some extra sauce to sweeten it; for the Punjabis he adds extra chilli.[7]

The range of culinary styles within India means that authenticity is more accurately tied to a region. But the regional subdivisions of Indian food are complicated by local patterns of consumption, as Francis Buchanan discovered when he was traveling across southern India in the early nineteenth century. He was observant of the minutiae of everyday life and noticed that in each locality the people relied on a different grain (rice, wheat, millet, sorghum) as the mainstay of their diet. "Habit," he wrote, "seems to be able to render every kind of grain sufficiently wholesome." But the peasants were unable to adapt to a different grain and when "compelled or induced to try another" their digestions became disordered. This was brought home to him by his servants, all suffering miserably from stomach complaints due to the constant changes in the staple grain as they traveled. Buchanan was surrounded by gloomy Indians homesick for their customary foods.[8]

The staple food of each locality still ties people to their land and their community today. Indians from Bangladesh to Tamil Nadu believe that the local qualities of the soil and the water are absorbed into the grain crop. When the grain is consumed it imparts these qualities to the population, giving them their strength. In Bangladesh, rice grown on village land is valued as more nutritious and more filling than rice bought at the market. Eating local-grown rice fills the villagers with the nature of their home and binds them to their community. Before setting out on a journey a traveler is required to eat large amounts of village-grown rice, to fill him with the essences of home.[9]

Each of the religious communities on the Indian subcontinent are distinguished by their particular food taboos, especially with regard to meat. Thus, for example, Christians will eat virtually any meat or fish. Muslims will eat most meats, including beef, but avoid pork. Jains are usually strict vegetarians, and sometimes even avoid red foods because they are the color of blood. Hindus will not eat the flesh of the sacred cow. Under certain circumstances, however, these apparently rigid restrictions on diet are ignored. Phillip Ray was a police officer in India from 1939 to 1946. He worked with a mixed force of Hindus, Muslims, and Sikhs. On one occasion he had taken his men out on a training exercise in the countryside. Each group had been given its own rations, but when he lit a fire and started cooking his sausages and bacon all the men gathered round to share his food. Back at work the next day, nothing was said about it.[10]

Below these broad religious divisions there are myriad different communities, castes, and religious sects, all with their own particular ways of preparing and eating food. Different groups are distinguished by particular customs and habits. For example, the Daudi Bohras of Bombay, members of a Shia Ismaeli sect, are known for the way in which they like to alternate between sweet and savory dishes throughout a meal.[11] Under the umbrella of Hinduism there exists great diversity in eating practices. The people we label as Hindus come from many different cultural backgrounds and have a variety of food taboos and culinary styles. The Hindu food of Rajasthan, for instance, includes both the frugal vegetarian dishes of the Marwari Banians (merchants) and the Rajput cuisine of roast meats.

In theory, Hindu food consumption is governed by a set of purity rituals. This is due to the fact that eating makes a person particularly vulnerable to pollution. Sharing food with someone who is immoral, or eating in an impure place, can transfer these impurities into the diner's body. Ideally, a Hindu should eat after a bath and wearing clean clothes. Men and women should eat separately, the women serving the men, before eating themselves.[12]

The actual preparation of food is also a delicate and potentially dangerous operation. The moral qualities of the person cooking the meal can be transferred into the food and imbibed by the eater. This is especially true of *kacca* foods, such as boiled rice, which are prepared with water. Water softens the food, opening it up to contamination. *Pakka* foods are fried in ghee, a product of the sacred cow, which makes them less open to pollution. *Pakka* foods can therefore sometimes be eaten even if they have been prepared by someone of a different caste.[13] Meat is regarded as an impure food, while grains and vegetables are higher-ranking foodstuffs.

These rules represent an ideal of good practice. By following these principles an individual can strive to achieve a state of purity. However, in practice, individual Hindus adapt these rules according to their circumstances and lifestyle.[14] Thus, a normally vegetarian Brahman might well drink a strengthening meat broth when suffering from a debilitating illness. Brahmans in Kashmir have adapted notions of purity to suit their food preferences. Although they avoid onions and garlic, they happily eat mutton. Similarly, Bengali Brahmans eat fish.

In theory, the caste position of a particular group is determined by the amount of impurity they encounter while working in their traditional occupation.[15] Thus, as scholars and priests, Brahmans occupy the highest position on the scale, while leather workers and sweepers (garbage and sewage collectors) are classed as untouchables. Indian villagers in Uttar Pradesh informed the anthropologist McKim Marriott that the higher caste position of the Brahmans, Jats, and Banians living in their villages was reflected by their diet. He was told that they maintained their purity by eating only the finest *pakka* foods, while the lower service castes (washermen, barbers, etc.) ate ordinary *kacca* foods, including meat. But when he investigated further he found that "all castes prepared and consumed food of both types on the same sorts of occasions." He also found that Brahmans frequently washed only their hands and faces before sitting down to a meal. Rather than being based on the actual observation of purity rituals, caste position in the villages was based, in practice, on the exchange of food. An accurate social map of all the different groups in the village (including the Muslim as well as the Hindu groups) could be constructed by working out which groups gave and accepted food from each other. Those giving food occupied a superior position to those who accepted it. Even then, *kacca* food was seen as an inferior food, not so much because it was open to impurity but because it was not prepared with highly valued ghee.

Thus, caste rules and regulations are far more malleable than they seem. On a daily basis, the observation of rules of purity and pollution are used as a way of maintaining the social status quo. They can be disregarded in certain circumstances or ostentatiously observed in others, in order to exercise social authority or to demonstrate respect.[16]

What an Indian eats depends on his region, religion, community, and caste. It also depends on his wealth. A vast proportion of the Indian population is made up of the rural poor who subsist on a diet that meets only about 80 percent of their nutritional requirements. Many of the poor, unable to find work all year round, and therefore unable to buy food everyday, have to manage their hunger by fasting on alternate days. In Bengal, the meals of the poor are made up of rice, a little dhal flavored with salt, chillies, and a few spices, some potatoes or green vegetables, tea, and paan. Paan, which is an areca nut mixed with spices and rolled up in a betel leaf, is chewed after the meal. Although it seems a luxury, in fact, the poor use it to stave off hunger.[17]

There are clearly numerous ways of eating an authentic Indian meal. However, there are certain underlying principles governing Indian food. These are derived from Ayurvedic (science of life) medicine, which is still practiced today in India and many other places throughout the world.

The founding texts of Ayurveda were two ancient medical treatises, known as the *Caraka-samhita* and the *Susruta-samhita*, first written down sometime in the first century BC.[18] These medical texts outlined the principles governing a correct diet. They argued that the body needed to be kept in a state of equilibrium with its environment. This translated into a recommendation that people living in marshy damp areas should eat hot heavy iguana meat and those living in the plains should eat the light and nutritious black antelope.[19] Diet also had to be adjusted to the seasonal variations in the Indian climate. During the hot weather, when the body needed to conserve energy, the *Caraka-samhita* advised a diet of cold foods such as milky gruels.[20] In the cold months, when the body could spare the energy to digest a heavy meal, it recommended a greasier diet of fatty meat, accompanied by wine and honey. The foods for each season were chosen according to a system of classification that divided foodstuffs into two principal divisions of either hot or cold. Within these categories foods were subdivided into six tastes (*rasa*). Hot foods, such as meat and pepper, were pungent, acidic, or salty. They had to be treated with caution as they could induce thirst, exhaustion, sweating, inflammation, and accelerated digestion. Cold foods, such as milk and most fruits, were sweet, astringent, or bitter. They were far less dangerous as they promoted cheerfulness and a calm contented mind.[21]

The Ayurvedic physician needed to be a proficient cook.[22] It was essential that he was able to choose foods with complementary properties, suitable for the time of year. The dishes were designed to bring out the therapeutic qualities inherent in the food and the principles of Ayurvedic medicine shaped Indian cookery across the regions. The staple grain (rice or wheat) was accompanied by a variety of dishes designed to heighten their taste and create a mixture of savors.[23]

The idea of mixing hot and cold foods to achieve a sublime blend of the six essential tastes (pungent, acidic, salty, sweet, astringent, and bitter) still lies at the heart of Indian cookery today. The imaginative use of spices to create a range of flavors, the judicious balancing of salt with a little sugar in many vegetable dishes, the combination of black pepper with cooling yogurt, the addition of a little tamarind to cut a cloying sauce with a hint of sharpness, all these techniques are derived from the Ayurvedic principles governing the combining of foods. Thus, Ayurvedic medical law provides the basis for the principles of Indian cookery that ensure its delectable taste.

If Ayurvedic medicine provided a culinary foundation for Indian food, over time layer upon layer of various influences have been laid down on to this base. The Indian subcontinent has accommodated a great variety of immigrants, all of whom brought with them their own cuisines. The curries that we eat today are the product of India's long history. Each recipe tells the tale of the different people who prepared and ate the dish.

In 1498, the first Europeans arrived off the Malabar coast, when the Portuguese explorer Vasco da Gama opened up the sea route to the Indies. Twenty-eight years later Babur, the first great Mughal, invaded India from the north. These two events were to have a lasting impact on India's culinary culture. This book tells the story of how central Asian, Persian, and European styles of cookery and ingredients were brought to the subcontinent, where over the next four centuries they interacted with Indian food to produce the Indian cuisine that we know today.

Chicken tikka masala

This restaurant curry should ideally be made with chicken cooked in a tandoor oven. You could buy ready-prepared chicken tikka pieces from a supermarket or try to simulate the effect of the tandoor oven at home by first marinating the chicken and then grilling it, or cooking it on a barbecue. The bright red color in restaurants comes from food coloring, which is not included in this recipe. Serves 3–4.

1¼ lb. chicken, cut into bite-size pieces

Marinade
¾ in. piece of fresh ginger, finely grated
5 cloves garlic, crushed
¼ teaspoon turmeric powder
¼ teaspoon chilli powder
1 teaspoon garam masala
½ teaspoon cumin powder
1 teaspoon coriander powder
salt to taste
juice of 1 lemon
6 tablespoons of yogurt

Combine the ginger, garlic, turmeric, chilli powder, garam masala, cumin, coriander, and salt with the lemon juice and yogurt. Mix well and add to the chicken in a bowl. Make sure all the chicken pieces are coated in the marinade. Cover and leave in the fridge to marinate overnight (or longer).

Thread the chicken pieces on to skewers and then cook under the grill or on a barbecue.

Sauce
4–6 tablespoons vegetable oil
1 large onion, finely chopped
¾ in. piece of fresh ginger, finely grated
4 cloves garlic, crushed
¼ teaspoon turmeric
¼ teaspoon chilli powder
1 teaspoon garam masala
1 teaspoon coriander powder
1 tablespoon tomato purée
salt to taste
2 tablespoons ground almonds, mixed to a paste with warm water
2 tablespoons thick cream
fresh coriander leaves, chopped

Heat the oil in a large pan. Add the onion and sauté until browned. Add the grated ginger and crushed garlic, stir and fry for 5–8 minutes. Add the turmeric, chilli powder, garam masala, and coriander powder. Fry for 1–2 minutes, stirring. Add the tomato purée, salt, and the almonds. Fry for 1–2 minutes, stirring. Then add the chicken and leave to simmer gently for 15–20 minutes. You may need to add a little water to prevent burning. When the meat is tender add the cream, and sprinkle on the coriander leaves just before serving.

Bakers

2

Biryani: The Great Mughals

IN THE SPRING of 1641, two Portuguese priests were taken to a gallery overlooking the principal reception room of a palace in Lahore. The palace belonged to Asaf Khan, one of the most powerful men in the Mughal Empire.

That evening Asaf Khan and his wife had invited the Emperor Shahjahan to a banquet. From their hiding place the priests looked down into the hall "adorned with rich carpets of silken silver and golden embroidery." Ambergris, eaglewood, and civet burned in perfume holders arranged around the room. At its center was a fine white muslin tablecloth with cushions arranged around it. As they watched, the Mughal emperor, adorned with strings of pearls and chains of gold, entered the room, followed by his hosts and two other members of the Mughal family. The party settled themselves on the cushions and washed their hands in bowls held out to them by beautiful serving girls. Then "the dishes were brought in . . . to the deafening sound of instruments . . . not unlike our trumpets, but of uncertain and mournful tone." The food was served "by eunuchs, richly attired in . . . trousers of different coloured silks and white coats of the finest transparent muslin." They passed the golden bowls of food to "two most lovely damsels who knelt on either side of the Emperor [and] . . . placed the dishes before him, similarly handing him his drinking water and removing dishes no longer wanted." The priests were surprised to observe that the Muslim "barbarians" possessed impeccable table manners. The meal lasted more than four hours. Once it had been cleared away dancing girls entered in "lascivious and suggestive dress" and entertained the party with "immodest behaviour and posturing." But Shahjahan was more interested in three vessels of jewels that were set before him. While the emperor was engrossed in examining the rubies and emeralds the eunuch, who had guided the priests to the gallery, returned to say that it was time for them leave. "We got up and followed our guide, who, in order not to take us through the body of the Imperial guards, took us by subterranean passages until he put us on the road."[1]

The priest who left us this description of the Mughal emperor at dinner was Friar Sebastien Manrique. His claim to have penetrated a Muslim nobleman's palace is audacious. The private quarters at the center of each palace complex were surrounded by high walls and guarded by soldiers. Muslim women were kept in strict seclusion and only members of the family and their servants were allowed to enter this sanctum. It seems extremely unlikely that a Portuguese priest would have been granted permission to enter to gaze upon the women of the household.

Manrique may have constructed the entire scene from stories circulating at the court. Seventeenth-century travel writers would often insert themselves into scenes as a device to assert authorial authority. Their readers derived a frisson from the sense that they, along with the author, had witnessed events that were strictly private. In this case, however, Manrique claimed that his adventure was made possible by the special relationship he had forged with Asaf Khan.

Manrique had been traveling across India on his way to Rome. He had stopped in Lahore to plead for a Jesuit priest who had been imprisoned by Shahjahan for over nine years. The nobleman who listened to his case was Asaf Khan, who, as well as being one of the most influential men at the Mughal court, was an uncle of the emperor. Manrique must have combined impressive negotiating skills with great charm. Not only did he secure the release of the unfortunate priest but at the end of their meeting the khan "ordered a eunuch to warn the doorkeepers that I should be given free entry whenever I came to see him, which was no small favour." As soon as Manrique heard that Asaf Khan planned to entertain Shahjahan he resolved to make the most of his advantage and sought "permission to exceed these limits." Asaf Khan himself may have arranged for Manrique to watch the meal from the gallery.[2] But even if he was aware of the priest's presence, the secrecy surrounding the visit, the hidden vantage point from the gallery, and the return journey through secret tunnels would suggest that the emperor had not been told.

The Emperor Shahjahan, whose dining habits so intrigued Manrique, was the fifth Mughal to rule India. The first was Babur, or "the Tiger," a contemporary of Henry VIII. Babur (1483–1530) was a Timurid prince from the central Asian kingdom of Fergana in what is now Uzbekistan. His goal in life was to reestablish the Timurid line as the major power in the region. And to this end, aged 15, he conquered the city of Samarkand that had been the capital of Timur's empire. It was a beautiful city, a center of Muslim learning, where Turkish and Persian traditions blended with those of central Asia and Afghanistan to create a sophisticated Islamic culture. Known as "the pearl of the Eastern Muslim world," Samarkand was the ultimate central Asian prize. But Babur was unable to hold the city and he was deposed by the Uzbeks. Many years of living rough in the mountains followed. But this experience did not crush Babur's ambition. He set his sights on Kabul, the capital of Afghanistan, and eventually gathered together a large enough fighting force to capture the city. Then, in 1526 (while Henry VIII was falling in love with his wife's maid of honor, Anne Boleyn), Babur launched his decisive attack on Hindustan, as northern India was then known.

Babur was not the first Muslim to invade Hindustan. His ancestor Tamur had sacked Delhi in 1398, and the city had been ruled by a series of Muslim sultans since the twelfth century. During this period, Muslims from Turkey, Persia, and Afghanistan had settled in northern India and the Deccan. Alongside Rajput and Jat high-caste rajas and chiefs, these Muslim warriors had established themselves as a landed aristocracy. They ruled over the peasants, village artisans, and laborers, some of whom, especially the untouchables or lower castes, converted to Islam in the

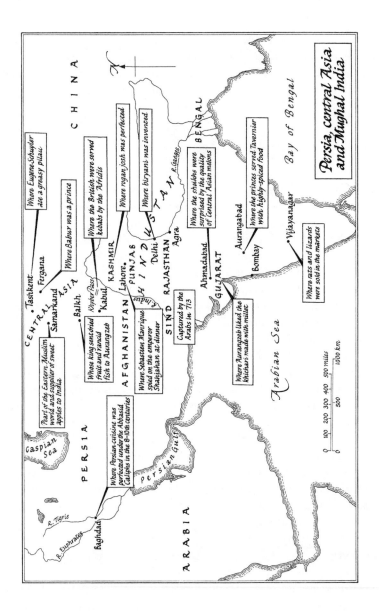

Persia, central Asia and Mughal India

CHINA

Bay of Bengal

BENGAL

R. Ganges

Where Eugene Schuyler ate a greasy pilaw

Where Babur was a prince

Fergana

Tashkent

CENTRAL ASIA

Samarkand

Balkh

Pearl of the Eastern Muslim world and supplier of sweet apples to India

Where Persian cuisine was perfected under the Abbasid Caliphs in the 8–10th centuries

Where king sanctified fruit and iranied fish to Aurangzeb

Whose king sanctified fruit and iranied fish to Aurangzeb

PERSIA

Caspian Sea

R. Tigris

R. Euphrates

Baghdad

ARABIA

Persian Gulf

Arabian Sea

Where the British were served kebabs by the Afridis

Where rogan josh was perfected

Where biryani was invented

KASHMIR

PUNJAB

Lahore

Khyber Pass

Kabul

AFGHANISTAN

Where Sebastien Manrique spied on the emperor Shahjahan at dinner

HINDUSTAN

R. Indus

Delhi

Agra

RAJASTHAN

SIND

Captured by the Arabs in 713

Ahmadabad

GUJARAT

Where Aurangzeb liked the khichari made with millet

Aurangabad

Bombay

Where the shaikhs were surprised by the quality of central Asian melons

Where the princes served Tavernier with highly-spiced food

Vijayanagar

Where rats and lizards were sold in the markets

100 200 300 400 500 miles
500   1000 k.m.
0
0

hope of escaping their lowly status. Northern India was thus divided into a patchwork of miniature kingdoms. Many of these paid tribute and allegiance to an assortment of Muslim sultans and Hindu kings who ruled over larger territories. In the urban commercial and trading centers, Hindu and Muslim merchant communities thrived.

"Hindu" was originally simply the Persian name for a person who came from Hindustan, which lay east of the River Indus. The Mughals lent the term religious meaning as they used it to refer to any Indian who had not been converted to Islam. But Hinduism was not an organized religion with a clear doctrine. The Indian population in the early sixteenth century was made up of a medley of sects and communities, most of whom loosely subscribed to a number of central beliefs such as the endless cycle of life and the need to propitiate a pantheon of gods. But religion in India at this period was more a matter of orthopraxy, or, in other words, how the individual behaved, rather than a matter of orthodoxy that implies subscription to a defined set of beliefs. This allowed for a certain fluidity of practice across the Hindu and Muslim communities. Muslims joined Hindus in ceremonies to appease Sitla, the goddess of smallpox. Hindus worshipped at the shrines of Sufi saints, although they were not necessarily prepared to share food with their fellow Muslim worshippers.[3]

Babur was disappointed by his new conquest. "Hindustan is a place of little charm," he wrote, "the cities and provinces ... are all unpleasant." Despite the Muslim influence in the region for over three centuries he was surprised to discover how different India was from central Asia and Afghanistan. "Compared to ours it is another world ... once you cross the Indus, the land, water, trees, stones, people, tribes, manners, and customs are all of the Hindustani fashion." The people paraded about naked apart from grubby loincloths and lacked beauty; society was devoid of grace or nobility, manners or etiquette. No one possessed any poetic talent, a sign of the highest cultivation in his homeland. He and his lieutenants retreated to the bathhouses to escape "the heat, the biting wind ... and the dust." The one good thing about Hindustan was that it was "a large country with lots of gold and money."[4] Babur planned to consolidate his hold over India and then return, saddlebags bursting with treasure, to his beloved homeland in central Asia where he intended to recapture Samarkand. His plans came to nothing and he died in India. Instead of reestablishing the Timurids in central Asia, he founded a new dynasty of Indian rulers: the Great Mughals. This was the name given to them by the Europeans who were hazily aware that on his mother's side Babur was descended from the great Mongol, Ghengis Khan. Babur, who held the Mongols in contempt as barbarians, would have been horrified.[5]

One of Babur's chief complaints against Hindustan was that the food was awful. "There [is] no good ... meat, grapes, melons, or other fruit. There is no ice, cold water, good food or bread in the markets," he grumbled.[6] Babur came from a culture that took great pleasure in eating. One of the earliest Muslim cookery books from Baghdad described food as "the noblest and most consequential" of the six pleasures (the others were drink, clothes, sex, scent, and sound).[7] Having spent much of his life after he lost Samarkand hiding out in the mountains, Babur was used to the hearty meat-based diet of the nomadic horse-riding shepherds of the central Asian steppes. This consisted of dishes that could be prepared easily over a campfire. At a garden party at Khyber in the 1920s, a British civil servant sampled the sort of kebabs Babur would have eaten in the early sixteenth century. The local Afridis, a warlike nomadic mountain people, had invited the British to watch a display of guns, fireworks, and "an exhibition of how they attack an enemy's position." As the guests stood around in a marquee, genteelly sipping cups of tea, an "old Afridi came up and offered us lumps of sheep's flesh strung along a skewer and freshly roasted. These had to be pulled off and eaten in the fingers."[8] Pilau was the other dish essential to any central Asian cook's repertoire. It made good use of the fatty tails of the local sheep. Arminius Vambery, a Hungarian professor of oriental languages who traveled widely in central Asia in the 1860s, described the method of preparation:

A few spoonfuls of fat are melted (... the fat of the tail is usually taken) in a vessel, and as soon as it is quite hot, the meat, cut up into small pieces, is thrown in. When these are in part fried, water is poured upon it to the depth of about three fingers and it is left slowly boiling until the meat is soft; pepper and thinly sliced carrots are then added, and on top of these ingredients is put a layer of rice, after it has been freed from its mucilaginous parts. Some more water is added, and as soon as it has been absorbed by the rice the fire is lessened, and the pot, well-closed, is left over the red-hot coals, until the rice, meat, carrots are thoroughly cooked in the steam. After half an hour the lid is opened, and the food served in such a way that the different layers lie separately in the dish, first the rice, floating in fat, then the carrots and the meat at the top, with which the meal is begun.[9]

Vambery pronounced it excellent, although Eugene Schuyler, an American diplomat who dined with the Muslims of Tashkent, had his reservations: "pleasant but...too greasy and insipid to be long agreeable to an European palate."[10]

In central Asia meat was strongly associated with masculinity. Hunting for game was regarded as a way of keeping fit and well trained for battle. In India, too, meat was associated with strength and valor. In the Indian epics such as the *Mahabharata*, the gods sit down to gargantuan meals of roast meat, and Ayurvedic medical thought regarded meat as the prime form of sustenance and the most efficacious medicine. It was considered that environmental essences contained in the soil were transferred from plants and then into herbivores, which, in turn, were eaten by carnivores. Each transference created a more powerful distillation of essences. Meat was thus the most intense of foods. Kings, who were expected to excel as hunters and warriors, to display sexual prowess with their numerous wives and concubines, and to deal decisively with the burdens of government, all relied on a meaty diet.

One of the best records of Hindu courtly cuisine has been left to us by the twelfth-century King Somesvara III. He belonged to the Western Chalukyan dynasty of kings who ruled over parts of present-day Maharashtra and Karnataka. Unusually for a king, he was more interested in the arts and literature than in waging war. Although parts of the kingdom were slipping out of Chalukyan hands, he busied himself with writing an encyclopedic account on the conduct of kingly affairs. Delightfully entitled *Manasollasa*, meaning refresher of the mind, it paid some attention to the conduct of affairs of state and the qualities needed by a king. But most of the space was devoted to kingly pleasures and enjoyments, from hunting, massage, and sex, to jewelry, carriages, royal umbrellas, and, one of his favorite preoccupations, food.[11] Meat-based aphrodisiacs and concoctions to promote youthfulness in kings often featured in Ayurvedic medical treatises.[12] Somesvara had paid attention to such texts and noted that a king needed to eat a "suitable, healthy and hygienic" diet. This might include lentil dumplings in a spicy yogurt sauce, fatty pork fried with cardamoms, or roast rump steak. Some of Somesvara's other favorite dishes sound less appetizing: fried tortoise (said to taste like plantain) and roasted black rat.[13] Five centuries later the habit of eating fabulous meats was still being kept alive by the kings of Vijayanagara, one of the largest and most powerful Hindu kingdoms in the south. Alongside mutton, pork, and venison, "sparrows and rats, and cats and lizards" could all be found on sale in the markets of the capital city.[14]

> *Recipe for roast black rat from the kitchens of King Somesvara III, Chalukyan king, 1126 to 1138*
>
> The rats which are strong black, born in the fields and river banks are called maiga; these are fried in hot oil holding with the tail till the hair is removed; after washing with hot water, the stomach is cut and the inner parts are cooked with amla [sour mango] and salt; or the rat is kept on iron rods and fired on red hot coal, till outer skin is burnt or shrinks. When the rat is cooked well, salt, jeera [cumin] and sothi [a flour made from lentils] are sprinkled and relished.[15]

However, this positive attitude toward meat had been complicated by a countermovement toward vegetarianism. Both Buddhism and Jainism, which were founded in the fifth century BC, promoted vegetarianism as a way of demonstrating compassion.[16] The practice of vegetarianism had been given an additional boost by the Emperor Asoka, who ruled a large proportion of the Indian subcontinent from 268 to 231 BC.[17] Asoka, influenced by Buddhist teachings, exhorted his subjects to adopt the path of dharma, which can loosely be translated as humanitarian conduct.[18] He communicated with his subjects by the unusual method of engraving a series of edicts on rock faces and specially constructed rock pillars. One of these regretted the wanton slaughter of "several thousands of animals" that had been made into soups in the ruler's kitchens and declaimed: "Here no animal shall be killed or slaughtered." Various other rock messages reminded Asoka's subjects which animals it was prohibited to slaughter or castrate, on which days fishing was banned, and urged them to remember that it was meritorious to abstain from slaughter.[19]

By the time Babur conquered Hindustan, vegetarianism had become a powerful statement of one's position in Indian society. Brahmans, who as the priestly caste had once performed rites of sacrifice, were now firmly vegetarian. They condemned meat because it heightened the passions and encouraged the virile, animal side of human nature. Orthodox Brahmans avoided all foods that were thought to stimulate the passions (which were known as *rajasic*). These included meat, onions, and garlic. Instead, they made a virtue of their light, nutritious, and easily digestible, vegetarian (*sattvic*) diet that enabled their bodies to channel the energy that would otherwise have been used to digest food into the improvement of the mind.[20] Vegetarianism introduced a new principle into the Indian social hierarchy. Unlike political power (which was based on physical strength and violence, sustained by an impure diet rich in meat), religious power was predicated on the principles of purity symbolized by vegetarianism. This conveniently placed the now strictly vegetarian Brahmans firmly at the top of the social pile.

A high place in the caste system was not always based on a vegetarian diet. The aristocratic Italian wanderer, Pietro della Valle, noticed that the Rajputs, the ruling warrior caste of Rajasthan, ate meat "without thinking themselves prejudic'd, as to degree of nobility." Hunting was an important part of Rajput culture. The essences of the landscape were thought to be found in even greater concentration in the flesh of undomesticated animals. Game was therefore highly valued. Rajasthani cuisine still has an important branch of shikar (hunting) recipes, such as boar cooked with fried onions, coriander, cumin, garlic, and ginger over an open fire.[21] And wild meat is still said to increase a man's "virility by helping him acquire semen, and with it, the qualities of courage and strength."[22]

However, the majority of Indians appeared to newcomers to be vegetarian, either through religious conviction or poverty. European visitors to Mughal India were as disgruntled as Babur had been about the quality of the available food. Jean-Baptiste Tavernier, a French jeweler who traveled through India buying precious stones, found that in the large villages with a Muslim governor it was possible to find "sheep, fowl and pigeons for sale" but in villages populated by the Hindu merchants known as Banians stores were very limited. Pietro della Valle grumbled, "I found much trouble in reference to my diet . . . as these Indians are extremely fastidious in edibles, there is neither flesh nor fish to be had amongst them; one must be contented only with Rice, Butter, or Milk, and other such inanimate things."[23]

In sixteenth- and seventeenth-century Hindustan the staple food of the rural peasants, who formed the majority of the population, and also of the urban artisans and laborers, was khichari, a simple dish of two grains, usually rice and lentils, boiled together in a little water. Every region had a variation on the recipe according to which grain they grew as a staple crop. Thus, millet sometimes replaced the rice, or chickpeas were used instead of lentils. Tavernier noticed that Indian soldiers made the meal more luxurious by dipping their fingers in a bowl of melted ghee (clarified butter) as they ate. Pickles or salt fish also went well with khichari. The very wealthy displayed their purchasing power by employing cooks who were heavy-handed with the spices. Tavernier wrote of the food prepared for the princes of Aurangabad: "Their rice and vegetables, which constitute, as I have said, all their dishes, were so full of pepper, ginger and other spices that it was impossible for me to eat them, and I left the repast with a very good appetite."[24]

For all "Hindus, of whatever station of life," there was a taboo on the consumption of beef. The Venetian Niccolao Manucci described how to eat beef was regarded as "a very low thing, a defilement, and sinful beyond all imagination." This had not always been the case. Ayurvedic medical texts discussed the qualities of cow's flesh and warned that it was "heavy, hot, unctuous and sweet," difficult to digest and to be eaten with caution. Yet beef broth was considered the most effective of medicines, especially for emaciatory diseases, and people with active occupations were advised to eat a beef-rich diet.[25] Well into the first century AD, Indians routinely sacrificed cows and ate the meat. The *Mahabharata* even mentions Brahmans enjoying good beef dinners, though it also includes a passage where "a cow complains about the wanton carnage committed on her relatives." This was an early sign of growing uneasiness about the killing of cows. The epics were originally oral folk tales but they were set down in writing by Brahman scholars who inserted religious and didactic sections. The resulting contradictions in the text reveal the way attitudes toward the consumption of beef altered over time.[26] A practical explanation for this change is that as the country became increasingly agrarian, Indians relied more heavily on cows as draught animals and producers of milk and became more reluctant to slaughter them.[27]

By the time Babur conquered Hindustan, the cow had become a sacred animal. Manucci was astonished to discover that not only did "these people hold it an abomination to eat of the cow," they held the products of the cow sacred and would drink a mixture of milk, butter, cow dung, and urine in order to drive out sin. He was disgusted to find that "they hold out two hands and receive the cow's urine of which they take a drink. Then, turning the cow's tail into a sort of holy-water sprinkler, they immerse it in the said liquid, and with it they daub their faces. When this ceremonial is over, they declare they have been made holy."[28]

The Mughals' hearty appetite for beef and mutton clashed with the dietary habits of many of their new subjects. Muslims regarded food as a pleasure. According to the Koran one of the activities the pious could look forward to in the gardens of paradise would be eating and drinking with relish.[29] This attitude was in conflict with the solemn approach that many Hindustanis took to their food. For them, eating was more a medico-moral activity than an enjoyable bodily pleasure. Food was an integral part of man's relationship with the gods. Propitiatory food offerings were customarily made before a meal and men were thus seen as eating the leftovers (*prasadum*) of the gods. In the villages, the position in the caste hierarchy of each particular occupational group was determined by which neighbors the group would accept food from and whether they would consent to eat in each other's company. Within the family, the superior position of the oldest male was demonstrated by the fact that he was served meals first and often ate on his own. On an individual level, Indians attempted to keep their bodies in balance with the environment by adjusting their diet to the climate, the season, and their occupation. When he ate, what he ate, and who he ate with, was thus a significant statement of a Hindu's position in the natural, moral, familial, and social order.[30]

In the kitchens of the Mughals these apparently mismatched culinary cultures came together to produce a synthesis of the recipes and foods of northern Hindustan, central Asia, and Persia. The result was the superb Mughlai cuisine that, for many people outside India, is synonymous with Indian food. The Mughal encounter with Indian food got off to a bad start, however. Although Babur was disappointed with the provisions in the markets he decided, "since I had never seen Hindustani food," to keep on four of the Hindustani cooks who had worked in the kitchens of India's defeated sultan, Ibrahim Lodi. Babur was to regret his curiosity. In his memoirs he described how he began vomiting after a Friday-evening meal of rabbit stew, saffron-flavored meat, and one or two titbits from a Hindustani dish of meat dressed in oil, served on a thin chapatti. Worried that he had been poisoned, he forced a dog to eat his vomit. The dog soon showed signs of feeling unwell, as did the pages who had shared Babur's meal. It was discovered that one of the Hindustani cooks had been bribed by the ousted sultan's mother to sprinkle poison on the meat. Everyone survived, including the dog. But the cook, having confessed under torture, was skinned alive and the taster was hacked to pieces. Given the brutality of these punishments, the instigator of the plot, the sultan's mother, got off very lightly. She was simply imprisoned. The incident did Babur little harm, merely renewing his zest for life. His memoirs do not tell us whether he continued to employ Hindustani cooks in his kitchens.[31]

We know, however, that Humuyan, Babur's son and the second Mughal emperor, did employ Hindustani cooks. When he was in Persia he entertained the shah in Indian style, providing Hindustani food at his request. The shah particularly liked the Indian "dish of rice with peas," a version of the ubiquitous khichari.[32] Humuyan was in Persia because he had lost the Indian throne to the Afghan ruler of Bengal, Sher Shah. He spent 15 long years in exile in Afghanistan and Persia, before he mustered enough strength to reclaim the Indian throne for the Mughals in 1555.

On his return, Humuyan brought with him a strong preference for Persian culture and a large number of Persian cooks. These cooks imported into India a Persian cuisine, developed five centuries earlier under the Abbasid caliphs of Baghdad. Between the eighth and tenth centuries, when they were at the height of their power, the caliphs had lavished vast sums on their kitchens. Their expenditure on food was matched by their gluttony—Caliph al-Mansur (754–775) is supposed to have died of overeating.[33] Cooks from all over the Muslim world— Turkey, Arabia, Egypt—gathered at Baghdad and incorporated their own local dishes into the courtly culinary repertoire. Even Indian cooks arrived from Sind (the southern part of what is now Pakistan), which had been conquered by the Arabs in 713. They were known for their trustworthiness, their ingenuity, and their extremely spicy dishes.[34]

The pièce de résistance of Persian cuisine was pilau. At the caliphs' court, the pilau that the nomadic shepherds prepared over their campfires was transformed into an exquisite and delicate dish. In Persia barley and wheat were the staple crops while rice, often imported from India, was relatively expensive and regarded as a luxury. Tavernier remarked in the seventeenth century that the Persians particularly liked the rice that grew southwest of Agra. "Its grain is half as small again as that of common rice, and, when it is cooked, snow is not whiter than it is, besides which it smells like musk, and all the nobles of India eat no other. When you wish to make an acceptable present to any one in Persia, you take him a sack of this rice."[35] When rice was eaten in Persia, it was therefore prepared as the centerpiece of the meal rather than as a side dish.[36]

The Persians judged the quality of a pilau by the rice, which was supposed to swell up completely, but without becoming sticky and forming clumps. A good pilau was also highly aromatic, filling the room with the delicate scent of its spices. Their cooks developed numerous variations: fruit pilaus, turmeric and saffron ones, chicken pilaus for special occasions; some varied by the addition of onion and garlic, or with raisins and almonds, and others varied by the color of the rice. The Persians would soak the rice in salted water for many hours to ensure that, when it was cooked, the grains were gleaming white, providing a striking contrast to colored grains that ranged from coal black to yellow, blue, green, and red.[37] All, as John Fryer, a seventeenth-century East India Company surgeon, scornfully put it, so that "you may know their Cooks are wittie."[38] An echo of their wit lives on in the stray grains of pink and green rice mixed into what Indian restaurants today call pilau rice. From Persia, pilau spread throughout the Muslim world. In Turkey it was called pilav. In Spain, with the addition of seafood and an emphasis on saffron, it became paella. In Italy, butter transformed it into risotto.[39] In India, where Persian and central Asian culture fused with that of Hindustan, pilau was to undergo yet another transformation in the kitchens of the next Mughal emperor.

Akbar, the third Mughal emperor (1555–1605), was the first to feel at home in India. Unlike his grandfather, Babur, he found the manners and customs of the Indian people pleasing. Rather than continually looking over his shoulder toward his lost homeland in central Asia, he focused on consolidating Mughal rule over Hindustan. In order to achieve this, Akbar implemented a policy of inclusiveness that sought to integrate his Indian subjects rather than simply impose Muslim rule upon them. Central Asians and Persians dominated the government, as they had done under Babur and Humuyan, but Akbar greatly increased the number of Indian ministers. He abolished the *jiyza*, a discriminatory tax on non-Muslims, and the Rajasthani princesses he married were allowed to worship their own gods behind the walls of the harem. He even joined his Indian wives in celebrating their religious festivals, such as Diwali. While

Babur strengthened India's cultural links with central Asia and Humayun introduced Persian influences, Akbar ensured that the two were melded together with Hindustani culture to create a Mughlai culture that was a synthesis of all three. At his court, Sanskrit epics such as the *Mahabharata* and *Ramayana* were translated into Persian. The poet laureate was an Indian, and the Rajasthani musician Tansen entertained the emperor after dinner. In Akbar's atelier the Persian artist Abus Samad, whom Humuyan had brought to India from Persia, trained over 100 Indian painters in the art of Persian miniatures. The geometric designs of the Persians merged with the bright, vigorous northern Indian painting style to produce an elegant Mughlai school of miniature painting.[40]

The same process of synthesis went on in the kitchens. Here, the delicately flavored Persian pilau met the pungent and spicy rice dishes of Hindustan to create the classic Mughlai dish, biryani. One of the most distinctive Persian culinary techniques was to marinate meat in curds (yogurt). For biryani, onions, garlic, almonds, and spices were added to the curds, to make a thick paste that coated the meat. Once it had marinated, the meat was briefly fried, before being transferred to a pot. Then, following the cooking technique for pilau, partially cooked rice was heaped over the meat. Saffron soaked in milk was poured over the rice to give it color and aroma, and the whole dish was covered tightly and cooked slowly, with hot coals on the lid and around the bottom of the pot, just as with pilau. The resultant biryani was a much spicier Indian version of the Persian pilau. Nowadays, it is a favorite dish at Indian wedding celebrations.

In the kitchens of Akbar's court, the chefs were expected to be able to serve up a meal of a hundred dishes within an hour. This army of cooks came from all over the Islamic world and northern India.[41] Each brought with him his own regional techniques and recipes. The cooks learned from each other and out of this vibrant synthesis of culinary styles, emerged a core repertoire of dishes that constituted a new Mughlai cuisine. Our information about Akbar's kitchen comes from the *Ain-i-Akbari*, an extraordinary book written by the courtier known as Abu'l Fazl. It is a gazetteer of the Mughal Empire, detailing every aspect of Akbar's government. Among the intricate expositions of the workings of land revenue and bureaucracy is a fascinating chapter devoted to the imperial kitchen. In it Abu'l Fazl provides a list of recipes for some of the most common dishes, which show that the Mughal cooks relied heavily on rice, gram (legumes such as lentils and chickpeas), crushed wheat, and sugar. Supplies of these staples were increased by improvements in agriculture. Under the Mughals the amount of cultivated land was extended. Reservoirs were cleaned, new wells were dug, and irrigation systems were improved. Sugar production rose and many areas were now able to harvest two crops of grain a year. A French visitor to Delhi in the seventeenth century described how the shops were stacked high with "pots of oil or butter, piles of baskets filled with rice, barley, chickpeas, wheat, and an endless variety of other grain and pulse, the ordinary aliment not only of the Hindoos, who never eat meat, but of the lower class of Muhammedans, and a considerable portion of the military."[42]

The Persian and central Asian influence on Mughlai cuisine is evident in the *Ain-i-Akbari* recipes. They called for large quantities of saffron and asafetida, favorite Persian flavorings, and the Mughals cultivated these plants in India to provide their cooks with a ready supply. *Hing* (the Indian name for asafetida) became popular with the Indian vegetarian population. When it was cooked in oil it took on a garlicky flavor that made it a good substitute for onions and garlic, which were avoided by devout Hindus. Asafetida was also known for its digestive properties and was therefore compatible with the vegetarian staples of pulses and beans that are difficult to digest. European visitors to Mughal India complained that the Indians ate so much *hing* that it made them smell odiously.[43]

Many of the recipes, like the one for zard birinj, used large quantities of raisins and pistachios. Combinations of meat and dried fruit were common in Persian dishes. Cartloads of sultanas, dried apricots, figs, and almonds were imported into India along the new roads that were constructed to facilitate trade throughout northern India, central Asia, and Persia. Indeed, the development of Mughlai cuisine was sustained by the availability of a wide variety of new and imported ingredients. such as the ducks and green vegetables from Kashmir.

Recipe for zard birinj from the Ain-i-Akbari by Akbar's courtier Abu'l Fazl

10 *seers* of rice; 5 *seers* of sugar candy; 3 ½ *seers* of ghee; raisins, almonds and pistachios, ½ *seer* of each; ¼ *seer* of salt; ⅛ *seer* of fresh ginger; 1½ *dams* saffron, 2½ *misqals* of cinnamon. This will make four ordinary dishes. Some make this dish with fewer spices, and even without any: and instead of without meat and sweets, they prepare it also with meat and salt.

One seer was equivalent to about 2⅓ lb. and a dam was about ¾ oz.

The meat dishes relied heavily on *qima* (minced meat), a favorite ingredient among Persian cooks. Mincing meat was a good way of dealing with it in hot countries where it tended to be tough because it had to be cooked soon after the animal had been slaughtered. The Muslim roots of many of the dishes can be seen in their heavy-handedness with onions and garlic. Abu'l Fazl gives a recipe for dopiaza, now familiar on British Indian restaurant menus, which calls for 4½ lb. of onions to 22 lb. of meat. Dopiaza is said to mean "twice onions" in Bengali and the key to the dish lay in the preparation of the onions: one portion was sliced then sautéed, and the other was ground into a fine paste. Thus, although the dish tasted overwhelmingly of onion, it combined two strikingly different textures.[44] The quantity of spices in the recipe given by Abu'l Fazl suggests that the Hindustani cooks had made an important contribution to the Mughlai dopiaza. The recipe calls for 4 oz. of fresh pepper, ¾ oz. each of cumin, coriander, cardamoms, and cloves, plus an additional 1 ³⁄₁₀ oz. of pepper and a large quantity of salt.

Besides synthesizing the different cuisines by creating new dishes, Mughlai cuisine brought together the cookery of central Asia, Persia, and Hindustan by combining different dishes from each of these traditions in one meal. In the pantry of the imperial kitchen, bakers made thin chapattis of Hindu provenance as well as the thick wheat breads, stuffed with honey, sugar, and almonds, loved by the Persians. Persian cooks prepared sugar-coated almonds, pastries, and quince jams, while Indian cooks made pickles and chutneys, sweet limes, curds, and green vegetables.[45] These accompaniments of varied provenance were served with the main dishes to create a Mughlai meal.

Although large quantities of fine food were produced in his kitchens every day, Akbar himself ate very little. For a man who had been a glutton in his youth, as emperor he demonstrated a surprising level of restraint. His friend and faithful courtier, Abu'l Fazl, tells us that Akbar ate only once a day, and then "leaves off before he is fully satisfied." As he grew older Akbar ate less and less and devoted an increasing number of days to fasting. He also developed a distaste for meat and became virtually vegetarian.[46] Babur and Humuyan had occasionally renounced meat or alcohol as a sign of the purity of their intent when going into battle, but such levels of renunciation were unusual in a Muslim ruler. Akbar's asceticism betrayed his growing affinity with the religious sensibilities of his Indian subjects. Every Friday Akbar held religious gatherings when a selection of holy men were invited to discuss religious subjects. These were initially confined to Islamic scholars, but he soon widened the invitations to include Brahmans, Jains, Parsees, and even Portuguese Jesuits. To the dismay of the Muslim holy men at his court, it became clear that Akbar was falling under the sway of the Brahmans and Jains. It was rumored that each night a Brahman priest, suspended on a string cot pulled up to the window of Akbar's bedchamber, would captivate the emperor with tales of Hindu gods. Akbar, in acknowledgement that his subjects held the cow sacred, renounced beef and forbade the slaughter of cows. He even banned the sale of all meats on certain holy days and advised his subjects to avoid onions and garlic.[47] Indeed, Akbar gradually adopted a diet more suitable for a Hindu ascetic than for a Muslim ruler.

The emperor even began to look a little like a Hindu. Rather than cropping his hair short in the Muslim style he wore it long in the fashion of his Indian subjects. He allowed Brahman priests to "tie jewelled strings round his wrists by way of blessing and, following his lead, many of the nobles took to wearing *rakhi* (protection charms)."[48] Akbar's religious tolerance, his acceptance and interest in Hindustani religion and customs, and his eating habits, did much to make the Mughals into Indian rather than foreign rulers. Both his son Jahangir and his grandson Shahjahan maintained many of Akbar's concessions, such as the ban on cow slaughter. They also continued to restrict themselves to vegetarian dishes on specified days of the week.[49] One particularly Indian habit that all the emperors maintained was to drink only Ganges water.

The Mughals did bring with them to India Persian sherbets of crushed ice mixed with fruit juice, but they were drunk between meals. Food was accompanied by plain water. Akbar referred to Ganges water as "the water of immortality," and he insisted on drinking it exclusively, no matter how far away from the river he was.[50] Jean-Baptiste Tavernier observed a string of camels that did nothing but fetch water from the river in order to supply the court. Even when Akbar was in the Punjab, about 200 miles from the Ganges, the water was sealed in large jars and then transported to the court by a series of runners. Tavernier did not share the emperor's high opinion of Ganges water. He described how a glass of wine mixed with water drawn from the river "caused us some internal disturbance; but our attendants who drank it alone were much more tormented than we were."[51] When it arrived at the court the water was cooled by means of saltpeter. Water in long-necked bottles was placed in another vessel where water mixed with saltpeter had been stirred about until it became cold. When the court was at Lahore the water was cooled with ice, brought by runners from the foothills of the Himalayas.[52]

The noblemen at the Mughal court formed a large group of adventurous eaters. In their palaces cooks from a wide variety of countries could be found experimenting with new dishes and refining old ones. In their restless search for social mobility, the courtiers did their best to ape and outdo the imperial kitchen. Thus they encouraged and spurred on the invention and discovery of new dishes and delicacies.[53] When Asaf Khan entertained Shahjahan he provided "European style . . . pastries, cakes, and other sweet confections made by some slaves who had been with the

Portuguese at Ugulim."[54] No doubt the khan obtained these novelties in an attempt to demonstrate the inventiveness of his own kitchen.

A description of a Mughlai banquet given by Asaf Khan has been left to us by one of his guests, Edward Terry, chaplain to Sir Thomas Roe. Roe was in India (from 1615 to 1619) as the ambassador of King James I. He had been sent at the instigation of the recently founded British East India Company to plead with Emperor Jahangir to grant the company a royal firman that would regulate their trading rights in India. In competition with the Portuguese and the Dutch, the British were trying to gain control of the valuable East Indian spice trade.

The food was served on a *dastarkhwan* (tablecloth) around which the three men sat in a triangle. Roe, as the honored guest, was presented with ten more dishes of food than his host. Terry, as the least important person present, was served with ten less. Nevertheless, 50 silver bowls were placed before him. Terry possessed a curious nature and he tasted a little from each one. He was particularly impressed by the rice that came in a variety of fantastical shades, including green and purple. He observed that Indian cooks were far better at cooking rice than the English, "for they boyl the grain so as that is full and plump and tender, but not broken in boyling; they put to it a little green Ginger and Pepper, and Butter, and this is the ordinary way of their dressing it, and so tis very good."

Not all the food served at the banquet would have been unfamiliar to Terry. Medieval European cookery was strongly influenced by Arab food and, like Mughlai cuisine, featured ground almonds, lots of spices, and sugar in both sweet and savory dishes. However, the Hindustani method of preparing meat was novel to Terry. He observed that, rather than eating large joints of boiled, baked, or roasted meat, the Indians preferred to cut it into slices or small pieces and then stew it with "Onions and Herbs and Roots, and Ginger (which they take there Green out of the earth) and other Spices, with some Butter, which ingredients when as they are well proportioned, make a food that is exceedingly pleasing to all Palates." This is one of the first European descriptions of what we now think of as curry. Sadly, Terry did not differentiate between the different curries he was served. He was delighted by the sophisticated gastronomic skills of the Mughal cooks, and concluded that although the dinner lasted "much

longer than we could sit with ease cross leg'd . . . all considered our feast
. . . was better than *Apicus*, that famous *Epicure of Rome*, with all his witty
Gluttony . . . could have made with all the provisions had from *Earth* and
Air, and *Sea*." [55]

It was under Akbar's successors, Jahangir (1605–1627) and Shahjahan
(1627–1658), that Mughal power and wealth reached its zenith. Shahjahan
was the wealthiest of all the emperors, with an annual revenue in 1647
of 220 million rupees, 30 million of which was spent on his private
household. Painting, poetry, and architecture (most famously Shahjahan
built the Taj Mahal as his wife's tomb) all prospered. In this atmosphere
of opulence and conspicuous consumption, huge sums were spent on
the imperial kitchens. Jahangir's Persian wife, Nur Jahan, is credited with
having invented some very fine dishes and Jahangir himself introduced
Gujarati khichari into the Mughal repertoire.[56] While traveling through
the province of Gujarat, he sampled a local version of this dish that
used millet instead of rice. He pronounced that it "suited me well" and
ordered that on his vegetarian days "they should frequently bring me
this khichari."[57] No doubt a Gujarati cook was immediately recruited to
work in the imperial kitchen. In this way a simple regional peasant dish
was integrated into the courtly cuisine. Other more elaborate versions of
khichari were incorporated into the Mughlai repertoire. During the reign
of Shahjahan, Sebastien Manrique was served a "far more costly" khichari
that he was told the Bengalis ate at their feasts. It was flavored with
expensive ingredients such as "almonds, raisins, cloves, mace, nutmeg,
cardamom, cinnamon and pepper."[58]

Jahangir discovered Gujarati khichari while traveling around his
empire, something the Mughals did a great deal to remind their subjects
of their power and authority. When they traveled, the imperial kitchen
traveled with them. "It is the custom of the court when the king is to
march the next day, that at ten o'clock of the night the royal kitchen

should start." This ensured that the kitchen was set up, and breakfast already prepared, by the time the emperor arrived the next morning. Fifty camels were needed to carry the supplies and 200 coolies, each with a basket on his head, to carry the china and the cookware. Fifty well-fed milk cows made up part of the procession, to provide sufficient milk, cream, butter, and curds.[59] One of the Mughals' favorite destinations during the hot weather was the mountainous province of Kashmir. There they escaped from the unrelenting heat of the plains in enchanting lakeside gardens. The presence of the Mughals encouraged a blossoming of Kashmiri cuisine and it was here that rogan josh, familiar to all customers of Indian restaurants, was perfected.

Rogan josh originated in Persia. In Persian the name implies a stew of meat cooked in butter (rogan means clarified butter in Persian) at an intense heat (josh means hot). In Kashmir the dish is flavored with regional spices. These vary according to the religion of the cook. Kashmiri Brahmans are unusual in that they eat meat without any qualms but they do avoid onions and garlic, so their version of rogan josh uses fennel seeds (commonly used in Kashmir) and asafetida to flavor the lamb. The Muslim version uses lots of garlic and onion and the dried flower of the cockscomb plant (maval). This is a plant indigenous to Kashmir that produces a furry red flower shaped like a cockscomb. Kashmiri Muslims have a particular liking for this herb and it imparts a bright red color to the food. Some food historians claim that this redness is the source of the dish's name as rogan in Kashmiri means red.[60]

One of Babur's main disappointments with India was that there was no decent fruit. Toward the end of his life he discovered that it was possible to cultivate sweet grapes and melons in India but the taste of a melon made him feel so homesick that it reduced him to tears.[61] Akbar set up an imperial fruitery, staffed with horticulturists from Persia and central Asia.[62] Jahangir wrote at tedious length on the merits of apples from

Samarkand and Kabul; exactly how many cherries it was possible to eat at one sitting; his uncle's apricot trees; and the astonishment of the sheikhs of Ahmadabad at the superiority of Persian melons over those grown in their native Gujarat.[63] Both Jahangir and Shahjahan took particular delight in having fruit weighed in front of them.[64] This obsession was more than mere gluttony. These fruits invoked the Mughals' lost homeland in central Asia. Their discussions were a coded expression of their homesickness. The delicate flavor of a Persian melon, the sweetness of a Samarkand apple symbolized the sophisticated culture that was their birthright and that they could no longer enjoy in its rightful setting. Their introduction of these fruits into India was an exquisite reminder of the central Asian civilization they had bequeathed to barbarous India.

The entire Mughal court was conversant with the political language of fruit. Foreigners were astonished to discover the proportion of their income that the Mughal noblemen and administrators spent on fruit.[65] Thomas Roe, always prickly about his dignity, failed to recognize the compliment he was paid when Asaf Khan sent him a basket of 20 musk melons. Instead, he complained that the Indians must "suppose our felicity lyes in the palate, for all I have ever received was eatable and drinkable."[66] In fact, so important and powerful a metaphor of power and prestige was fruit within the Mughal world, that it was one of the best gifts one could send or receive. When the King of Balkh sent ambassadors to Shahjahan's son, the Emperor Aurangzeb, they brought with them 100 camels loaded with fresh and dried fruit and nuts. (They also, intriguingly, gave him a seventeenth-century form of Viagra: boxes of rancid fish that were said to increase desire.)[67]

All the Mughal emperors were misty eyed about central Asian fruit. But Jahangir and Shahjahan both demonstrated a love of Indian fruit that suggested that, while their homeland had not lost its romantic image, their hearts now lay with their empire in Hindustan. After all, neither man had ever set foot in central Asia. Their favorite fruit was the Indian mango. Babur had been willing to admit that mangoes were the best fruit in Hindustan but he did not think they warranted much praise. Jahangir, 80 years later, declared that "notwithstanding the sweetness of the Kabul fruits, not one of them has, to my taste, the flavour of the mango."[68] On one occasion when Shahjahan was angry with his son, he accused him of eating the best mangoes from Shahjahan's favorite tree in the Deccan, rather than sending the fruit to him.[69] The conversion to mangoes is a telling sign that the Mughals were now Indians at heart. This became clear during the wars Shahjahan waged on the Uzbeks, the same people who had driven Babur out of Samarkand and deprived him of what he saw as his birthright. In contrast to Babur and his men who had felt unhappy and homesick in Hindustan, Shahjahan's soldiers, about a hundred years later, felt completely out of their element in central Asia. A contemporary chronicler of the Mughal regime described, in language reminiscent of Babur's first reaction to Hindustan, how " 'the natural love of home, a preference for the ways and customs of Hindustan, a dislike of the people and manners of Balkh, and the rigours of the climate, all conduced to' a desperate desire among the Mughal nobles to return to India."[70]

Shahjahan's campaign in central Asia was spectacularly unsuccessful. According to European observers this was due to the Mughals' decline into a luxurious and corrupt despotism that had thoroughly undermined their authority and military might. They argued that the rot had begun with Shahjahan's debauched father, Jahangir. Thomas Roe had never "seen a man so enamord of drincke." On the rare occasions when he was able to gain an audience with the emperor, the British ambassador was frustrated by the fact that Jahangir was often so far gone in his cups that he was incoherent, and would fall into a befuddled sleep halfway through the conversation.[71] In his memoirs Jahangir frankly admitted to his debauchery and cheerfully detailed his destructive and uncontrollable addiction to alcohol. After his first taste of wine on a hunting trip he progressed to arrack, Indian schnapps distilled from toddy, the sap of the palm tree. He was soon greedily imbibing 20 cups a day of this distilled spirit and became so permanently inebriated that his hands shook uncontrollably. William Hawkins, an Englishman who was a favorite with Jahangir for a short while, described how by the end of the day the emperor was so drugged with liquor and opium that his supper had to be "thrust into his mouthe by others."[72] It was only after the strongest of warnings from his physician that Jahangir found the willpower to wean himself down to a relatively healthy six cups a day of arrack diluted with wine, supplemented by generous doses of opium.[73] His jade drinking cup can now be seen in the Victoria and Albert Museum.

Jahangir frequently indulged in drinking parties with his courtiers, and throughout the reign of the next emperor, Shahjahan, the vice of drinking continued unabated. Little is known about the character of Shahjahan. He checked everything the chroniclers of his reign wrote about him, thus ensuring that few indiscretions were recorded for posterity. Niccolao Manucci, who was an artilleryman in the army of Shahjahan's son, commented that although he did not drink he "left everyone to live as he pleased, contenting himself with passing his days among women."[74] The French doctor François Bernier claimed that his "antics and follies" with his troupe of dancing girls transgressed the bounds of decency. He was even said to have had an incestuous affair with his daughter, Jahanara. Bernier claimed that she loved her father passionately and took great care of him, even personally supervising the preparation of all his food.[75]

Shahjahan's love of luxury ensured that Mughlai culture flourished. Artisans were busily employed constructing the jewel-encrusted peacock throne that he commissioned on his accession. Builders and architects created the beautiful city of Shahjahanabad (now known as Old Delhi) as well as the Taj Mahal at Agra. In Shahjahan's ateliers Mughal artists painted the exquisite series of miniatures known as the *Padshahnama*. His chefs concocted banquets consisting only of dishes with white sauces. For these they used white cumin, which cooks in Delhi refer to nowadays as *shahi jeera* (royal cumin).[76] The culinary culture of the court filtered down to ordinary people, and in all the major towns there were bazaars filled with cookshops. When Manrique visited Lahore in 1641 he found that the court had spread out into the countryside: "more than half a league of the adjoining country was covered by a handsome, well laid out, moving town, composed of a variety of tents and pavilions of many colours." This city of tents contained

> market-places, filled with delicious and appetising eatables ... Among these dishes the principal and most substantial were the rich and aromatic Mogol Bringes [biryanis] and Persian pilaos of different hues ... Nor did

these bazaars lack the simple foods of the native and superstitious pagan; as to meet their taste many tents held different dishes of rice, herbs and vegetables, among which the chief place was taken by the Gujerat or dry bringe . . . Bread was not lacking . . . of the ordinary and poor people . . . entirely of flour, baked on iron plates or clay dishes which are put upon live embers; [and] a very fine bread, delicate in flavour and made from wheat flour and the purest ghi so as to come out in thin leaves . . . Of these and other kinds of food there was such abundance in this moveable suburb that the curious Reader can imagine what would be met with in the bazaar and markets within the City itself. What struck me most were the low prices at which these things were sold, for any man could fare fully and sumptuously all day for two silver reals.[77]

Shahjahan's beautiful buildings, his peacock throne, his glorious banquets, were all paid for by an increasingly hard-pressed Indian peasantry.[78] In 1630, a terrible famine struck the inhabitants of Gujarat. European merchants from Surat observed with horror Indians scrabbling for food in dunghills. The villages were desolate and corpses piled up on the outskirts of the towns.[79] In response, public kitchens were opened, and revenue collection from the peasants was suspended.

Shahjahan was a poor administrator. Rather than consolidating his power at home he waged unnecessary wars in central Asia. The empire began to fray at the edges. His ruthless and excessively pious son, Aurangzeb, took drastic steps to remedy his father's mistakes. In an attempt to restore Islam to the court of the Mughals, Aurangzeb forbade the distillation of spirits within the city walls of Delhi and any Muslim or Hindu found to be selling alcohol lost a hand and a foot.[80] He discontinued many of the Indian practices that had crept into the Mughal emperor's way of life and, in a characteristic spirit of self-sacrifice, he banned music, which he loved, from the court. Aurangzeb's one indulgence appears to have been food. He spent a lavish 1,000 rupees a day on the imperial kitchens and he sought out good cooks. When his son refused to send "Sulaiman, who cooks biryani" to work in the imperial kitchens, Aurangzeb was frustrated and asked him to look out for a pupil of this skillful cook as "the desire [for eating] has not entirely left me."[81]

Under Aurangzeb the Mughal Empire reached its furthest extent. But when he died in 1707, his successors were unable to prevent provincial governors from breaking away and establishing themselves as virtually independent rulers of new satellite states. It was at these regional courts that Mughlai cuisine continued to flourish in the eighteenth century.

دضع علم كماى ومحموى وقت نى غمى طهر عناره ش فه خلاط الشافعى رح فاته اليومع
لمه عنده م لكل سعنه ثمانىة واربعون درنمان كل باخد فى لكم شهر اربعة دراهم

These very simple kebabs are the sort Babur might have eaten in camp or that the Afridis would have served at the tea party they held for the British. Serves 3–4.

1½ lb. tender beef or lamb steak
3 cloves of garlic, crushed
1 teaspoon fresh ginger, finely grated
1–3 green chillies, finely chopped
¼ teaspoon freshly ground black pepper
¼ teaspoon salt
3–4 tablespoons oil (olive or vegetable)

Spices (choose according to the flavors you prefer)
1 teaspoon ground cumin
1 teaspoon ground coriander
½ teaspoon garam masala

If you prefer a creamy marinade, add:
2 tablespoons yogurt
1 tablespoon lemon juice

And if you like a granular texture, add:
1–2 tablespoons ground almonds

Cut the meat into small chunks. Combine the garlic, ginger, chillies, pepper, salt. Add the spices of your choice. Add the oil (use less if you want a yogurt marinade). Add the yogurt, lemon juice, and (optional) the ground almonds. Mix well. Combine with the meat. Cover and leave in the fridge overnight.

Thread on to skewers and roast under a grill, or on a barbecue.

Khichari

Khichari is the simple peasant dish eaten all over India. The key to getting it right is to add just enough water so that the rice and lentils are well cooked without being sticky. Serves 4.

¼ lb. red split lentils
2 cups water
½ teaspoon turmeric
½ lb. basmati rice
salt to taste
1 oz. butter
1 small onion, finely chopped

Put the red split lentils in a pan with 1 cup of water and the turmeric. Bring to a boil. Skim off the scum that rises to the surface. Turn the heat very low and cook gently for about 10 minutes. Add the rice, another 1 cup of water, salt to taste, and bring to a boil. Then reduce the heat, cover the pan, and cook over a very low flame. Once all the water has been absorbed, take the pan off the heat and wrap in a towel. Leave in a warm place for 10–20 minutes to allow the rice to expand fully. Meanwhile, fry the onions in the butter until browned and sprinkle over the rice and lentils when it is served.

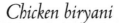

Chicken biryani

Biryani is a celebratory dish, eaten at weddings. It is the Mughal version of pilau. A pilau was supposed to be aromatic rather than spicy, allowing the sweet or nutty flavor of the rice to dominate. Mughal biryanis were extremely spicy, much spicier than biryanis tend to be nowadays. Serves 5–6.

1 whole chicken about 3½ lb., washed and jointed into 8–10 pieces

Marinade:

¾ in. piece of fresh ginger, finely grated

6 cloves garlic, crushed

2–3 fresh green chillies, pounded in a pestle and mortar

½ teaspoon cardamom powder

1 teaspoon cumin powder

1 teaspoon coriander powder

4 whole green chillies, slit down the side

¾ in. cinnamon stick

2 whole cloves

salt to taste

1 tablespoon of lemon juice

2 tomatoes puréed

6–8 prunes

Mix all the ingredients together in a bowl, add the chicken and mix again. Make sure all the pieces of chicken are coated in the marinade. Cover and leave in the fridge overnight.

12 oz. red split lentils, presoaked in water for 15 minutes

2 cups water

4–6 tablespoons vegetable oil

2 large onions, ¼ of one onion should be sliced, the rest should be chopped

1¾ cups yogurt

¼ teaspoon saffron, crushed and steeped in 2 teaspoons of hot milk

1¼ lb. basmati rice, presoaked in water for 20 minutes

salt to taste

¾ in. cinnamon stick

3 cardamom pods

3 cloves

3½ pints water

6 small new potatoes, boiled until just cooked

3 hard-boiled eggs, shelled and cut in half

a few sprigs of mint

¼ lb. blanched slivered almonds

Put the lentils and water in a large pan. Bring to a boil. Turn down the heat and then simmer for 10 minutes. Drain and set aside.

Heat the oil in a pan and fry the chopped onions until golden brown.

Take the meat in its marinade out of the fridge and add the onions, with their cooking oil, to the bowl.

Add the yogurt and mix well. Now pour in the saffron soaked in milk.

Drain the rice and put in a cooking pot with salt, cinnamon stick, cardamom pods, whole cloves, and 3½ pints of boiling water. Simmer for 10 minutes and then drain.

Meanwhile, fry the cooked potatoes.

Take a large casserole and put the marinated meat mixture in the bottom of the pot. Nestle the hard-boiled eggs in among the meat, and sprinkle with a few sprigs of mint. Spread the red lentils over the meat. Then place the potatoes in a layer over the lentils. Spread the rice over the potatoes.

Fry the slices of onion and the slivered almonds in a little oil and scatter over the rice. Sprinkle a little water over the contents of the casserole. Close the lid tightly and put over a high heat for 5 minutes. When the contents begin to sizzle, turn the heat to low and simmer for 1 hour.

Green mango sherbet

For a long time the Mughal emperors mourned their lost homeland in central Asia and pined for melons. But by the time the third emperor, Jahangir, came to the throne he had switched his allegiance and thought Indian mangoes sweeter and better than any central Asian melon. Mangoes, the Mughals found, made good sherbets. Serves 3–4.

2 raw green mangoes
6 tablespoons of sugar
1 teaspoon of salt
½ teaspoon roasted, and then ground, cumin seeds
sprig of fresh mint
1 cup cold water

Roast the whole mangoes in a hot oven until they are soft. Allow them to cool and then make a hole in the skin and squeeze out the pulp. Put the pulp in a blender and process with the sugar, cumin, salt, and mint. Add cold water and pour into chilled glasses.

*View of the fortified city of Goa in 1509, showing the
Portuguese war fleet in the East Indies*

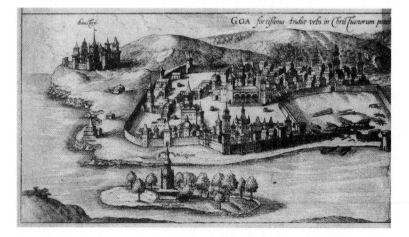

3

Vindaloo: The Portuguese and the Chilli Pepper

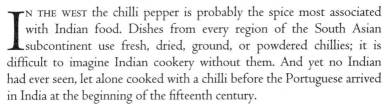

IN THE WEST the chilli pepper is probably the spice most associated with Indian food. Dishes from every region of the South Asian subcontinent use fresh, dried, ground, or powdered chillies; it is difficult to imagine Indian cookery without them. And yet no Indian had ever seen, let alone cooked with a chilli before the Portuguese arrived in India at the beginning of the fifteenth century.

Before 1500, pepper was the hottest spice in the Indian culinary repertoire. It came in two forms. The most widely used was the long

catkinlike fruit of the hot and sweet *Piper longum*, known as long pepper. (The English word pepper is derived from *pippali*, its Hindi name.) This plant is native to Bengal but by the sixteenth century it grew wild along the southwest Malabar coast.[1] The jeweler Jean-Baptiste Tavernier noticed that the Muslims threw long pepper into their pilaus "by the handful."[2] The other form was the small round fruit of the *Piper nigrum, gol mirch* in Hindi, or the black pepper that is familiar to us in the West.

Ayurvedic physicians used both kinds of peppers extensively in their medicines to cure patients afflicted with phlegm and wind, and long pepper was valued as a means to increase semen, the source of a man's strength according to Ayurvedic reasoning. One of the more outlandish Ayurvedic recipes to be found in a nineteenth-century pharmacopoeia recommended frog boiled with black pepper and turmeric as a cure for madness. More appetizing was a recipe for lark cooked with long pepper, turmeric, and salt, used to treat severe fevers.[3]

The ancient Greeks and Romans used both peppers for similar medical purposes (to cure impotence, for example) and they greatly valued pepper for flavoring meat and fish. Ships loaded with gold and silver were sent from Roman Egypt to India's southwestern coast and returned heavy with pepper, which the Caesars stored like precious metals in their treasury.[4] Medieval Europeans had an equally strong hunger. Along with ginger and cinnamon, pepper accounted for 93 percent of the spices annually imported into Venice between 1394 and 1405.

In Europe, spices were initially prized for their medicinal properties. They were thought to ward off the plague, stimulate the appetite, and aid digestion. Cooks also found that they helped to liven up the bland vegetarian and fish dishes that were consumed on the numerous fast days of the Christian calendar. The use of spices increased significantly during the thirteenth century. At this time French, Catalan, and Latin translations of an Arabic folk-tale about a Garden of Delights were in circulation. Fascinated by the Muslim attitude toward food as a source of pleasure, Europeans found the idea of heaven as a place of Epicurean indulgence an inviting contrast to severe Christian teachings that valued self-denial. The influence of the spicy Arab cuisine on European cookery can be seen in the increasing number of recipes that called for sugar, ginger, grains of paradise, and pepper. Many Europeans thought spices, because they came from such faraway exotic places, possessed magical powers. Thus they merited an important place in the conspicuous consumption of the wealthy.[5] By the fifteenth century virtually every recipe contained spices of some sort. However, the idea that medieval cooks were heavy-handed with spices in order to disguise the taste of rotten meat is misguided. Those wealthy enough to afford spices would have been able to buy good fresh meat. Rather than throwing spices into dishes in a random fashion to disguise rancid ingredients, the cooks used spices with great care, to enhance the flavor of the food. Pepper was the king of spices and the apothecary of an affluent medieval household would have always had some in store, while in the kitchen the cooks would have kept some ready-ground, close to hand in a special leather pouch. It was the one spice that seems to have been used by medieval people on almost all levels of the social scale.[6]

For their supply of spices, medieval Europeans relied on a chain of traders, which began with Chinese and Malayan merchants who toured the spice islands of the Pacific. They brought the goods back to China and Malaya, from where they were taken across the Indian Ocean to the ports of India, and then on over the Arabian Sea to the African continent. Arab traders transported them across Africa and the Mediterranean until they finally reached the European entrepôts of Venice and Genoa. Other Europeans had always resented having to pay whatever price the Italians chose to charge, but when the Ottomans captured Constantinople in 1453, and then invaded Egypt at the end of the fifteenth century, prices began to spiral out of control. Throughout the fifteenth century the price of pepper was fairly stable but between 1496 (when it cost 42 ducats the hundredweight) and 1499 it nearly doubled in price. By 1505 pepper in Cairo cost 192 ducats the hundredweight. Such prices provided a great incentive to find an alternative route to the Indies that would enable the successful nation to capture the lucrative spice trade.

When he set sail in 1492, Christopher Columbus was convinced that by sailing west he would eventually reach the spice islands and open up a direct sea route to China. In particular, he hoped to find a cheap source of pepper. On landing in the Caribbean, he firmly believed that he had reached his goal and that he was in the outer reaches of the Indies. In a letter written after his return to Europe, he described how the islanders ate their food "heavily seasoned with hot spices." In particular they used a vegetable which they called *aji*. This was the first European encounter with the chilli pepper. Columbus was certain that *aji* was a form of the pepper plant he was looking for and he named it "pepper of the Indies."[7] In fact, it was one of the many varieties of capsicum that the native American peoples had been cultivating to flavor their food since 4000 BC. The capsicum plants of America are unrelated to the pepper plants of Asia. But the name has stuck and the fruits of all capsicums have become known as peppers. The word chilli itself comes from Mexico where, some years later, the Spaniards came across a wide variety of cultivars of the *Capsicum annuum* that the Aztecs called chilli.

Although Columbus insisted until the end of his life that he had discovered the offshore islands of Asia, it quickly became clear to the Spaniards that he had in fact discovered a New World, which they set about incorporating into their own. Despite the complaints of an early Spanish soldier about the horrible diet of maize cakes, prickly pears, and chillies, the majority of the Spanish settlers in the Americas took to munching chillies with enthusiasm.[8] A Spanish physician writing in the 1570s attributed to chillies medicinal properties similar to those of black pepper: "it dooeth comforte muche, it dooeth dissolve windes, it is good for the breaste, and for theim that bee colde of complexion: it doeth heale and comforte, strengthenyng the principall members." The Spaniards used chillies in much the same way as black pepper. They flavored pork dishes with them and invented spicier versions of staple Iberian recipes. It was claimed that the sweet pork from the Toluca Valley, west of Mexico, when combined with chillies, made a chorizo sausage to rival any found in Old Spain.[9] In the home country their compatriots were less enchanted, however, and on the Iberian Peninsula chillies were grown more as curious ornamental plants than as sources of a fiery flavoring.[10]

In May 1498, six years after Columbus crossed the Atlantic, three Portuguese vessels anchored off the town of Calicut on India's Malabar coast. Funded by King Emanuel of Portugal, and under the command of Vasco da Gama, these vessels had succeeded where Columbus had failed and discovered the sea route to the Indies. They had followed a more cautious approach and, following in the wake of previous Portuguese explorers, had made their way down the west coast of Africa, round the Cape of Good Hope, and then sailed across the Arabian Sea to India.

The Portuguese relationship with the Indians did not begin auspiciously. An audience with the king of Calicut was arranged but the meeting was not a success. The king's courtiers laughed at the presents da Gama had brought: "cloth, a dozen coats, six hats, some coral, six basins, a bale of sugar, and two barrels each of butter, probably rancid from the long journey, and of honey." He departed three months later under a cloud.[11] Nevertheless, his ship was loaded down with pepper, bought for three ducats the hundredweight. On da Gama's triumphant return to Lisbon a gloomy Venetian observed that although the price of pepper had fallen to 22 ducats, the Portuguese were still able to make a profit of 100 percent on their pepper. He predicted correctly that from then on Europeans would turn away from Venice and look to Lisbon for their spices.[12]

Within three years the Portuguese were back in India. In 1505, Lopo Soares's fleet of nine vessels departed from the Malabar coast with a cargo that included 1,074,003 kilograms of pepper, 28,476 kilograms of ginger, 8,789 kilograms of cinnamon, and 206 kilograms of cardamom.[13] By 1530, the Portuguese had established a capital at Goa, a string of 50 forts around the Gulf of Cambay and along the west coast of India, outposts on the Coromandel coast and in Bengal, all protected by a fleet of 100 ships.[14] They had wrested control of the spice trade from the Arabs (who turned to vicious piracy) and had begun their ruthless domination of the East Indies trade that was to last for most of the sixteenth century.

It was by means of the Portuguese that the chilli pepper found its way to India. It is not known exactly when chillies arrived on the Malabar coast, but 30 years after Vasco da Gama first set foot on Indian soil, there were at least three different types of chilli plants growing around Goa. In India, the confusion with the pepper plant that Columbus had initiated continued. Chillies were known as "Pernambucco pepper," a name that indicated that the initial imports probably came from Brazil via Lisbon. Further afield, in Bombay, they were known as *Gowai mirchi*, or Goan

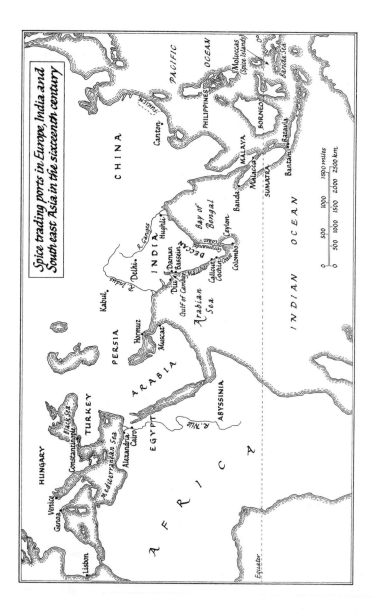

Spice trading ports in Europe, India and South east Asia in the sixteenth century

pepper, a label suggesting that Goa was their point of entry into India.[15] The south Indians, who used black and long pepper abundantly in their dishes to create fiery, piquant sauces, took to chillies straight away. The chilli was very similar to long pepper in appearance and therefore did not look too unfamiliar. It had a similar hot taste and was much easier to grow and store than long pepper, which was susceptible to mold. Chillies were soon cheaper than long pepper and eventually supplanted it.[16]

It is surprising how quickly chillies became essential to the south Indian diet. Indians were often slow to accept new foodstuffs, but only a few years after chillies had been introduced a south Indian poet declared them the "Saviour of the Poor." They provided a cheap and easy way to give taste to a simple meal of rice and lentils. Even Ayurvedic physicians, who rarely incorporated foreign foods into the cosmic world of diet and health, replaced pepper with chillies in many of their remedies. While the ancient recipes prescribed pepper water for those afflicted with cholera, nineteenth-century Ayurvedic physicians often used chilli both in plasters and in soups to treat the cholera patient.[17] By this time they were a staple of the Indian diet and, "ground into a paste between two stones, with a little mustard oil, ginger and salt, they form[ed] the only seasoning which the millions of poor can obtain to eat with their rice."[18] Even today, chillies are still often the sole flavoring many can afford and therefore constitute a vital source of vitamin C for the poor of India. South Indian cooking in particular is now notorious for its heavy-handed use of chillies to create dishes, the heat of which numb the tongue. A Keralan recipe, for example, uses green chillies and chicken in proportions of 100 grams of chillies to 700 grams of chicken, plus generous helpings of ground red chilli powder.[19]

Northern Europeans became familiar with chillies by means of an unexpected and circuitous route. There was some awareness that Columbus had discovered a pungent "Spanish pepper" and examples of South American chilli peppers would almost certainly have traveled from Lisbon and Seville to the ports of Antwerp and London by the 1540s. But the majority of Northern Europeans believed that chillies were native to India. Indeed, India was almost certainly the source of most chilles to be found in Germany, Holland, or Britain in the sixteenth century. They were introduced by the Turks, whose source of supply is uncertain, though it seems likely that capsicums grown on the west coast of India were dried or ground into powder and then traded along the medieval spice routes across the Arabian Sea into Persia. From there dried chillies, cayenne pepper, and paprika would have found their way north along the trade routes connected to the Black Sea ports, where they were incorporated into Turkish cuisine. In 1526, the Turks conquered Hungary and paprika, later the hallmark spice of Hungarian cookery, was introduced into the region. This complicated migration engendered a confusion as to the origins of the chilli. A herbal published by the German physician and botanist Leonard Fuchs in 1542 described its different varieties. He had obtained the seeds from Hungary but referred to them as "Calicut" and "Indian" pepper, thereby indicating his belief that they were native to India.

It took a long time for chillies to become popular in Northern Europe. They did supplant the long pepper (which began to fall out of use during the sixteenth century) but Europeans continued to prefer black pepper, which remained the most commonly used spice. It was not until the nineteenth century that chillies began to appear in British recipes. And then they entered the cookery books in Indian curry recipes, further conflating them in the British mind with the Indian subcontinent rather than with the Americas.[20]

When the Dutchman Jan Huyghen van Linschoten arrived in Goa in September 1583, almost a century after Vasco da Gama landed at Calicut, he was surprised to discover the wives of the Portuguese eating Indian food. A typical meal was boiled rice with a thin watery soup poured over it, salt fish, mango pickle, and a fish or meat sauce. These were dishes strange to a sixteenth-century European whose staple diet was wheat bread and roast meats. Not only did the Portuguese in India eat unfamiliar food, they ate it with their hands in the Indian manner. Indeed, the women laughed at anyone they observed using a spoon.[21]

Many of the Portuguese settlers had adopted a variety of Indian habits. The men had discarded their tight knee-length hose for "a sort of breeches, called Candales, the like whereof I never saw in any part of Europe; for when they are ty'd they leave something like the tops of Boots on the Leg. Others under a short Doublet, wear wide silk Breeches; and some have them hang down to their Ankles."[22] Even more peculiar, they regularly changed their underclothes. In Europe, it was customary to rub oneself down with one's old linen underclothes before putting on a fresh undershirt, and a bath was out of the question. In contrast, the Portuguese in India were scrupulously clean. Besides regularly changing their linen, they took a bath at least once, and sometimes twice, a day. Nor did the women ever fail to wash "as often as they ease themselves or make water, or use the companie of their husbands." These were habits unusual in Europe.

The women observed purdah, and wore veils when they went outside. Although the wealthy hung themselves with "jewels, and rosaries of Gold and Silver many times double," to indicate their Christian faith, they wore Indian clothes: thin, almost transparent, swathes of material above the waist and petticoats, bare legs, and colorful slippers below. "Being nurtured up in a lowly Bashfulness, whereby they are render'd unfit for Conversation," the wives were said to spend their days idly chewing betel nut, and washing and rubbing themselves with sweet-smelling perfumes and sandalwood. These were all practices, Linschoten observed, they had learned and "received of the Indian Heathens, which have had these customs of long time."[23]

Linschoten had come to India in the suite of Vincente de Fonseca, the newly appointed Bishop of Goa. During his childhood in the Netherlands (then under Spanish rule) Linschoten, his imagination fed by adventure stories and histories, had dreamed of traveling the world. At the age of 16 he followed his two elder brothers to Seville and six years later one of his brothers, who was a clerk on board a ship in the India fleet, managed to get him the position with the bishop. Goa was by now the capital of the Portuguese *Estado da India* (State of India), the Indian territory that the Portuguese used as their base for their trade in spices. Here, Linschoten discovered a lively colonial society, which he described in his *Itinerario* published 13 years later in 1596.

The Portuguese colonial empire was based on the control of trade routes. The Indian ports had always been strategically important. Here, the Arab trading world, which, at the end of the fifteenth century, reached from North Africa and the Mediterranean to the Bay of Bengal and Malacca in Southeast Asia, overlapped with the trading world of China and Malaya and the spice islands of the Pacific Ocean. By dominating the oceans with their warships, the Portuguese now monopolized these trading networks. Linschoten noted that the Arabs required a passport from the Portuguese in order to conduct trade and that, despite a friendly manner, they regarded the Portuguese as deadly enemies.[24] Nevertheless, the Portuguese were still dependent on a network of non-European merchants and money brokers. The Portuguese towns were filled with Gujarati Banians, Tamil, and Telugu Chettis and Syrian Christians from southwestern India, all trading with Chinese from Fukien province, and Arabs from Hormuz and Aden.

Goa was distinguished from other Indian towns by the houses built "after the Portingall manner," surrounded by gardens and orchards full of Indian fruit trees, and by "all sorts of Cloysters and Churches." But the commercial areas looked just like any other Indian port. Linschoten described how the streets were lined with the shops of rich Indian merchants, each street specializing in particular wares. In one, the stores were piled with silks, satins, damasks, and Chinese porcelain; in another, precious stones and lacquer furniture in every color. Gold- and silversmiths shared their street with coppersmiths, carpenters, and craftsmen. Corn and rice merchants heaped up their wares in huge piles, and Brahman merchants sold spices craftily mixed with dust and rubbish. All around could be heard the tongues of the "Heathen Brokers very cunning and subtill in buying and selling." In the galleries above the shops the "Barragios . . . or great bellies" sat with their shirts open, their toenails being pared by slaves, while they nibbled dishes of conserves or took a nap. The Portuguese owned shops and workshops where their slaves made hats, shoes, sails, and barrels. The streets were filled with diverse peoples —"Heathens, Moores, Iewes, Persians, Arabians, Abexijns [Abyssinians] ... Armenians (Christian), Banianes of Cambaia, Gusarates and Decanijns." The Portuguese, swamped by such diversity, were just one group among many, even in their own territory.[25]

Portuguese society was itself made up of a number of layers. The upper stratum was composed of a small group of Portuguese officials who came to India only for a short term of three years. They enjoyed lives of great luxury in grand houses "with covered Balconies, and large Windows two Stories high, with panes of Oister shell."[26] Whenever they left their houses, they moved through the streets "very slowly ... with a great pride and vainglorious maiestie, with a slave that carrieth a great hat or vaile over their heads, to keep the sunne and raine from them."[27] The officials wore elaborate and expensive European clothes, employed large numbers of Indian servants, and owned many Bengali, Chinese and East African slaves. The viceroy at their head set the tone for their behavior. He used his first year in India to repair and furnish his palace in Goa. The second year he spent amassing a fortune. The third year he prepared for departure. When the next viceroy arrived he found a palace with "not a stoole or a bench within, nor one pennie in the treasure." On discovering his "bare and naked" palace the viceroy would renew the cycle. Linschoten concluded that no one in India could "looke for any profit or furtherance of the commonwealth by any Viceroy" and that "the same is to bee understoode of all the Captaines in the Fortes, and of all officers in India," who simply repeated his example on a smaller scale.[28]

Below the layer of official Portuguese, a small army of *soldados* and sailors protected the trading posts and manned the ships. Their presence made the towns of Portuguese India rough and dangerous places. From June to September, when the monsoon winds meant that it was impossible for ships to put to sea, mobs of unpaid and hungry sailors would roam the town of Goa. Many of the sailors were former beggars and vagrants who had been impressed in Portugal, or they were convicts sentenced to serve out their time in India rather than in a Portuguese prison. Their quarrelsome presence meant that "everyone walks the City with his naked

Sword in his Hand for his own defense at evening."[29] Often they were taken under the care of a nobleman, who would feed them and use them as a personal army. This meant that disputes between gentlemen often escalated into armed conflicts as they fought out their differences using bands of followers.[30]

The bulk of the permanent Portuguese population in India were *casados*: merchants, money exchangers, shopkeepers, and craftsmen. Some of these men had been attracted to India by the promise of making their fortunes, many were soldiers and sailors who had married and settled down in India. Very few Portuguese women emigrated to Asia and most *casados* married either Indian women who had converted to Christianity, or *mestiços* born to a Portuguese father and an Indian mother. It was the *casados* whom European visitors persisted in thinking of as Portuguese, even though the women were Portuguese only by virtue of their marriage. Living in intimacy with the locals, the men had picked up many Indian habits and customs. Indeed, the disapproving argued that they had "adopted the vices and customs of the land without reserve."

A Jesuit padre was most disturbed by the Portuguese settlers' licentiousness, which he attributed to the influence of the Indians. He complained that they had acquired the "evil custom of buying droves of slaves, male and female, just as if they were sheep," sleeping with the girls, and then selling them.[31] If their morality was in question, so were their religious sensibilities. Linschoten observed that, despite being Christians, the Portuguese had incorporated certain Hindu practices into their behavior. When they drank, they held the vessel "on high, and touch it not with their mouthes, never spilling a drop."[32] This technique ensured that they never came into contact with another person's saliva, which, in the eyes of a Hindu, was polluting. Their adoption of this manner of drinking indicated that the Portuguese men had adopted their Hindu wives' religious scruples about purity.

Cross-cultural exchange was hardly surprising, given that the majority of the Portuguese second generation had been brought up in a *casado* household organized by an Indian mother along Indian lines. As Linschoten observed, the women preserved their preference for rice over bread, and for eating with their hands rather than a spoon. When the family entertained, they maintained the Hindu custom of keeping the genders separate while eating, women serving the men first and then consuming the leftovers. Although their refusal to eat with guests irritated the visiting British East India Company surgeon, John Fryer, he nonetheless thought Portuguese women excellent cooks. They made the best mango pickle, he enthused, "and dress Meat exquisitely, not to put the Stomach to much trouble, but such as shall digest presently; Supoes, pottages, and varieties of Stews, in little China dishes or Plates, which they shift before you are cloy'd, and at a common Entertainment after half a dozen Modes: Their relishing Bits have not the Fieriness of ours, yet all the pleasure you can desire; and to speak truly, I prefer their ordinary way of ordering Victuals before any others."[33] The food served in Portuguese households was not all Indian, however. Like most emigrants, the men preserved a taste for the dishes of their home country and they introduced a variety of Portuguese dishes to India.

Although Portugal was a small country, its cuisine combined influences from a wide range of cultures. The ecology of the Iberian Peninsula was suited to the cultivation of wheat, pigs, sheep, olive oil, and the various manifestations of the grape, that is, must (grape juice), verjuice (the juice of unripe grapes), vinegar (soured wine), and wine. But Portuguese cooking also incorporated foodstuffs and recipes from a wide range of cultures. Jewish settlers and Moorish rulers had introduced rice, almonds, pomegranates, citrus fruits, and sugar from the Near East. The European spice trade provided a steady supply of important flavorings such as black pepper, cloves, and cinnamon. And, after Columbus's voyage of 1492, Spain and Portugal were supplied with curious new ingredients from the Americas, such as tomatoes, potatoes, maize, cashew nuts, and turkeys. A stew of chicken simmered with cloves, cinnamon, black pepper, saffron, and a little vinegar and thickened with ground almonds was standard Portuguese fare during the sixteenth century.[34]

In southern India rice was the staple crop. Cardamom bushes, pepper vines, and clove trees thrived in the lush green forests. Ralph Fitch, one of the first Europeans to reach India overland, described black pepper growing in the fields around Cochin, "among the bushes without any labour, and when it is ripe they go and gather it. The shrubbe is like unto our ivy tree; and if it did not run about some tree or pole, it would fall down and rot. When they first gather it is greene; and then they lay it in the sun, and it becommeth blacke."[35] South Indian sauces were thick with these spices. They were also marked by a sour note, derived from the tamarind, which had been introduced into India from Africa by Arab traders. Groves of coconut palms lined the coast and coconut milk was used as a base for many sauces while ground coconut was used as a thickening agent. The marriage of these two culinary styles produced Goan cuisine.

The Portuguese in India particularly missed leavened wheat bread. South Indians sometimes used wheat to make unleavened flat chapattis, but they preferred soft rice breads made with a fermented batter of ground rice and lentils. This batter produced a surprising range of breads: idlis, which are soft and puffy (like light doughnuts) and eaten with chutney; appams, which have a spongy center and a crispy fringe and, soaked in coconut milk flavored with cardamom, make a good breakfast; and dosas, thin rice pancakes that are wrapped round a variety of spicy vegetable fillings. But for the Portuguese it was not simply a matter of missing the taste of crusty loaves. Wheat bread was of enormous religious significance to sixteenth-century Europeans. It was the only substance with which it was permitted to celebrate Mass and the Portuguese settlements were populated by large numbers of Catholic missionaries. The Portuguese therefore went to great lengths to make bread in a country where this was very difficult. The problem was that yeast, essential to the success of a white wheat loaf, was unavailable. The ingenious Goan cooks used toddy (alcohol made from the sap of the palm tree) to ferment the dough, with, as a European traveler in Goa in the 1630s found, good results. He reported that "good white wheat bread" was available in Portuguese India.[36] In fact, the Portuguese added a variety of European breads—crusty white rolls, soft croissantlike breads called *burbuleat*, and the sweet milk bread *pao de lo*—to the Indian repertoire.[37] Even when India was under British rule in the nineteenth century, and many British foods had been introduced into India, according to a British soldier on leave, the Portuguese in Goa continued to make the best leavened bread in western India.[38]

One of the culinary legacies of Moorish rule on the Iberian Peninsula was the pride cooks took in preparing sweet dishes made from eggs and milk.[39] It was natural, therefore, for Portuguese bakers to introduce such confections to India alongside their wheat breads. The Portuguese specialized in pastries such as *dariols*, a favorite European sweet in the sixteenth century. A *dariol* was made of milk (although more often medieval European cooks used almond milk, which kept far longer), eggs, and sometimes fruit, fish, or bone marrow cooked in a pastry shell.[40] Their other speciality was fragrant egg custard, a style of dessert entirely new to India, where sweets were usually made of milk boiled down to the point where it solidified, or of ground lentils bound together with ghee and flavored with a spice such as cardamom.

In 1638 Albert Mandelslo, a young German on a tour of the East Indies, enjoyed Portuguese confections when he dined at the College of St. Paul in Goa. The Jesuit college educated young Indian converts in Christian doctrine, Latin, Portuguese, and music.[41] Its table was set with "fruit and bread" and they ate "several courses, both of flesh and fish, all excellently well dressed" served in "little dishes of Porcelain." The meal was brought to a close with a delightful dessert of "tarts, Florentines, Eggs drest after the Portuguez way, admirably well perfum'd, Marchpains [marzipan], and Conserves, both dry and liquid."[42] Portuguese bakers passed on their skills to their Indian wives, who soon acquired a reputation for making exquisite confections.

In Bengal, the Portuguese taught the art of confectionary to the Moghs: the latter were Bengali Buddhists who for centuries had been employed as deckhands and cooks on the Arab trading ships sailing across the Bay of Bengal to Southeast Asia. When the Portuguese established their base in Bengal at Hughli and took over the trade from the Arabs, they also took over the Arab tradition of employing the Moghs on their ships. Before long the Mogh cooks became accomplished bakers and confectioners.[43] Bengal was well supplied with bakers' shops selling light and crumbly pastries and delicately flavored egg confections to the eager Bengalis, who were renowned for their passion for sweets. Even the Frenchman François Bernier, who was generally scathing about the quality of food to be found in India, thought that Bengal was a "place for good comfits, especially in those places where the Portuguese are, who are dexterous in making them, and drive a great trade with them."[44] Two hundred years later, the same English soldier who praised Goan bread acknowledged that despite the debased state of the Portuguese, "in this one point their descendants have not degenerated."[45]

Over time Goan cooks replaced the European ingredients in Portuguese cakes with others more easily available in India. Coconut milk was used as a substitute for fresh cow's or almond milk. Jaggery, the hard lumps of raw sugar made from the sap of the palm tree, replaced the more refined sugars used in Europe. Ghee supplanted fresh butter. The far more common and cheaper rice flour took the place of wheat flour.[46] Goan confections were clearly derived from Portuguese cakes and pastries but they took on a distinctively Indian flavor. *Bebinca* is a typical example of the Goan adaptation of Portuguese cake-making traditions. It is made from a batter of coconut milk, eggs, and jaggery. A thin layer of the batter is poured into a pot and baked, then another layer is added, and so on until the cake forms a series of pancake-like layers. Ideally, it should be baked in an earthen oven fueled by coconut husks that impart a smoky flavor. *Bebinca* traveled with the Portuguese to Malaya, and from there to the Philippines, where the cooks dispensed with the time-consuming layers. From the Philippines *bebinca* continued on its extraordinary journey to Hawaii, where it transmuted into butter mochi, a fudgelike rice-flour dessert.[47]

Portuguese cooking was strongly meat based. Lamb, pork, and beef were the most favored meats. Pork was, of course, forbidden for Muslims, as was beef for Hindus, and many Indians were vegetarian. Indifferent to the feelings of the indigenous population, the Portuguese continued to eat all these meats whenever they could. This was not unusual. What is striking, however, is that they succeeded in changing the eating habits of the Indians living in their territories. By the 1650s Jean-Baptiste Tavernier reported that beef and pork were "the ordinary foods of the inhabitants of Goa," and Christian Goan cuisine today uses a great deal of meat, especially pork.[48] Nowhere else in India did European settlement have this impact. The British certainly did not persuade their subjects to relinquish their taboos on meat consumption. The Portuguese achieved this feat by a campaign of mass conversion to Christianity begun only a few years after they had established themselves in India in the 1540s.

The English ship's captain Alexander Hamilton declared that Goa at the end of the seventeenth century was "a Rome in India" it was so overrun with Catholic missionaries. He thought them "a pack of notorious Hypocrites" and the "most zealous Bigots" of the Roman Catholic Church to be found anywhere. While the Portuguese were establishing their Indian territory in the mid-sixteenth century, the Counter Reformation was just beginning in Europe. The Portuguese, heavily influenced by an aggressively Catholic Spain, brought their religious concerns with them to India. A number of religious orders established monasteries in Goa and throughout the 1540s the friars made vigorous efforts to convert the Indian population. In 1560 the Inquisition, which had been established in Portugal in 1531, was introduced to India to ensure that the Christian faith had been firmly established among the converts.[49] The Goa Inquisition gained a reputation for being terrifyingly severe and the announcement that the Inquisition was at the door was enough to turn most Portuguese householders pale.

One tale claimed that a man uprooted his prized mango tree after an encounter with the Inquisition. A messenger from the lord inquisitor had appeared at his door. The visit turned out to be innocuous—the lord inquisitor simply wanted to taste some of the fruit from the famous tree. A basket of mangoes was dispatched, but the feeling of dread that had overwhelmed the man had so shaken him that he did not wish to repeat the experience.[50] Hamilton claimed that the Jesuits were such bullies that the laity in Goa were confined to eating only "stale or stinking Fish." The fishermen dared not sell ordinary customers any fish until the churchmen had bought up all that they wanted. By way of illustration, Hamilton told the story of a gentleman friend who bought the last parcel of fresh fish from the fishermen. A priest arrived soon afterward and demanded that he hand over the purchase. When he refused, explaining that "he had some friends to dine with him, and could not spare them," the priest denounced the man using "scurrilous language." He gave a tart reply that so incensed the priest that he threatened to have the gentleman excommunicated. The matter was only resolved after Hamilton's friend paid a sum of money and suffered the humiliation of begging his pardon on his knees in front of the archbishop.[51]

As soon as it was established, the Inquisition instigated a series of harsh measures in an effort to root out Hinduism in the Portuguese-controlled areas. Seven years after arriving in India the Inquisition had destroyed almost all Hindu temples in the Portuguese territory. Edicts were issued ordering all Brahmans to sell their property and leave the territory. Those Hindus left behind were forbidden to perform many of their religious ceremonies and ordered to attend preaching on the Christian doctrine. An edict instructed that all public posts should be reserved for Christians. Orphans (defined as children whose fathers had died but whose Indian mothers were often still living) were seized by the Church and brought up as Christians. In response, Hindus deserted Portuguese India en masse.[52]

Those who remained were forced to convert to Christianity. In 1550 only one-fifth of Goa's population had converted, but by 1650 two-thirds were Catholic.[53] One priest at least was under no illusions as to the sincerity of these conversions. He wrote a despairing letter to his leader, Ignatio Loyola [sic], in Rome in which he acknowledged that "The people of this country who become Christians do so purely for temporal advantage . . . Slaves of the moors and Hindus seek baptism in order to secure their manumission at the hands of the Portuguese. Others do so to get protection from tyrants, or for the sake of a turban, a shirt, or some other trifle they covet, or to escape being hanged, or to be able to associate with Christian women. The man who embraces the faith from honest conviction is regarded as a fool. They are baptized whenever or wherever they express a wish for the Sacrament, without any instruction, and many revert to paganism."[54]

For those at the bottom of the Hindu social hierarchy, conversion was a means of escaping the oppressions of the caste system. The majority of converts were drawn from the downtrodden tribal communities, the lower castes, and untouchables. The Christian principle of equality before God appeared to offer them a means of improving their social and economic status. There were also a variety of incentives: widows and orphans who converted were entitled to inherit their husband's or father's property; the Church provided converts with food (including a Christmas lunch), clothes, dowries, medicines, and money to finance funerals.[55] The higher castes converted to protect their privileges and social status. They also found that, by bringing them closer to their new European rulers, conversion opened up new job opportunities.

After the initial success in terms of the number of conversions, the Inquisition found it hard to enforce its rule. Each time the edicts of the Church were enforced, the mass desertion of the Indian inhabitants from the Portuguese territories left the Europeans short of agricultural laborers, artisans, craftsmen, and sailors. The contradictions of Portuguese rule were evident in the letter of one official who reported thankfully that, despite the activity of the missions around the port of Bassein, they had still been able to recruit sailors for the Portuguese ships. In the vital areas of trade and finance, the Portuguese relied heavily on Hindu merchants, money lenders, and tax collectors. Even the important pepper procurement contracts were often handled by members of the elite Saraswat Brahman community.[56] The Church complained frequently (in 1559, 1582, and 1591 at least) that "many important government posts were held by Hindus even though this was not royally sanctioned." But for the sake of the economy the Portuguese were forced to make numerous exceptions to the law or to turn a blind eye to the religious convictions of their partners in trade and finance.

Among the converts, the battle to inculcate Christian habits and establish a Christian way of life was slow and difficult. The fact that for almost 200 years the Church regularly issued edicts banning the same Hindu practices demonstrates only partial effectiveness. In the 1580s a despairing order noted that "many Hindus keep reverting to their old rituals," and again in 1633 the Church complained that converts were still to be found worshipping idols. As late as 1736 the Inquisition issued a very lengthy edict outlawing hundreds of Hindu practices that had already been banned in the Portuguese territories in the sixteenth and seventeenth centuries. The list revealed that many of the Indian converts continued to revere the cow and to spread cow dung on their floors to purify them, and to observe Hindu strictures governing the preparation and consumption of food. The Church ineffectually reminded its subjects that they were not supposed to avoid pork and beef, neither were they to "bathe in their clothes before entering [the] kitchen for cooking food, in the manner which is customary among the Hindus." Nor were they supposed to cook their rice "without salt, adding salt subsequently according to taste, as the Hindus are accustomed to do."[57]

Goan villagers conducted a clandestine resistance to the Catholic Church. Although the majority of village temples were destroyed and replaced by churches, the villagers rescued the statues of the gods once resident in them. The deities were smuggled over the border to villages in the neighboring provinces where they were reestablished in new temples. The links between the gods and their old villages still survive today. Some of the deities have since returned to their original villages, others are taken on an annual visit to their old homes. Both Catholics and Hindus frequently visit the temples of the escaped gods when looking for advice or solace.[58]

In the face of often brutal coercion, the Goans were able to retain aspects of their Hindu culture and identity within the Christian framework.[59] To the frustration of the priests, the Indian converts tended to embrace Catholicism as a form of Hinduism. The Church was often able to eradicate some of the pagan trappings, such as the ceremonial use of betel and areca nuts, but it was unable to suppress many of the actual rituals. A Jesuit letter described how recent converts in the parish of Divar insisted that the priest should take on the role of the Hindu astrologer who blessed the rice harvest each year. The villagers arrived at the church carrying a banner with the names of Jesus and St. Paul on it and laid the sheaves of rice on the steps of the altar.[60] Similarly, the Hindu mixture of milk, turmeric, coconut oil, and rice powder that was used to bathe the bride and groom at weddings was replaced with more acceptable coconut milk. Crosses of palm leaves substituted for the betel leaves and areca nuts that were usually placed underneath the new *choolas* (stoves) at a wedding.[61] High-caste converts continued to socialize and marry within their castes, and they maintained their caste names, adding them after their new Christian names and surnames.

Nevertheless, by the nineteenth century the majority of the Goan population attended Mass on Sundays, wore European clothes, shaved their beards, and lived in Portuguese-style bungalows. Most strikingly, they drank alcohol and happily ate pork and beef. Indeed, the stranger approaching the town of Panjim (new Goa) in the 1850s could instantly tell that it was a Christian town "from the multitude and variety of the filthy feeding hogs, that infest the streets."[62] The adoption of the Portuguese attitude toward meat is not particularly surprising among the lower-caste converts, who would have been lax about food restrictions and, even before conversion, would not necessarily have found the consumption of meat abhorrent. But what is extraordinary is that it was the wealthier Catholics with an upper-caste background who placed the greatest emphasis on the consumption of pork and beef. This was due to the fact that within their own society they were now regarded as outcastes. The only way in which they could hold on to their high status was to associate themselves as closely as possible with the Portuguese rulers. Hence, they not only embraced the faith of their colonizers, but also wholeheartedly embraced the Portuguese language, education, clothes, and diet. Thus, in Goa a meal of pork or beef was surrounded by an aura of prestige.[63] Although the Inquisition had been dismantled in India in 1812, it had finally won the battle.

Not only did the Portuguese persuade their Christian converts to eat pork, they taught them how to cook it. The most famous of all Goan dishes is undoubtedly vindaloo, now a standard dish in almost every Indian restaurant: the curry that (until the advent of the even hotter phal)

British men would choose after a few lagers in the pub to prove their machismo; and that British 1998 World Cup football fans included in their chant, alongside cups of tea, knitting, and cheddar, as a symbol of Englishness.

The British discovered vindaloo in 1797 when they invaded Goa. By then the British, Dutch, and French had joined the Portuguese in India and were jostling for control of the lucrative spice trade. The British were worried that the French would use the homeland of these fellow Catholics to launch an attack on British bases in southern India. During their 17-year-long occupation of Portuguese India, the British discovered the delights of Goan cookery. They were relieved to find that the Catholic cooks were free from the irritating caste or religious restrictions that prevented Hindus and Muslims from cooking beef and pork and, when the British left in 1813, they took their Goan cooks with them.[64] In this way vindaloo made its way to British India, and from there back to Britain.

Vindaloo is normally regarded as an Indian curry, but in fact it is a Goan adaptation of the Portuguese dish *carne de vinho e alhos*, or meat cooked in wine vinegar and garlic.[65] The name vindaloo is simply a garbled pronunciation of *vinho e alhos*. The Portuguese particularly savored the sour, but fruity, taste of meat marinated and cooked in wine vinegar.[66] When they arrived in India, however, they found that Indians did not make vinegar, though a similar sour-hot taste was produced by south Indian cooks using a combination of tamarind and black pepper. Some ingenious Franciscan priests are said to have solved the problem by manufacturing vinegar from coconut toddy, the alcoholic drink fermented from the sap of the palm tree. This, combined with tamarind pulp and plenty of garlic, satisfied the Portuguese cooks. To this basic sauce they added a garam masala of black pepper, cinnamon, and cloves, some of the spices in search of which Vasco da Gama had made his way to the Malabar Coast in 1498. But the key ingredient, which gave bite to the granular sauce of vindaloo, was the chilli. Like their Spanish counterparts in South America, the Portuguese in India had developed a liking for the fiery taste of the chilli pepper and they used it in excessive quantities in a vindaloo. Some recipes call for as many as 20 red chillies.

Recipe for Vindaloo or Bindaloo—a Portuguese Karhi from
W. H. Dawe, The Wife's Help to Indian Cookery,
a British Indian cookbook

The best Vindaloo is prepared in mustard-oil ... Beef and pork, or duck, can be made into this excellent curry. The following ingredients are employed in its preparation: Ghee, six chittacks,* lard or oil may be used; garlic ground, one tablespoonful; garlic, bruised, one tablespoonful; ginger, ground, one tablespoonful; chillies, ground, two teaspoonful; coriander-seed, one teaspoonful; coriander-seed, roasted and ground, half a teaspoonful; bay leaves, or Tej-path, two or three; peppercorns, quarter-chittack; cloves, half a dozen roasted and ground; cardamoms, half a dozen roasted and ground; cinnamon, half a dozen sticks; vinegar, quarter-pint. Take a seer of beef or pork, and cut it into large square pieces, and steep them in vinegar with salt and the ground condiments given above, for a whole night. Warm the Ghee, lard, or mustard-oil, with the ingredients in which it has been soaking over-night and add the meat with peppercorns and bay leaves, and allow the whole to simmer slowly over a gentle fire for a couple of hours, or until the meat is quite tender. When preparing pork into vindaloo, omit the cloves, cardamoms, and cinnamon.[67]

* One chittack was equivalent to about 1 ounce.

In fact, chillies became central ingredients in Goan cuisine. Almost all fish and vegetable recipes, sausages and pork dishes contain them. Many of these were adaptations of Portuguese recipes. Thus, a Portuguese sorpotel of pork meat, offal, and blood was made more piquant with the addition of toddy vinegar and spices. Enthusiastic about their discovery of these new ingredients, south Indian cooks created *ambot-tik* (meaning sour and hot) made of mackerel, eel, and shark cooked with red chilli, black pepper, tamarind, vinegar, and dried fruit peel.[68] The result of this culinary interchange was a pleasing fusion of Portuguese ingredients (pork)—some of which were derived from Arab influences on Iberian cookery (dried fruit)—and Portuguese techniques (marinating and cooking in vinegar), with the south Indian spice mixtures, sour tamarind paste, shredded coconut, and coconut milk. Added into this already cosmopolitan blend were the recently discovered foodstuffs from the New World such as the chilli. Thus Goan dishes unite in their fiery sauces the culinary histories of three continents: Europe, Asia, and the Americas.

Chillies were only one of many new foods that the Portuguese brought to India from the New World. The turkey, for instance, was viewed as a great curiosity. On the orders of the Emperor Jahangir, one was purchased in Goa and brought to the Mughal court where an exquisite image of this peculiar bird was painted. Turkey meat did not, however, become popular until the British arrived.

More successful were New World fruits. The Portuguese introduced papayas, custard apples, and guavas from the Americas, all of which have since been incorporated into the Indian diet. But the most popular was the pineapple. Columbus came upon this fruit on his second voyage (1493) to the West Indies. The Spanish came to love pineapples. When Oviedo produced his *Natural History of the Indies* (1535), he enthused that "to taste it is so appetising a thing, so delicate, that words fail to give it its true praise for this . . . most beautiful [of] fruits I have seen wherever I have been in the whole world." Travelers to America were so captivated by the taste that they took fruits and plants with them to other countries and the Portuguese are said to have introduced the pineapples to India in 1550.[69] By the time Jahangir came to the throne in 1605, they were being grown at many of the European ports. As we have seen in the previous chapter, he was particularly fond of fruit and he had some pineapple bushes planted at Agra to supply his table.[70] Pineapples are now a familiar sight in Indian markets, but they are regarded with suspicion by many Kanarese. New foodstuffs are generally categorized using the Ayurvedic categories of hot or cold foods and integrated into the diet accordingly. Fruits are usually classified as cool, due to their sweetness. But, despite its sweet taste, the pineapple tends to be regarded as hot and dangerous because it is grown in arid areas with the application of fertilizers, which are seen as heating.

Kanarese villagers who have had the opportunity to taste a pineapple often claim to suffer from a sore mouth afterward.[71]

Although the Portuguese almost certainly introduced tomatoes and potatoes into India, these foods were not integrated into the Indian culinary world until the British showed their own cooks how to use them. Much more successful was the cashew nut. Cashew-nut trees still grow around Goa and further south along the Keralan coast. South Indians use the nuts whole with shrimps in their seafood pilaus, grind them to thicken sauces, powder them to make a succulent milky sweet called *kaju katli*, which is decorated with silver leaf, or crush the stems of the cashew plant to make a juice out of which they brew an extremely potent spirit called *feni*.[72] The backstreets of Panjim are dotted with dingy *feni* bars, where old men sit sipping this heady brew, listening to the cricket on the radio.

Of all the foods they introduced to India, chillies are undoubtedly the most important Portuguese culinary legacy. And yet, even at the end of the seventeenth century, chillies were still largely confined to the south of India. Two centuries after the Portuguese first landed at Calicut, the chilli had still not reached the northern plains of Hindustan. It arrived with the Marathas, a wild and unruly group of people from the Deccan in central India, who contributed to the decline of both the Mughals and the Portuguese. The Marathas had a reputation for being as restless and dangerous as the craggy mountainous country they inhabited. An English visitor to the area in the seventeenth century described them as "naked Starved Rascals; . . . accustomed to Fare Hard, Journey Fast, and take little Pleasure."[73] Akbar subdued the Marathas in the 1590s, but 80 years later they overthrew their Mughal masters and began to pillage the lands bordering their territory. The last great Mughal emperor, Aurangzeb, wasted many years of his life fighting the Marathas. He referred to their leader Shivaji as "his Mountain Rat." The Maratha cavalry would swoop down on the Mughals' long baggage trains and heavy guns, inflict a great deal of damage, and then disappear back into the mountains.[74] By 1735, the Marathas had encroached as far as Malwa in central India and they continued to rule large swathes of central and southern India until the British defeated them in 1818.

A north Indian scholar and poet argued that the Marathas' nature was "dry and hot" because they "put hot chillies in everything they eat." This custom, he claimed, accounted for their warlike and determined character. In contrast, it was said that the Mughals, accustomed to a diet of rice pilaus, almond sweetmeats, and central Asian fruit, had become soft and ineffectual. There was some truth in this observation. When they were posted to the Deccan, the Mughal officers were appalled by the life of tough military hardship they were forced to lead in the hill forts. They longed for their city lives, for lazing around on cushions, drinking wine, taking opium, feasting on pilau, listening to flowery poetry, and dallying with dancing girls. One Englishman commented with disgust that they would "miss of a Booty rather than a Dinner." Their bodies, he stated decisively, were "unfit for such barren and uneasy Places."[75] They were no match for the Marathas with their bellies on fire with chilli juice.

Chillies are still regarded as a potent food. The Jains classify them as a *rajasic* foodstuff. In contrast to *sattvic* foods such as cereals and pulses, fruits and vegetables, which are thought to encourage moderate behavior and feelings of peace, *rajasic* foods are said to induce anger and hatred.[76]

The Marathas were as much trouble to the Portuguese, who were responsible for introducing the spice that supposedly nurtured their angry natures. During the seventeenth century the Marathas wreaked havoc on the Portuguese settlements. By 1749 the Portuguese only had four territories left: Dui, Daman, Bassein, and Goa.[77] Cochin had been captured by the Dutch and the British had effectively wrested away control of the spice trade. Goa itself went into decline as its inhabitants were ravaged by epidemics of malaria and cholera, and by the mid-nineteenth century, the town was abandoned. The depleted population moved to the nearby settlement of Panjim, to leave a small community of monks to watch the grand houses, the cathedral, and churches, which gradually disintegrated into ruins. But while the Marathas helped to bring the Portuguese to their knees, they were also taking the Portuguese legacy of the chilli pepper with them to the northern plains of India. The poet who attributed their dry, hot natures to their chilli-rich diet also noted that "during the last ten or twenty years, ever since these people spread over Northern India, the inhabitants of that region have learnt to use hot chillies, a practice which was very rare previously."[78]

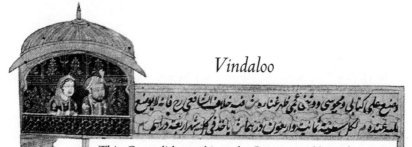

Vindaloo

This Goan dish combines the Portuguese liking for pork marinated, and then stewed, in vinegar with a south Indian spice mixture and lots of chillies. Many recipes for vindaloo call for as many as 20 fresh red chillies. The spiciness of vindaloo is a matter of taste. This recipe is hot but not eye-wateringly so. If you like very hot food, feel free to add more of either the dried or the fresh red chillies, or more black peppercorns. If you deseed the chillies first they will be less piquant; blending the red chillies with a little water in a mixer before adding them to the paste will increase their potency. Vindaloo is traditionally made with pork but the British liked it best with duck and so do I. If you can obtain palm vinegar or jaggery, these will add a particularly Goan flavor to the dish. Serves 3–4.

2–4 breasts of duck (or 1½ lb. stewing pork), cubed

Paste
2 large dried red chillies
1 teaspoon cumin seeds
1 teaspoon poppy seeds
4–6 whole cloves
10 black peppercorns
½ teaspoon turmeric
2 fresh red chillies, finely chopped
(or puréed in a blender with a little water)
1 tablespoon palm or wine vinegar
1 tablespoon tamarind paste
6 large cloves of garlic, mashed
¾ in. piece of fresh ginger, peeled and finely grated

In a cast-iron pan dry-roast the dried chillies, cumin seeds, poppy seeds, cloves, peppercorns, and turmeric for 1–2 minutes. Grind these spices into a fine powder in a coffee grinder. Put in a bowl with the fresh red chillies, wine vinegar, tamarind, ginger, and garlic and mix to a paste.

Add the meat and mix again. Make sure all the pieces of duck (or pork) are coated in the marinade. Cover and leave in the fridge overnight.

Sauce
4–6 tablespoons vegetable oil
1 teaspoon black mustard seeds
¾ in. cinnamon stick
1 large onion, finely chopped
1¼ cups water
salt to taste
pinch of jaggery (palm sugar) or soft brown sugar
a few curry leaves, crumbled

The next day, heat the oil in a large pan and when hot add the mustard seeds and cinnamon stick.

When the mustard seeds begin to pop, add the onions and fry over a medium heat until they begin to brown. Add the meat and its marinade and sauté until all the pieces are browned. Add the water, and a pinch of salt to taste. Cover, turn down the heat, and simmer for about 10 minutes (if duck, longer if pork).

Remove the lid, keep the heat very low and simmer gently until the meat is tender (about half an hour with duck, an hour with pork) and the sauce is thick (you may need to add a little more water to prevent burning).

When the meat is tender add the jaggery or sugar, the crumbled curry leaves, and simmer for another 3 minutes. Then serve.

Bebinca

This is the Goan pancake-layer cake adapted from a Portuguese recipe that used wheat flour and milk. It is laborious to make but the effect of the layered cake is striking. It should really be made over a fire fueled with coconut husks but a modern grill is a sufficiently effective substitute. Serves 10–15.

2⅓ lb. caster sugar (or jaggery if you can get it)
3 cups coconut milk
20 egg yolks
¼ lb. rice flour
½ teaspoon grated nutmeg
1 teaspoon cardamom essence (or about ⅛ teaspoon of cardamom powder)
1 cup melted butter

Mix the caster sugar with the coconut milk until it is dissolved.

Beat the egg yolks until creamy and mix the flour into them thoroughly until the mixture is smooth.

Add the egg yolks and flour to the mixture of coconut milk and sugar, along with the nutmeg and cardamom.

Heat the grill. Take a deep pan, about 4¾ in. in diameter, and put a tablespoon of melted butter in it. Place it under the grill. When it is hot take it out and pour enough batter into the pan to cover the bottom to the depth of about ⅝ in. Put under the grill for about 2 minutes and let it cook until it is deep brown in color.

Remove from the grill, put a dessert spoon of melted butter over the cooked layer, and heat under the grill. Then pour over enough batter to cover the first layer, to the depth of about ¼ in. Repeat this process until all the batter and melted butter has been used up. Make sure each layer of batter is the same thickness. The final layer should be of melted butter.

When cool, turn out on to a dish, keeping the first layer face down. Decorate with a few slivers of toasted almonds. Cut into slices and serve.

Yash Muthanna's appam

Although this is a complicated recipe I have included it
because the soft rice breads of southern Indian are not very
well known in the West. Appams are very good eaten with
fresh chutney, or dipped in warm milk flavored with almonds
and cardamoms. They also come in handy for mopping up
runny coconut-milk sauces. The idea is to aim for a thick soft
center and a thin crispy outer edge. As a child Yash Muthanna,
whose recipe this is, was persuaded to eat up her appam by the
addition of an egg that was cracked whole into the center of
the appam and became embedded in the mixture as it cooked.
Serves 4–6.

1 lb. rice
½ lb. cooked rice
½ lb. grated coconut
½ teaspoon baking powder
2 teaspoons sugar
a little milk
a little oil

One day in advance, soak the rice for at least 2 hours. Drain,
saving some of the water. Mix the soaked rice with the
cooked rice and ½ lb. of grated coconut. Add
some of the saved water and grind together in
a blender to make a paste. If necessary add more
of the water, until the paste has a batterlike
consistency. Cover and set this batter aside
overnight.

The next day, add to the mixture the baking powder, sugar, and enough milk to thin the batter.

Take a nonstick pan with a rounded base (or a wok). Smear with a tiny amount of a nontasting oil. Heat to a high temperature.

Coat the sides of the wok with the batter, using one large serving spoonful at a time. Pour ¼ of a serving spoonful straight into the center of the wok. Put the lid on tightly and cook for 2 minutes.

The edges of each appam should be brown, crispy, and very thin; the middle should be fat and soft and absorbent. (The sugar should help you to achieve the brown edges as it caramelizes.)

Remove the appam to a warm plate and repeat the process until the batter has been used up.

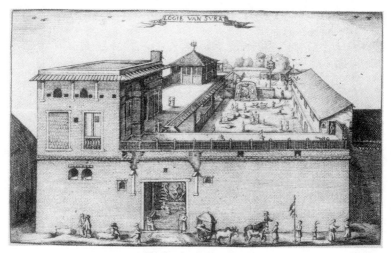

The Dutch factory at Surat

4

Korma: East India Company Merchants, Temples, and the Nawabs of Lucknow

VERY DAY AT twelve noon the East India Company merchants living at the English factory in Surat filed into the great hall and sat down at the dining table in order of their seniority. A servant brought round "a large Silver Ewer and Bason" and everyone washed their hands. In 1689 John Ovington, chaplain on board an East Indiaman that had sailed into the Indian port, joined the merchants at their dining table and savored the fragrant Mughal specialities that were served. There were pilaus of "rice boil'd so artificially that every grain lies singly without being added together, with Spices intermixt, and a boil'd Fowl in the middle"; "dumpoked" chicken, a rich and greasy dish that involved stuffing the bird with raisins and almonds and then baking it in butter in a tight-fitting pot; and beef and mutton "Cabob . . . sprinkled with Salt and Pepper, and dipt with Oil and Garlick" roasted "on a Spit, with Sweet Herbs put between every piece." Ovington observed that "several hundreds a Year are expended upon their daily Provisions which are sumptuous enough for the Entertainment of any Person of Eminence in the Kingdom."[1]

In 1689, when Ovington dined with the English merchants, Surat was the main port for the largely landlocked Mughal Empire, then ruled by the Emperor Aurangzeb. It was also an important hub in the European East India trade. By then the Portuguese monopoly of the spice trade had been broken by the Dutch, the British, and the French, all of whom had established factories in the town. These storehouses and living quarters were known by this name, as the representatives of the East Indian trading companies were called factors.

The Dutch were the first to capture a share of the lucrative East India trade from the Portuguese. Their long relationship with Spain (which ruled the Netherlands until 1581) and Portugal gave them an advantage. The Dutch merchant fleet had always played an important part in distributing the goods brought into Europe through the port of Lisbon. And men like Jan Huyghen van Linschoten, who had worked in the service of the Portuguese in India, provided detailed knowledge of their sea routes and trading practices. The first Dutch fleet sailed for Bantam on the island of Java in 1595 and returned loaded with pepper two years later. The Verenigde Oostindische Compagnie was founded in 1602.

The English were not far behind their Dutch rivals. A group of merchants gathered together a list of investors in 1599, and in 1600 the English East India Company was granted a royal charter. The next year four ships set sail for the spice islands of the Pacific. The voyage was successful and 11 men were left behind to establish an English factory at Bantam and gather together a cargo of pepper ready for the arrival of the next fleet.

Between 1604 and 1613 the British concentrated their efforts around Bantam, but it quickly became clear that bases in India would prove useful. The Europeans brought out broadcloth, woollens, tin, lead, copper, and some "fancy goods," such as swords and mirrors, to trade for spices. But the only really good currency were Spanish *reales de plato* (pieces of eight) that they bought in the European currency markets. However, they realized that the inhabitants of the spice islands were eager to trade cloves, pepper, and nutmeg in exchange for Indian textiles.

The Dutch had already (in 1608) established a factory on India's east coast at Masulipatnam in the territory of the King of Golconda. Here they were able to buy fine chintz that they then traded in Bantam. The British joined them at Masulipatnam in 1611. But they also wanted to break into the market at Surat. This was the hub for trade in "rich Silks and Gold Stuffs curiously wrought with birds and Flowers; . . . brocades, velvets, taffetas," exquisite muslins, chintzes, and calicoes, produced in the Gujarati hinterland. Here raw silk and carpets arrived from Persia, and a brisk trade in rhubarb and asafetida was conducted across the Arabian Sea. The British ship *The Hector* touched at Surat in 1608 to allow William Hawkins to disembark. Equipped with a letter from James I, he set off for the Mughal capital of Agra, where he petitioned Jahangir to grant the company a firman that would give them favorable terms of trade and allow them to establish factories in the Mughal territories.[2]

Hawkins was popular with the emperor. He had probably been a merchant in the Levant, and he was therefore able to speak Turkish. This meant that he could communicate with Jahangir without an interpreter. The emperor made him a permanent ambassador to the court and granted him a generous allowance. Hawkins settled into the life of a courtier, adopted Mughal dress, married an Armenian lady, and is reported to have "used altogether the custome of the Moores . . . both in his meate and drinke and other customes." But he was out of his depth when it came to intriguing at the Mughal court. He eventually fell out of favor, ostensibly for having been caught in the presence of the emperor with alcohol on his breath. Disgraced, he set off for Britain without having obtained a firman for the company.[3]

He was succeeded by Sir Thomas Roe, who, in contrast to Hawkins, was determined to preserve his English habits. Roe spent vast sums on suits of English clothes in crimson, sea green, and white damask, trimmed with gold and silver lace. His entourage wore green outfits with red taffeta cloaks and his chaplain, Edward Terry, was expected to walk abroad in a "long black Cassock." Terry commented with some humor that "the Colours and fashion of our garments were so different from theirs, that we needed not, wheresoever we were to invite spectators to take notice of us." At his house Roe dined at a table and chairs from silver-plated dishes and, although he kept an Indian cook on his staff, his main chef was English.[4] Although Roe was careful to preserve his dignity, he was no more successful than Hawkins in persuading Jahangir to grant the East India Company a firman. However, even before his arrival in India, the British

European trading posts in India:
The extent of the East India Company's
territory in 1804 ▦ and 1856 ▒

0   100   200   300   400   500 miles
0   200   400   600   800 km

KASHMIR

R. Indus

Delhi

RAJPUTANA

Karachi

Agra · OUDH

Lucknow

MALWA

r. Ganges Patna

Ahmadabad
Cambay

MARATHA

GUJARAT
Surat

STATES

Calcutta

Diu Daman
Bassein
Bombay

NIZAM'S
HYDERABAD

· Hyderabad

Arabian

Goa

Masulipatnam

Bay of

Sea

Bengal

MYSORE
Calicut

· Madras

Pondicherry

MALABAR COAST

COROMANDEL COAST

N

Cochin

CEYLON

Colombo

INDIAN   OCEAN

had gained an important foothold. In 1614, the Mughal governor of Surat, persuaded by the British defeat of several Portuguese ships, allowed them to establish a factory there.

In the spice islands, constant skirmishes with the Dutch made life difficult and dangerous for the British factors. But in India the English East India Company gradually put down firm roots. The popularity of Indian textiles in Britain shifted the company's focus toward India as the trade in cottons and calicoes began to overtake that in spices. By the time John Ovington visited the town, two or three British ships were arriving at Surat every year. Besides Surat and Masulipatnam, the British had established a number of other factories round the Indian coastline.[5] Indeed, Surat's heyday was virtually at an end when Ovington visited. Attacks by the Marathas on the town meant that the British moved the center of their west coast operations to Bombay. They were followed there by many of the wealthy Indian merchants.[6]

Before sailing to Surat, Ovington's ship had briefly visited Bombay. The town had been given to the company by Charles II, who received it in 1661 as part of the dowry of his Portuguese bride, Catherine of Braganza. At Bombay, the company had built a fort and a "barracks or soldier's apartment in imitation of Chelsea College." A half-finished church stood nearby and a small kitchen garden. However, the dominating feature was the British cemetery. In the short time that Ovington's ship was there they buried 20 out of 24 passengers, and 15 sailors. Another visitor commented that the British who lived there walked "in Charnel-houses, the Climate being extremely Unhealthy; ... whence follows Fluxes, Dropsy, Scurvy, Barbiers [elephantiasis] ... Gout, Stone, Malignant and Putrid fevers, which are Endemial Diseases: Among the worst of these, Fool Rack [arrack] ... and Foul Women may be reckoned."[7]

On the east coast the British moved their main base to Madras in 1640. It was not a sensible choice as offshore sandbanks, which often shifted their position, and a rolling surf made it extremely dangerous for shipping. But it was said that one of the factors favored the site as his Indian mistress lived nearby. The British built a fort (St. George) and a small town, populated mainly by cloth weavers, grew up next to the factory. Further east, in Bengal, the British, who had been trading there since the 1650s, settled for Calcutta as their base around 1690. Here, a collection of bungalows that looked like "thatched hovels," a stables, a hospital, a barracks, and a powder magazine could all be found huddled next to the imposing Fort William. Malaria was a problem, probably due to the "pools of stinking water" that gathered around the settlement.[8]

The three as yet unpromising settlements of Bombay, Madras, and Calcutta, were eventually to become the power centers of British rule in India. But the seventeenth-century merchants were uninterested in empire building. They were too busy making money, for the company and for themselves. During the busy season between September and November, when the East Indiamen were able to sail, the factory courtyards were transformed into bustling stock exchanges. The Indian middlemen, who the merchants employed to contract the weavers, would come in to negotiate with the British in corrupted Portuguese. The factors were kept occupied checking the quality of the cloth, loading it on to the ships and drawing up new contracts. Besides conducting the company's trade, the merchants engaged in small-scale commerce on their own behalfs. They used "country" (meaning Indian) ships to ferry musk, spices, cottons, and carpets across the Bay of Bengal or the Arabian Sea. Those East India merchants who survived the diseases that killed most men within two years were able to amass large fortunes.[9]

A description of life in the factory at Surat was written by Albert Mandelslo, who had been educated as a page at the court of the German Duke of Holstein. In 1638, the duke sent an embassy to Persia in order to try and find a way of carrying on the overland silk trade. Mandelslo was allowed to accompany the duke's ambassadors. In Persia, he met two English merchants whose tales of the Indies inspired him to continue traveling. He set off with three German servants and a Persian guide and interpreter. In April, he took an English boat across the Arabian Sea to Surat, where he was invited to stay with the English in their factory.

Korma

The factors led a collegiate life. Divine service, which everyone was
expected to attend, was held twice a day, at six in the morning and eight at
night, and three times on a Sunday. After prayers the merchants spent the
mornings working. Mandelslo commented that there was "no person . . .
but had his particular Function, and their certain hours assigned them as
well for work as recreation." All the factors took their meals together in
a "great Hall," and Mandelslo, like Ovington 50 years later, noted that
they "kept a great Table, of about fifteen or sixteen dishes of Meat, besides
the desert." Every evening after supper "the President, his Second, the
principal Merchant, the Minister and my self" retired to "a great open
Gallery [to take] the coolness of the Sea Air."

The merchants spent their leisure time in the Mughal fashion. "The
English have a fair Garden without the City, wither we constantly went on
Sundayes, after Sermon, and sometimes also on other dayes of the week."
Mandelslo described how they entertained themselves by shooting at
butts, eating "Collation[s] of Fruit and Preserves . . . bathing in a Tank
or Cistern which had five foot water, where some Dutch Gentlewomen
serv'd and entertain's us with much civility." The merchants also whiled
away their time playing board games, under the mellow spell of the
hookah (hubble-bubble pipe), or watching pretty Indian dancing girls,
who sometimes offered sexual favors to their admiring audience.

There was always plenty of arrack punch to drink. This was the Indian
schnapps or fire water that befuddled the Emperor Jahangir and left him
incapable of feeding himself. It was otherwise known as "Fool Rack" and
was viewed with disapproval by some as it fell "upon the nerves . . . causeth
shaking of the hands in those that drink a little too much of it, and . . .
casts them into incurable maladies." Despite its dangers, it was "drunk in
drams by the Europeans." At an entertainment to "commemorate the day
they left England and their wives," Mandelslo noticed that in drinking their
wives' healths several of the merchants "made their advantage of this meeting,
to get more than they could well carry away." They got drunk on "Palepuntz,
which is a kind of drink consisting of Aqua vitae [arrack], Rose-water,
juice of Citrons and Sugar."[10] Punch, the English name for this cocktail is
said to be derived from the Hindi word *panch*, meaning five, because the
drink usually combined five ingredients. But the Hindi pronunciation of

panch does not correspond with the seventeenth-century pronunciation of the word as "poonch." It is more likely that East Indian merchants picked up their taste for hard liquor mixed with milk, sugar, lime juice, and spices, as well as its name, on the voyage out to India when sailors were handed out a daily allowance of liquor from a cask known as the puncheon.[11]

Recipe for Milk Punch from the papers of Matthew Campbell,
Lieutenant in the Indian Army in the 1820s

Soak the rinds of thirty Limes in two Bottles of arrack for twelve hours—drain off this liquor, add ten bottles of arrack and six of Brandy or Rum, to this add two and half bottles of lime juice, eight nutmegs grated—twelve lb. of moist sugar—eight quarts of new milk boiling and 14 quarts of boiling [water]... The whole to be mixed in some large vessel and stirred about for half an hour and when perfectly cool, to be strained thro' flannel and bottled off.[12]

One habit that they did acquire from the Indians was chewing paan. Newcomers to India were often horrified to observe that "almost everybody was spitting something red as blood." This was the juice of paan that "the Indians champ[ed] and chaw[ed] on all day long." A little lime and some spices were added to a small areca nut, which was then wrapped up in a betel leaf, and popped into the mouth and chewed. The Mughals picked up this habit from their Hindustani subjects and the company merchants also became addicted to the grainy and astringent bite of paan. Moreover, it was said to preserve the teeth, strengthen the stomach, comfort the brain, and cure tainted breath.[13] It was also supposed to increase sexual pleasure, and a Persian ambassador suggested that betel chewing accounted for the "numerous harem" of 700 princesses and concubines belonging to the southern King of Vijayanagara.[14]

The mixture of Mughal and British habits that characterized the East India merchants' lives was evident at their dining tables. According to Ovington, "that nothing may be wanting to please the Curiosity of every Palate at the times of Eating, an English, Portuguese and an Indian Cook, are all entertain'd to dress the Meat in different ways for the gratification of every Stomach."[15] The British in India consumed stupendous amounts of meat. A surgeon who visited Surat in the 1670s calculated that in one month more animals were killed to supply the British table than were generally slaughtered for the entire year to feed the Muslims.[16] Seventeenth-century India abounded with game and British visitors were delighted by the diverse kinds of meat, which were plentiful and "because many of the Natives eat no kind of flesh at all . . . bought there at such easy [cheap] rates, as if they were not worth the valuing."[17]

Just as the English cook produced the kind of fare that was commonplace in wealthy seventeenth-century English households—roasting saddles of venison and preparing game pies—the Indian cook prepared the staple dishes eaten by wealthy Indian Muslims. In fact, during this period the Islamic and Christian worlds shared a similar culinary repertoire of "thick purées, lots of spices, sweet and sour sauces, cooked vegetables . . . warmed wines" and sugar as a flavoring in savory as well as sweet dishes.[18] At the Mughal banquet attended by the English chaplain Edward Terry in 1616, he praised most highly a dish that "the *Portugals* call *Mangee Real*, Food for a King." This was a concoction of breast of chicken stewed in a mixture of ground rice and almonds, sweetened with "*Rose-water* and *Sugar-Candy*, and scented with *Amber-Greece*." In fact, it closely resembled the European invalid's dish blancmange, made from chicken, rice flour, sugar, and almond milk.[19] It is possible that *Mangee Real* was the product of an exchange of recipes between Portuguese and Mughal cooks.

The power of the Mughal emperors, and the spread of their empire, ensured that Mughlai cuisine dominated in northern India. The Mughlai repertoire remained virtually untouched, however, by the distinctive techniques and recipes of southern India.[20] In the south during the sixteenth and seventeenth centuries there were a number of alternative centers of Indian culinary development. Among them were the Vaisnavite Hindu temples.

Vaisnavite Hindu temples acted as "landholder, employer . . . bank, school, museum . . . hospital, [and] theatre" to their surrounding areas. Towns sprung up next to the temples, populated by priests, donors, and temple servants. The shrines were often set upon hilltops with long stairways leading to them, up which the pilgrims filed.[21] These pathways, as well as the walls of the buildings on either side of them, acted, among other things, as stony recipe books. Men of influence and wealth would donate money, land, cowsheds, and food to the temples. The details of the donation were then inscribed on the stone tablets that paved and lined the way to the shrines. The tablets preserved not only the generosity of the donor but also the culinary arts of the temple cooks. Reading them today, it is possible to trace the development of a sophisticated vegetarian cuisine in the temple kitchens.[22] Alongside the name of the donor and the amounts of food he had presented, the details of its preparation were sometimes given. At the temple at Little Conjeeveram, one of the many stone tablets records that a private individual made an offering of rice and vegetables. It details that he also donated large quantities of salt, pepper, mustard, cumin, and sugar to add flavor. These were accompanied by plantains and curds, as well as enormous quantities of sugar candy and cardamoms with which to make rice cakes. Everything was provided for, right down to the firewood to light the cooking fires, and areca nuts and betel leaves to make paan to chew after the meal.[23]

Although they worked with a limited list of ingredients, the temple cooks produced dishes of variety and imagination, including numerous types of rice dishes, sauces, sweets, savories, and drinks. The food was first placed before the gods and then, once they had metaphorically eaten their fill, it was distributed throughout the community. The sauces and milky drinks, which would have been messy to divide and subdivide, were used to feed the priests and their assistants, as well as vast numbers of pilgrims who flocked to the temples each day. Today, the kitchens that serve the temple dining halls preserve these ancient vegetarian culinary traditions. Many cooks working in restaurants in south India learn their trade in the vast kitchens of the temples. At the Udipi temple, pilgrims enjoy meals of thick lentil soup mixed with white pumpkin pieces poached in tamarind water. The dhals are flavored with red chillies, ground chickpeas, coriander, fenugreek, mustard seeds, and curry leaves fried in hot oil. The food is prepared in huge pots and served on banana leaves on the floor of the long dining hall. After each shift of hungry pilgrims has been served and vacated the hall, the sacred temple cows are let into the room to eat up the banana leaves. Once the cows have finished, the dining hall is given a quick washdown and the next shift of pilgrims is ushered in.[24]

Another temple speciality was sweets. The Mughal revenue system had stimulated the cultivation of cash crops like sugar cane, and now that this highly valued product was more readily available it was donated to the temples in large quantities.[25] Sweets were much easier to subdivide and transport than sloppy dhals. Thus the food donor was often given his share in the form of sweets. He then distributed these among his followers, dependants, and kinsmen, as well as various monasteries and sects. In this way he affirmed his power, formed links with important social groups, and demonstrated his charity to the poor. The distribution of the donor's food has remained an important expression of social status in south Indian society. In the 1950s an irate donor complained to the authorities at the Sri Partasarati Svami temple in Madras that two dosas (rice-flour pancakes), two vadais (savory wheat-flour doughnuts), and two laddus (chickpea flour, ghee, and sugar sweets) had been "stolen openly and kept separately by the Temple Staff" instead of being distributed to the public.[26]

Temple sweets also became an important devotional food in northern India. The English ship's captain Alexander Hamilton noted that at the temple of Jaggerynatt (in Orissa): "There are in all, about 500 [priests] that belong to the Pagod, who daily boyl Rice and Pulse for the Use of the God. There are five Candies daily drest, each candy containing 1600 lb. weight. When some part has been carried before the Idol, and the smoke had saluted his Mouth and Nose, then the Remainder is sold out, in small Parcels, to those who will buy it, at very reasonable rates, and the surplus is served out to the Poor, who are ever attending the pagod out of a pretended devotion."[27]

For pilgrims, the production of temple sweets meant that they were able to carry the religious power embodied in the food home with them. The large quantities of sugar and tamarind used in the sweets acted as preservatives, ensuring that they kept for a long time before going rancid.

This tradition of distributing temple sweets to pilgrims is still alive. At the Tirupati temple in Andhra Pradesh, for example, the cooks use three tonnes of urad dhal, six tonnes of sugar, and two and a half tonnes of ghee, besides large amounts of raisins, cashew nuts, and cardamom, to make 70,000 hard, sweet, and powdery laddus that are given away to pilgrims every day.[28]

Southern India has a long history of outsiders bringing in culinary influences. Syrian Christians, who settled at St. Thomé near Madras in the first century AD, are said to have brought the recipe for stew with them, which they had been taught how to make by Irish monks. Along the west coast the Arab traders intermarried with the Indian population and showed their wives how to make seafood pilaus. Jewish settlers brought Middle Eastern tastes to Cochin and combined a liking for rice and nuts with pickled mangoes and smoked tamarind.[29] Further inland, in the area of India known as the Deccan, Persian Shi'ites found employment with the Bahmanid sultan during the fourteenth century. The Bahmanid kingdom eventually broke up into a number of satellite states, one of which was Golconda, which later became known as Hyderabad. Here, the pilaus of the Persians combined with Hindu Deccani cookery, in which shredded coconut and coconut milk are vital ingredients and the tang of curry leaves, the astringent bite of fresh fenugreek leaves, and the sharp sour note of tamarind impart flavor. The meeting of the two styles gave rise to an elegant cuisine with unusual combinations, such as lamb cooked with beans and tamarind.

Eventually, Mughlai cuisine spread south. Shahjahan conquered Hyderabad in the 1630s and installed a Mughal governor. But Mughal power was shortlived in the south and a century later the Mughal Empire began to break up into satellite states. Governor Nizam-ul-Mulk reestablished Hyderabad's independence and founded a new dynasty of rulers. By this time, however, the strong central Asian flavor of Mughlai cuisine had been imparted to the Hyderabadi blend, and kebabs coated in

1. *A banquet including roast goose given to Babur by the Mirzas* (1507) An open-air banquet much like the one given by Asaf Khan for Edward Terry and Thomas Roe when the many dishes of rice and meat were served in golden bowls on a *dastarkhwan* (tablecloth) around which the diners sat cross-legged.

2. *Harvesting of the almond crop at Kand-i-Badam* (1507) Cartloads of nuts and dried fruit were imported into India along roads constructed by the Mughals to facilitate trade throughout northern India, central Asia, and Persia. Under the Mughals, Indian cooks learned to thicken sauces with ground almonds.

3. *Portuguese man reading a book held by a servant* (ca. 1595) Portuguese officials enjoyed lives of luxury in India. While one servant holds this man's book for him, others prepare refreshments. Portuguese bakers were famous for their fragrant egg custards, tarts, and perfumed marzipan.

4. *Grain merchant in Pushkar* (1999) Corn and rice merchants in old
Goa heaped up their wares in huge piles in front of their shops much
like this modern grain seller.

5. *Sweet shop in northern India* (1980s) A sweet shop piled high with fudgy barfis,
powdery laddus, made from chickpea flour and sugar, and gulab jamans, crispy
on the outside with a soft and melting milky filling, coated in rose-water syrup.
Larger versions of these sweets were made at temples throughout India and
distributed to pilgrims.

6. *Nasir al-Din Haidar (King of Oudh, 1827–1837) at dinner with a British official and wife* (ca. 1831) The Nawabs of Oudh did their best to incorporate European culture into their court life. They entertained British guests in style, and the wife of a British army officer reported that French, English, and Indian food were all served at the Nawabs' table.

7. *Cooked food and kawab makers* (Kashmir, 1850–1860) The Mughlai art of kebab making was perfected at Lucknow where the cooks produced such soft, velvety shammi kebabs that even the toothless Nawab Asaf-ud-Daulah could eat them.

8. *Cook shop in northern India* (1980s) The streets of eighteenth-century Lucknow were lined with cook shops where the cooks could be seen "basting keebaubs over a charcoal fire on the ground with one hand, beating off the flies with a bunch of date leaves in the other; kneading dough for ... bread, or superintending sundry kettles and cauldrons of currie, pillau, [and] preparing platters and trays." These are modern-day descendents of such cookshops.

9. *Frying puris* (1996)

10. *Our burra khana* (1859) The British dinner party in India was a hot, crowded affair. Even a punkah swinging above the table could not cool the air. Nevertheless, guests tucked into great saddles of beef, enormous turkeys and bowls of curry and rice.

11. *The interior of the governor-general's traveling kitchen tent with numerous uniformed cooks engaged in cooking a meal* (1820–1821) British governor-generals traveled in great state. Lord Auckland's entourage in the 1830s consisted of a train of 850 camels, 140 elephants, 250 horses, and 12,000 personnel. This included his French chef, St. Cloup, and a small army of cooks who provided lavish entertainments when the governor-general entertained Indian rulers or British officers at the various towns he visited.

12. *A servant setting out a meal in camp* (1930s) The British loved camp life and developed a separate branch of shikari cookery characterized by incredibly fiery sauces.

13. *Grinding curry stuff* (Bangalore, 1901–1904) No Indian kitchen was properly equipped without a heavy flat grindstone on which the day's supply of spices was freshly ground each morning.

14. *Kitchen servants* (ca. 1880) "To destroy the illusion of effortless elegance, so carefully created in the British dining room, all one had to do was to step onto the back verandah of the bungalow. Here one would discover a host of servants pulling the punkah, sleeping, washing up, or boiling a kettle for tea."

15. *The breakfast* (1842) Fish was served for breakfast in Anglo-Indian households and accompanied by rice or khichari. Eventually these dishes were amalgamated and, garnished with fried onions and hard-boiled eggs, the combination of fish and rice became known as kedgeree. The couple in the picture have also been served a plate of sweet Syhleti oranges.

16. *Delivering tiffin boxes in Bombay* (1996) Painted on each tiffin box is a series of symbols that tell the dabba-wallahs where it needs to go at each stage of its journey. These are being delivered to Churchgate railway station.

17. *A dabba-wallah in New Delhi* (1990s) A group of residents living in a modernized slum of New Delhi in 1995 decided to set up their own tiffin-carrying business, along the lines already established in Bombay. Here a dabba-wallah has loaded boxes onto his bicycle ready to deliver to various offices in time for lunch.

18. *Packing tea for export* (1901) By the 1880s, planters in Assam were producing sufficient quantities of high-quality Indian tea to take on the challenge of Chinese tea, which had until then dominated the market.

19. *Madras tea shop* (1940) It was the British who energetically marketed tea within India itself by setting up tea shops in urban areas. Once the shops were established, hawkers equipped with kettles and cups moved in to sell sweet milky tea.

20. *Sadhu drinking tea in Pushkar* (1990s) After a long and successful campaign by the Indian Tea Association almost everyone in India now drinks tea, even the sadhus (holy men).

21. *Lovers' picnic* (1970s)

22. *Anglo-Indian picnic* (1930s) Eating in the open air has long been a favorite pastime in India. The Mughals enjoyed picnics while relaxing in their ornamental gardens. The East India Company merchants followed suit and drank punch and watched dancing girls in the gardens outside Surat. The British in India continued the tradition.

23. *Indian picnic* (1980s) Nowadays picnic parties can be seen at beauty spots all over India. The members of this party have removed their shoes to ensure that they do not pollute the area where they are eating.

24. *Vegetable market in Pushkar* (1990s) Here the women are selling beans, cauliflower, potatoes, tomatoes, and chillies—all of which were introduced to the Indian subcontinent by Europeans, and significantly widened the range available to a largely vegetarian population. "Simply boiled vegetables are never eaten" in India. European and American fruits and vegetables have been integrated into Indian cookery and are prepared according to Indian methods.

25. *Chicken seller in northern India* (1980s)
Indians prefer the taste of freshly killed
chickens, and in Birmingham in the
1950s the chicken sellers congregated
with the prostitutes on the Varna Road
on Sunday mornings.

26. *A village store selling curry powder and corned beef on the island of Savai'i, Samoa* (2001)
In Samoa, curry is a luxury food, made with expensive tinned ingredients bought
from the village store. But rather than eating it with rice many Samoans
consume their curry with boiled taro or breadfruit that they grow in their
gardens.

spicy yogurt had been incorporated into the repertoire, alongside sharper versions of Mughlai biryanis, flavored with the southern taste of curry leaves and chillies, tamarind and coconut.[30]

Some people would argue that it was in fact at Hyderabad that Mughlai cuisine reached its zenith. During the eighteenth century, as the Mughal emperors gradually lost their grip on their empire, the imperial kitchens ceased to act as engines of culinary change. They were surpassed by various successor states that became the new centers of innovation. Hyderabad was one such state, while another was Oudh in northern India.

In Lucknow a story is told of how the last nawab of Oudh, Waji Ali Shah (1847–1856), invited Mirza Asman Qadar, a prince from Delhi, to dine with him. The prince, a noted gourmet, chose a spicy conserve of vegetables called murrabba from the array of dishes set down before him. As he began to chew he discovered to his surprise that he was in fact eating a qaurama of meat. Waji Ali Shah's chef had taken great pains to disguise the qaurama, and the nawab was delighted that he had succeeded in tricking one of the great food connoisseurs of Delhi. Mirza Qadar went home feeling very embarrassed to have been caught out. He soon took his revenge. Waji Ali Shah duly received a return invitation. As he tasted each dish in turn he was stunned to discover that all the food—the pilau, the biryani, the meat curries, the kebabs, the chutneys and pickles, and even the breads—were all made of caramelized sugar. The nawab was defeated.[31]

The food trickery played out between the nawab and the prince was part of a political power game. The nawab wished to demonstrate to his guest the existence of an autonomous courtly culture at Lucknow that was sufficiently elaborate to outdo even the sophistication of the Mughal court at Delhi. In this case, Delhi, represented by the prince, won the battle. But by the time the two men were sparring over dishes made of sugar, the nawabs of Oudh had in fact already won the war. As the Mughal Empire began to break up during the eighteenth century, the nawabs of Oudh set about establishing Lucknow as a center for high culture to rival the old Mughal capital. At first there was skepticism. The Delhi poet Meer Taqi Meer declared:

The ruins of Delhi were ten times better than Lucknow / I wish I were dead before I came to Lucknow.[32]

But the stupendous salaries the Lucknavis was prepared to pay eventually proved too great a temptation. Artists, poets, musicians were all attracted to the Oudh court, which grew into something more than a replica of Mughal Delhi, developing its own distinctive style of architecture and its own schools of poetry and music.[33] Cooks also flocked to Lucknow and were rewarded handsomely. One nobleman was rumored to pay his cook as much as 1,200 rupees a month, "an amount greater than the salary of any cook in the highest courts in the history of India."[34] In the 1770s, the nawab spent four times more on his cook room than on his poor house.[35] Even the disgruntled Meer Taqi Meer had to change his mind, eventually admitting,

Lucknow is better than Delhi even / So my heart has wandered hither.[36]

In Lucknow, Mughlai cuisine was transformed by the incorporation of the products of the lush agricultural region of Oudh. The Lucknavis loved cream, and in the eighteenth century used it to perfect the Mughal dish qaurama or what we would call korma. Qaurama was made with only the tenderest pieces of lamb or chicken and the name referred to the cooking technique of gently braising the meat in oil. Under the Mughals the Persian method was applied, first marinating the meat in yogurt mixed with ginger, garlic, onions, and spices before simmering it gently in the yogurt sauce. The mixture was thickened with ground almonds, another Persian trick. In Lucknow, they added large dollops of cream to the sauce to create a dish that was voluptuously rich.[37] Even the simple lentil dish of dhal was transformed in Lucknow in to a rich, thick velvety mixture of milk, yogurt, and cream, flavored with saffron.[38]

Aside from dairy products, Oudh was famous for the "whiteness, delicacy, fragrance and wholesomeness" of its rice. It is unsurprising that the dish that the Lucknavis most prided themselves on was pilau. In Delhi, biryani (the much spicier Mughal version of a pilau) was the most admired dish. In Lucknow, they were willing to concede that "a good biryani is better than an indifferent pilau," but biryanis were considered to taste too strongly of spices that overwhelmed the delicate floral flavor of the rice. Lucknavi gourmets considered a biryani a "clumsy and ill-conceived meal in comparison with a really good pulao."[39] Bishop Reginald Heber, who traveled through India in the 1820s, could not help but agree. While breakfasting with the nawab of Oudh, Heber was invited to taste a "pillaw" that he did with much "secret reluctance" as vivid memories of the greasy offerings of the nawab of Dacca were still in his mind. He was "surprised, however, to find that this was really an excellent thing, with neither ghee nor garlic, and with no fault, except, perhaps, that it was too dry and exclusively fowl, rice and spices." Heber noted that "the high-bred Mussulmans of this part of India affect to dislike exceedingly, as vulgar, the greasy and fragrant dishes of the Bengalees and Hindoos, and that the aim of their cookery is to be dry, stimulant, and aromatic."[40]

In pursuit of the stimulant and the aromatic, the Lucknavi chefs sometimes cooked the rice for their pilaus in a broth made from chickens fed on musk and saffron. The scent of this absurdly expensive concoction was said to permeate every corner of the room. The rulers of Lucknow displayed their wealth and luxury at their tables, and encouraged their cooks to invent ever more artful dishes. They produced pilaus that were supposed to look as if a plate of jewels had been placed on the table rather than a plate of rice. Using a technique developed in the kitchens of the caliphs of Baghdad, they soaked some of the rice in salt water before cooking it, to make it sparkle like crystals. Other rice was dyed fiery red or bright green to give it the look of rubies and emeralds. Never content with simplicity, the cooks transformed the plain peasant dish of khichari into an elaborate joke. Almonds were painstakingly cut to resemble grains of rice, and pistachios were shaped to look like lentils. It was said that "once savoured [this dish] . . . could never be forgotten."[41]

Just as Mughlai cuisine had incorporated peasant cookery into the courtly repertoire, the Lucknavi court kitchens adopted the dishes of the ordinary Oudh people. Different types of pancakes and rissoles made from chickpea or lentil flour, cooked in rich gravies, were adapted from the peasant cooking of the region.[42] One of Lucknow's most famous cooking techniques was perfected as a result of the need to provide food for the poor. In 1784, Oudh was struck by famine and Nawab Asaf-ud-Daulah responded by paying the hungry to work on the building of the Great

Imambara (the Shia form of a mosque). Thus, he was able to prevent his subjects from dying on the streets while he continued to beautify the city to his own glory. *Nanbais* (bazaar cooks) were charged with the difficult task of supplying the workers with warm food at any time of day or night. They used the Mughal technique of *dum pukht* (meaning to breathe and to cook), a recipe for which can be found in the *Ain-i-Akbari*. The Indian cook also served a "dum poked" chicken when John Ovington dined with the English merchants in the factory at Surat. In Lucknow, the *nanbais* set up enormous cooking pots filled with meat and vegetables that were sealed with lids of dough and placed on hot coals. In this way the food cooked slowly and hungry laborers could be fed at a moment's notice with tender pieces of meat that fell from the bone. When he went to inspect the work, the nawab is said to have found the smells rising from the steaming pots so inviting that he ordered the palace cooks to learn the recipe from the *nanbais*. *Dum pukht* was also applied to good effect to a dish of mutton and turnips that was brought to Lucknow by Kashmiris, looking for alternative sources of employment now that the Mughal court was in decline. The Lucknavi cooks made mutton meatballs that were put in a pot known as a *deg* with the turnips. The pot was sealed with a pastry lid (*dum pukht*) and cooked on a slow fire through the night (*shub*). Lucknavis still eat *shub deg* for breakfast, tender after a long night of slow cooking.

Nawab Asaf-ud-Daulah's love of food is also said to have led to the invention of the shammi kebab. This is one of Lucknow's many contributions to kebab cookery. In contrast to the Mughal emperors, most of whom ate sparingly, the nawabs of Oudh were gluttons. Indeed, Asaf-ud-Daulah became so fat that he could no longer ride a horse.[43] He managed to gain vast amounts of weight despite the fact that his ability to chew was compromised by the loss of his teeth. Shammi kebabs are supposed to have been created in order to accommodate this problem. They were made out of finely minced and pounded meat, known as *qima*. While Westerners tend to mince meat as a way of using inferior grades, the Mughals would often mince the best cuts. *Qima* is frequently referred to in the recipes given by Akbar's courtier, Abu'l Fazl, as an ingredient for pilaus.[44] The Mughals liked minced beef but in Lucknow the cooks preferred lamb, which produced a softer mince. They would grind the meat into a fine paste and then add ginger and garlic, poppy seeds and various combinations of spices, roll it into balls or lozenges, spear them on a skewer, and roast them over a fire. The resulting kebabs were crispy on the outside but so soft and silky within that even the toothless Asaf-ud-Daulah could eat them with pleasure.[45]

The best kebabs were made by the *nanbais*. Large Muslim families, where the parents, several sons, and their wives and children all lived in one house together, were too big to cater for in one kitchen. Instead, a few choice dishes were made at home and the rest were ordered from the trusty bazaar cooks. The food was sent to each house set out on a large tray with a dome-shaped cover, secured with a seal to ensure that the food could not be tampered with en route. Each *nanbai* specialized in a particular dish and the streets of Lucknow were lined with shops where the cooks could be seen "basting keebaubs over a charcoal fire on the ground with one hand, beating off the flies with a bunch of date leaves in the other; kneading dough for sheermaul or other bread, or superintending sundry kettles and cauldrons of currie, pillau . . . &c . . . preparing platters and trays, in order to forward the delicacies at the appointed hour to some great assembly."[46]

Bread was an essential accompaniment to every meal and a *nanbai* named Mahumdu is said to have invented the Lucknavis' favorite shir mal in the 1830s. This bread is a happy marriage of Indian and Persian bread-making techniques. Indians liked to add ghee to everything, and the Muslim cooks noticed that the Indian cooks would fry their chapattis, which made them puff up (producing puris). Muslim cooks added the ghee to their bread dough before the baking stage. This created parathas, when the dough was cooked on a griddle, and baqar khani, when it was cooked in a tandoor oven. Mahumdu improved on the latter by adding milk and eggs, as well as ghee, to the dough, which he then rolled out into paper-thin sheets. Layered on top of each other and baked in a tandoor, these sheets of dough were transformed into rich but flaky and delicate bread. Lucknavis ate shir mal with everything from vegetable and meat dishes to sweet rice puddings, and they claimed that "when efforts are made to bake it anywhere else, it is not the same."[47] After the meal, the family might send out to one of the men who wandered the streets selling ice creams and sherbets delicately flavored with pomegranate or rose water.[48] *Nanbais* still preserve the traditions of Lucknow cuisine at their stalls and Lucknavis will often stop to savor their flaky shir mals and soft, silky shammi kebabs, even when they are on their way out to dinner.

At the beginning of the nineteenth century the wife of a British army officer passing through Lucknow noticed that "three distinct dinners" were served at the nawab's table. "One at the upper end, by an English cook; at the lower end by a French cook; and in the centre (where *he* always sat,) by a Hindoostanee cook." This was a sign of things to come. Even though the merchants of the East India Company were not at first interested in empire building, their trading activities progressively enmeshed them in the economic fabric of India. As a result they were drawn into Indian politics. Initially, they were motivated by a desire to protect their commercial interests but they gradually began to see the benefit of acquiring territory. This would enable them to collect taxes, which would replace the precious bullion that currently paid for Indian textiles.

By the beginning of the eighteenth century, Bengal had become a thriving commercial center. In 1717, the Mughal Emperor Farrukhisyar had been persuaded to grant the company a firman that, in return for 3,000 rupees a year, gave the merchants the right to trade free of dues in Bengal, Bihar, and Orissa. Bengali weavers were found to be as skilled as their counterparts in the south and west, and on their own behalfs the factors engaged in lucrative "country" trade along the River Ganges. When Calcutta was captured by Siraj-ud-Daulah, the nawab of Bengal, in 1756, the city was too valuable to abandon and a few months later Robert Clive retook Calcutta and defeated Siraj-ud-Daulah at the Battle of Plassey. From then on the company became embroiled in intrigue, placing first one then another nawab on the throne in return for substantial payments. They also began to prepare for conflict by building up a permanent army, recruited from declining Brahman and Rajput landholding families, headed by a British officer corps. The machinations in Bengal culminated in the Battle of Buxar when the company defeated Mir Kasim, who they had in fact installed as nawab of Bengal. In acknowledgement of the British victory, the emperor granted the diwan (governorship) of Bengal to the British.

The East India Company was now in an unusual position for a trading venture. It was a virtually autonomous ruling power in one of India's richest provinces. The merchants were transformed into civil servants, in charge of collecting revenue, and administering the law. The East India Company's private army expanded, to about 155,000 in the 1790s, making it one of the largest European-style armies in the world. Company influence spread beyond the borders of the regions it officially administered, and a network of British residents was installed at Indian courts. A resident arrived at Lucknow in 1774 and gradually, what was in effect a rival court was established under the noses of the nawabs. It was clear that a new power had arrived in India and the nawabs did their best to keep up by incorporating elements of British culture into court life. But in 1856 the British deposed Nawab Waji Ali Shah and annexed Oudh.

In the south matters were complicated by the fact that the British and the French played out their European rivalry on Indian soil. The French were latecomers to the East India trade. Their company was only founded in 1664. But from the 1740s onward they struggled with the British for supremacy in southern India. The nizam of Hyderabad and the sultans of Mysore were drawn into the power struggle. Hyderabad eventually allied itself with the British, but Haider Ali and his son Tipu Sultan, of Mysore, held out against the East India Company with the aid of the French. But the arrival of Arthur Wellesley in India as governor-general in 1798 secured the foundations of the British Empire in India. He began his campaign by defeating Tipu Sultan in 1799. This blow eradicated the French challenge and put the East India Company in control of almost the entire tip of southern India. Not satisfied with this coup, Wellesley waged war on the Marathas in 1803–1804 and brought Delhi, Agra and the surrounding provinces into the British sphere of control. Such naked and expensive warmongering was not to the taste of the company directors in London. Territorial control was supposed to bring in revenue rather than lead to costly battles. Nevertheless, by the time they had recalled Wellesley, in 1805, a large swathe of India was either directly under their control or under indirect British rule by means of a resident established at the court.

Lamb korma

Persian cooks introduced to India the idea of marinating meat in yogurt. At the Mughal court spices were added to the marinade, and in Lucknow the chefs added dollops of cream. The Mughals would not originally have used chillies but by the eighteenth century chillies, spread by the Marathas, were becoming popular among northern Indians. They were eventually incorporated into Mughlai and Lucknavi dishes. Serves 4–5.

1¾ lb. tender lamb, cut into pieces

Marinade
3 tablespoons vegetable oil
¾ in. cinnamon stick
10 cardamom pods
10 whole cloves
8 bay leaves
1 large onion, finely chopped
2 oz. ground almonds
6 tablespoons yogurt

Heat the oil in a pan and when it is hot add the cinnamon stick, cardamom pods, cloves, and bay leaves. Stir in hot oil for 30 seconds. Turn down the heat and add the onions. Fry until browned and then add the almonds. Fry, stirring for 5–6 minutes. Remove from the heat and allow to cool. Add to the yogurt in a bowl and mix in the lamb. Cover and put in the fridge overnight.

Sauce
4–6 tablespoons vegetable oil
¾ in. fresh ginger, finely grated
6 cloves garlic, crushed
2 green chillies, finely chopped
1 teaspoon coriander powder
1 teaspoon cumin powder
½ teaspoon garam masala
salt to taste
1 teaspoon sugar
1 cup single cream

The next day remove the meat from the fridge and allow to come to room temperature. Heat the oil in a pan and add the ginger, garlic, and chillies, and fry for about 10 minutes. Add the cumin, coriander, and garam masala and fry for another 1–2 minutes, stirring.

Add the lamb and its marinade to the pan and fry vigorously for about a minute. Add the salt and sugar. Turn the heat low and simmer gently until the lamb is tender. You may need to add a few more tablespoons of yogurt or some water to prevent the mixture from burning.

Once the meat is tender, add the cream and simmer for another 10 minutes.

Shammi kebabs

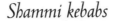

These are a refined version of the central Asian and Afghani kebabs Babur ate. It is said that they were made with a soft fine mince (ideally like velvet) so that the nawab Asaf-ud-Daulah of Lucknow could eat them despite the fact that he had lost all his teeth. Serves 4–6.

1¼ lb. finest minced meat (the Mughals preferred beef, the Lucknavis lamb)
2 tablespoons vegetable oil
2 onions, sliced
1 teaspoon cumin seeds
4 cloves
1 teaspoon black peppercorns
⅜ in. cinnamon stick
4 cardamom pods
2 dried whole red chillies
2 oz. red split lentils
¾ in. piece of fresh ginger, chopped
2 green chillies
a sprig of mint
a bunch of fresh coriander, chopped
3 tablespoons of yogurt
salt to taste
1 tablespoon raisins
1 tablespoon sliced almonds

Heat the oil in a frying pan and sauté the onions until they are transparent. Add the cumin seeds, cloves, peppercorns, cinnamon, cardamom pods, and red chillies. Fry for 3–4 minutes. Set aside.

Put the lentils in a pan with water and cook until soft (about 20 minutes).

Put the meat, the onion and spice mixture, the lentils, the ginger, green chillies, mint, fresh coriander in a food processor and purée.

Add the yogurt and salt. Process again.

Mix the raisins and almonds together.

Take the mixture and form it into balls. Press a few almonds and raisins into each ball.

Thread the balls on to skewers and grill or barbecue, turning occasionally, until the meat is cooked all the way through. They should be crispy on the outside and soft inside.

Besan laddu

This is an easy version of the temple sweets produced at the Tirupati temple for the pilgrims to take home. If you like, you can add raisins or nuts to the mixture. Makes 10–15.

9 oz. ghee (or melted butter)
1¼ lb. besan (chickpea flour)
1¼ lb. powdered (icing) sugar
½ teaspoon cardamom powder

Heat the ghee or melt the butter. Add the besan and fry, stirring. Remove from heat and add the sugar and cardamom powder and mix. Form into balls and allow to cool and harden.

A gentleman's khidmutgars, or table servants, bringing in dinner

5

Madras Curry: The British Invention of Curry

IN 1824 FANNY PARKS and her husband, a civil servant in the service of the East India Company, invited some friends to dinner. Despite the fact that they were a "small party of eight . . . including ourselves . . . two-and-twenty servants were in attendance! Each gentleman," she wrote, "takes his own servant or servants, in number from one to six, each lady her attendant or attendants, as it pleases her fancy." Thomas Williamson's handbook to Indian life, written as a *Guide to Gentlemen Intended for the Civil, Military or Naval Service of the Honourable East India Company* in 1810, informed the novice that the *aub-dar* (water cooler) would generally arrive at the house well before the party began, to ensure that the water, champagne, Madeira, claret, or pale ale were all well chilled. In Calcutta, the host could be expected to possess sufficient china and silverware to set the table but Williamson noted that "at all military stations, each guest sends his servant" with "two plates, a soup plate, a small bowl for bones &c., a tumbler, a glass for Madeira, [various cutlery] . . . and a napkin." At the dinner, the servants, "delicately dressed all in white muslins and white or figured turbans and large gold earrings" would stand behind the chairs of their masters attending to their needs. The *khansaman* (butler) would change the plates and hand round the dishes, another more menial servant might employ a small *chowrie* (fan) of peacock's feathers to beat away the flies.

Underlying the noise of clinking dishes and conversation would be the hiss and bubble of the hookahs. Fanny Parks noted that "the *Hooqû* was very commonly smoked at that time in Calcutta: before dinner was finished, every man's pipe was behind his chair." Crouching beside each chair were the hookah *burdars* who attended to the tobacco and the functioning of the pipe. What with the hot Indian climate, "the steam of the dishes, the heat of the lamps, and the crowd of attendants," the atmosphere could be oppressive. Matters were made worse by the disagreeable smell of coconut oil that the servants rubbed into their skin. If you had the misfortune of sitting next to a man from the Mofussil (remote countryside), then the fumes from the spices his "country" servants used to prepare the tobacco for his hookah could also be unpleasant. Other, less happy reminders that the dinner party was being held in India were the insects and the dust. Fanny Parks was too genteel to refer to such things but Thomas Williamson jovially mentioned that "the alighting of cock-roaches on the face while at table" was simply a matter of course that one had to put up with. He did acknowledge that "the number of flies at times found in the sauces will occasion a disposition to enquire how they got there, and whence they came!" But flies could be picked out of the food. On the whole he seems to have found the "shoals of dust which skim during the middle of the day" far more annoying as they were likely to "render the whole dinner unacceptable." Efforts were made to relieve the heat with punkahs. Fanny described these as "monstrous" fans made of "a wooden frame covered with cloth, some 10, 20 or 30 or more feet long, suspended from the ceiling of a room, and moved to and fro by a man outside by means of a rope and pulleys, and a hole in the wall through which the rope passes." Despite the breeze they provided, there were frequent complaints that it was "scarcely . . . possible to sit out the melancholy ceremony of an Indian dinner."[1]

Now that the East India Company was the de facto ruler of large tracts of India, the factories at Madras, Bombay, and Calcutta expanded into proper towns, from which British power radiated out into the rest of India. By 1800, the company employed 681 civil servants who replaced the old Mughal administrators. They collected revenue and administered justice in the Indian courts. Fanny Parks was one of a tiny number of women who accompanied their husbands out to India. As the company conquered more territory they needed an ever-larger army, Indian sepoys were supplemented by British troops directly recruited by the company, and by regiments from the British or Queen's army that were sent on tours of duty in India. Thus, by the turn of the century there were 20,000–30,000 British soldiers in India. This meant that the presidency towns, as they were known, were now home to sizeable British communities.

The scruffy thatched bungalows huddled around the factory of Fort William, which had confronted the new arrival in Calcutta in the seventeenth century, had been replaced by a town of "Greek-like pillared mansions" and churches, all laid out in elegant wide streets and squares with "the superb colonnaded and domed residence of the Governor-General of India" dominating over it all.[2] In the cool of the evenings the dusty parade ground, known as the maidan, was crowded with British gentlemen taking the air on horseback and a scattering of ladies in *tonjons* (open carriages, carried by four to six bearers on long poles). If it had not been for the Indian shacks in the background, the adjutant storks gloomily surveying the scene from the rooftops, and the numerous Indian servants and hawkers milling about, the stranger might have thought he had arrived in Jane Austen's Bath. Indeed, Frederick Shore arriving in Calcutta in November 1818, aged 19, found the society very much like that of "a country Town in England."

Frederick Shore began his career as a civil servant by spending a year at Fort William College dutifully studying Persian and Hindustani and attending lectures on religion and good government. In a letter he wrote to his aunt back in England, he assured her that he did not "wish to have a name among the idle ones of this place of which there are a good many." Calcutta boasted all the temptations of an English town. There were European shops selling "liquors of all kinds, guns, pistols, glass ware . . . crockery, stationery, shoes and boots, hosiery, grocery and an infinity of articles" on which a young man could waste his money. There were taverns, some where he might respectably hold a dinner for his friends, and others where he was likely to fall prey to inebriety and the charms of "sable beauties." There were pleasure gardens and assembly rooms where young men could dance and flirt pleasurably with young ladies who had come out, as Shore put it, "for the [marriage] market." Shore avoided dancing—he did not wish to become ensnared in marriage before he could afford it. Nor did he indulge in gambling at cards or at the races, two of the pursuits most favored by young recruits. He was aghast at the foolhardiness of those "mad" young men who bought 16 horses, bet on them crazily, and ruined their prospects forever.

At all their settlements, even the remote military cantonments in the Indian countryside, the British created a simulacrum of British society. But their little Englands in India were always fragile, as India insinuated itself into every aspect of daily life. British racial and cultural arrogance meant that they set out to shape Indian society and culture to their own ends. However, they discovered, just as the Mughals had done before them, that India's impact on the culture of its rulers was inescapable. At first the British were fairly unconcerned by this and to some extent they embraced India and allowed it to become an integral part of their identities. Indeed, East India Company officials referred to themselves as Indians, East Indians, or Anglo-Indians. The latter name stuck and throughout this book Anglo-Indian is used to refer to the British in India. It was only in 1911 that the meaning of the term changed and it was used to describe the people of mixed British and Indian parentage, who until then were known as Eurasians.

Besides enthusiastically adopting the Indian hookah, in the late eighteenth and early nineteenth century, company officials smoked the Indian form of cannabis known as bhang, drank arrack, interlarded their conversations with Indian words like *pukka* (proper) and bundobust (contract), took regular shower baths, adopted lightweight nankeen jackets and white linen waistcoats, and sometimes even wore Indian-style loose pyjamas, which were more comfortable in the heat. Indeed, they allowed India to get under their skins and were transformed into hybrid figures, neither British nor Indian but a blend of the two.

The scarcity of European women meant that many British men lived with Indian mistresses, in semi-Indian style. These unions were not heartless matters of convenience, many men were deeply attached to their consorts and whiled away their leisure hours in the purdah quarters of their compounds. Such intimate contact with Indian women educated the British in the "syntaxes of native life" and the women taught their partners the local language and customs, and how to enjoy Indian food.[3] The children of these unions also created an enduring bond between the company servants and India. The fact that their lifestyle lent British society in India a rakish, slightly dissolute air seems not to have perturbed the majority of company officials.

In fact, in the early days of company rule in India the British administrators actively set about constructing themselves as a new *Indian* aristocracy. The British were conscious of the fact that although they had replaced the Mughals as the ruling elite, in the eyes of their Indian subjects they were still low-class traders. They therefore concentrated on projecting an image of themselves as an impressive ruling class. The Reverend James Cordiner, who visited India in the 1820s noted that "all classes of society here live sumptuously and many individuals expend from 2 to 10,000 pounds each annually, in maintaining their households." In Britain this level of expenditure would have been beyond the means of any but the wealthiest levels of the upper classes. Even if the figure is an exaggeration, it was true that in India the sons of ordinary middle-class commercial families, and of the declining British gentry, were able to live like aristocrats. If James Munro Macnabb had remained in the Lowlands of Scotland, where he was born, he might have expected to earn between £500 and £1,000 a year as a minister or doctor. He would have been able to afford between four and six servants, and might have spent between £20 and £30 a month on his table.[4] In Calcutta, where he was Acting Mint Master and Magistrate of the City, he lived in "an excellent three-storied house . . . attached to the Mint," employed ten bearers to carry him about town in his palanquin (a coffinlike box in which the passenger reclined and that was carried on poles by four to six bearers) and two *hurkarrahs* to run in front carrying silver sticks, which were marks of status. He also owned a coach and employed a coachman, as well as six syces (grooms) to care for the horses. Dining and entertaining were central to maintaining his place in Calcutta society, and a high proportion of the 41 servants he employed were associated with the table. Apart from a cook, a cook's mate, and a *masalchi* (spice grinder and dish-washer), James Macnabb employed a *khansaman* and a second butler to wait at table, assisted by an *aub-dar* and a *khidmutgar* (waiter). He spent 400 rupees, or approximately £55, a month on food bought at the bazaar, as well as bread, butter, wood for the kitchen fire, and wine and beer. This was a princely sum that ensured that his table would always have been well supplied with "delicious salt humps, brisket and tongues . . . superb curry and mulligatawny soup."[5]

The *burra khana* (big dinner) was the focus of Anglo-Indian social life. It was on their dinner tables that the British in India most extravagantly displayed their wealth and status. Amazed commentators remarked that there was always so much food "that no part of the table-cloth remains uncovered."[6] "The receipt for an Indian dinner appears to be, to slaughter a bullock and a sheep, and place all the joints before the guest at once, with poultry &c. to match," wrote the ever-critical Emma Roberts. She was in India as the companion to her married sister, a position that she described as one of unmitigated ennui, which perhaps accounts for her persistently disgruntled tone.[7]

East India Company merchants had brought the eating habits of the British squirearchy with them to India. In Britain, a gentleman might consume as much as 74 kilograms of meat a year (compared to the average amount of about 40) and reach the incredible weight of 40 stone. The diet of fashionable society was reflected in caricatures of the time that featured obese and gouty men.[8] Tables piled high with huge meat pies, saddles of mutton, and enormous hams were vivid demonstrations of the upper class's ability to command vast quantities of a scarce resource. Anglo-Indians gained a reputation for consuming immense amounts of meat, in contrast to the vegetarian Indians, and even the meat-eating Mughal nobility. Once the British were established in India, they continued to replicate the consumption patterns of the wealthy at home and loaded their tables with "Turkies that you could not see over—round of Beef, boiled roast Beef, stewed Beef, loin of Veal for a side dish and roast big capons as large as Hen Turkies." Large bowls of curry and rice were placed along the table, in between the turkeys and beef. This was just the first course. After the outsized joints had been cleared, a second course of beef steaks, pigeon pies, chicken drumsticks, more curry, and rice, "quails and ortolans . . . piled up in hecatombs," fruit and nuts, was placed on the table.[9]

Moreover, East India Company officials sat down to a table thus burdened with food twice a day. Frederick Shore was disgusted. He described to his sister Anna the "absurd, universal practice in this country, viz. to eat a tiffin as it is called, though it is nothing more or less than a regular dinner, at 3 o'clock after which they sit down to another dinner in the evening though they cannot eat anything, yet there is always a tolerable portion of wine and beer drank, the doing of which twice daily cannot be very conducive to health."[10] An army captain confirmed Shore's impression and noted that due to eating too much at tiffin most people "only go through the form of dining; . . . condescend[ing] to taste some Yorkshire ham, coast mutton . . . hot curry and English cheese." It was impossible for the diners to consume all that was set before them. In Calcutta, poor Christians were given the leftovers, but elsewhere the food had to be thrown away. Only the lowest caste of Indians would consider eating unclean British leftovers and in the Indian climate it was difficult to keep the food for the next day. Thus, *burra khanas* engendered an extravagant level of waste.

The servants were invariably blamed. The Reverend Cordiner complained that Indians "estimat[ed] the goodness of a dinner by the quantity which they crowd upon the board." Emma Roberts acknowledged that "the servants would be ready to expire with shame at their master's disgrace" if the number of dishes were reduced, or smaller joints of meat were chosen, although she also blamed the Anglo-Indians' lack of elegance and refinement for the vulgar splendor of the *burra khana*. Indian servants certainly collaborated with their masters' and mistresses' efforts to display their wealth on their tables. The status of their employers had a direct effect on the servants' own standing in the Indian social world. During dinner parties the silent, and apparently subservient, servants of the guests were in fact quietly assessing the display of wealth on the table and ranking their colleagues accordingly. Elizabeth Gwillim, the wife of a judge at Madras, noted that her servants took "great pride in setting out the dinner." Fortunately, Elizabeth's "plate and figurines were just to their taste." "I am glad I brought our China dessert set," she wrote, "both that and my Wedgwood have been admired beyond everything."

Elizabeth did discover that the servants' pride in the dining arrangements could have certain drawbacks. For one particular occasion she was pleased to have obtained a hare and she carefully instructed her cook on how to prepare it. During the evening the hare failed to appear on the dining table and when she ordered her butler to fetch it he ignored her. Afterwards, when she asked for an explanation, "he said he was very sorry but the cook and he had both agreed that all the company would laugh if a country hare was brought to so handsome a dinner . . . I believe [they] are perfectly convinced that it is from stinginess that I order them and I have never so far prevailed as to have one for company." Hares were cheaper than rabbits and therefore considered inferior. Elizabeth was sufficiently good-humored to simply laugh at her servants' "extraordinary notions of grandeur."

The Gwillims continually ran into the distinction their servants made between high- and low-status foodstuffs. They both particularly liked fish and Elizabeth would often take a trip down to the beach when the fishermen were bringing in their catch. Here she came across all sorts of fish she had never encountered before and she and her husband would try them for supper. But many of their favorite dishes, such as the tiny whitebait-like fish that the Indians fried whole, were never served at other British dining tables. Her servants explained: "Gentlemen cannot eat that fish." "Then we ask them if *they* can eat it, yes they say, black people very much like that but gentlemen can't eat, no custom to bring gentlemen." Their servants served the British with the food of the previous ruling class: the Mughlai pilaus and dum poked chickens that the company merchants had eaten at Surat. These were the high-status dishes familiar to the Muslim cooks the Anglo-Indians usually employed.[11]

What the British in India ate, for breakfast, lunch, and dinner, was curry and rice.[12] Anglo-Indian dining tables were not complete without bowls of curry that, eaten like a hot pickle or a spicy ragout, added bite to the rather bland flavors of boiled and roasted meats. No Indian, however, would have referred to his or her food as a curry. The idea of a curry is, in fact, a concept that the Europeans imposed on India's food culture. Indians referred to their different dishes by specific names and their servants would have served the British with dishes that they called, for example, rogan josh, dopiaza, or quarama. But the British lumped all these together under the heading of curry.

The British learned this term from the Portuguese who described as "caril" or "carree" the broths that the Indians "made with Butter, the Pulp of Indian Nuts ... and all sorts of Spices, particularly Cardamoms and Ginger ... besides herbs, fruits and a thousand other condiments [that they] ... poured in good quantity upon ... boyl'd Rice."[13] The Portuguese had adopted these terms from various words in south Indian languages. In Kannadan and Malayalam, the word *karil* was used to describe spices for seasoning as well as dishes of sautéed vegetables or meat. In Tamil, the word *kari* had a similar meaning (although nowadays it is used to mean sauce or gravy). As the words *karil* and *kari* were reconfigured into Portuguese and English they were transformed into "caril" and "caree" and eventually into the word curry, which the British then used as a generic term for any spicy dish with a thick sauce or gravy in every part of India.[14]

Although they used the word curry to describe dishes from every Indian region, the British were aware of regional differences in the cooking of the subcontinent. In his cookery book on *Curries and How to Prepare Them* (1903), Joseph Edmunds stated decisively that "in India there are at least three separate classes of curry, the Bengal, the Madras and the Bombay." Most cookery books also incorporated two other types of curry from outside India's borders and gave recipes for Ceylon and Melay (Malayan) curries. The Anglo-Indian understanding of regional differences was, however, rather blunt. They tended to home in on distinctive, but not necessarily ubiquitous, features of a region's cookery and then steadfastly apply these characteristics to every curry that came under that heading.

"The Bengal artist," wrote Edmunds, "is greatest in fish and vegetable curries. Bombay boasts of its peculiar gifts in its bomelon fish and its popedoms."[15] Ceylon curries were usually piquant with chillies and made with coconut milk.

These broad categorizations missed out much of the subtle variety of dishes within each region and the strong sense among Indians of local, often minute, differences in food. Even within one region the variations in soil, water, and air from one locality to another are thought to produce subtle distinctions in the taste of the grains, vegetables, and grazing animals. Thus Punjabis "in a strange part of the Punjab [regard themselves] . . . as exiles, and comment on the air, water, milk, vegetables, the size and sweetness of cabbages and cauliflowers, dialect and everything else as not being quite what [they are] used to."[16] Tiny differences in the way basic foodstuffs are prepared, which may seem irrelevant to an outsider, are of great significance to Indians who pay close attention to the nuances of food. When south Kanarese villagers are asked how they differ from the people living in the neighboring villages they will often respond by explaining "they eat . . . raw rice" and "we eat parboiled rice."[17]

The British insensitivity to these details was matched by their hazy awareness of the endless variations in flavor that were achieved by adding spices to the food in different combinations and at different stages in the cooking process. This was partly the result of the fact that Indian cooks gradually altered and simplified their recipes to suit British tastes. For example, Lucknavi quaramas were transformed into Anglo-Indian "quoremas" or "kormas," which were different in substance as well as name. A "thirty-five years' resident" of India who wrote an Indian cookery book explained that korma "without exception, is one of the richest of Hindoostanee curries, but it is quite unsuited to European taste, if made according to the original recipe." He gave both the original and a diluted British version of the curry. The latter greatly reduced the amount of ghee and yogurt, as well as the aromatic spices such as the cloves and cardamom. It omitted the cream altogether and, instead, produced a more generic curry sauce by adding coriander, ginger, and peppercorns, which were basic ingredients in a British curry.

The "original" and the British recipe for Kurma or Quorema Curry from Thirty-Five Years' Resident, The Indian Cookery Book

The original recipe:—

Take two pounds of mutton, one pound of tyre or dhye [yogurt], two chittacks of garlic, one dam of cardamoms, four chittacks of bruised almonds, four mashas of saffron, the juice of five lemons, one pound of ghee, four chittacks of sliced onions, one dam of cloves, one chittack of pepper, four chittacks of cream, and a quarter of a teaspoonful of ground garlic.

The following is the recipe of the quorema curry usually put on a gentleman's table:—

Two chittacks and a half or five ounces of ghee, one cup or eight ounces of good thick tyre, one teaspoonful of ground chillies, four teaspoonsful of ground onions, one teaspoonful of coriander seed, six small sticks of ground cinnamon, two or three blades of lemon-grass, one teaspoonful and a half of salt, a half a teaspoonful of ground ginger, a quarter of a teaspoonful of ground garlic, eight or ten peppercorns, four or five ground cloves, five or six ground cardamoms, two or three bay leaves, a quarter of a cup of water, the juice of one lemon, and twelve large onions cut lengthways into fine slices.

Take two pounds of good fat mutton, and cut it into pieces nearly one inch and a half square. Warm the ghee, fry in it the sliced onions, and set aside; then fry all the ground condiments including the ground hot spices. When quite brown, throw in the mutton and salt, and allow the whole to brown, after which add the tyre, the hot spices with peppercorns and bay leaves, the lemon-grass, the water, and the fried onions, finely chopped; close the pot and allow to simmer for about an hour and a half or two hours, by which time the kurma will be quite ready. The blades of lemon-grass are never dished up.[18]

Curry became not just a term that the British used to describe an unfamiliar set of Indian stews and ragouts, but a dish in its own right, created for the British in India. One surgeon described curry as "a most heterogeneous compound of ginger, nutmeg, cinnamon, cloves, cardamoms, coriander, Cayenne pepper, onions, garlic, and turmeric, ground to a powder by a pestle and mortar, made into a paste by ghee, . . . and added to a stewed kid or fowl."[19] And this was the formula that provided a template for Anglo-Indian curries, most of which were variations on this basic recipe. The Madras curry epitomized this attitude toward Indian food. It was simply a spicy sauce for meat, made from a spoonful of curry powder, some onions and tomatoes. Joseph Edmunds described it as "the high old curry made perfect."

Recipe for Madras Karhi from W. H. Dawe's The Wife's Help to Indian Cookery

Cut a part of a neck of mutton into small pieces, taking out the bones; fry in its own fat until brown. Let it stew for two hours in some water or good stock. Add some fried onion, pepper and salt to taste, season it, and a few minutes before serving put a tablespoonful of curry-powder on the meat, mixing well, letting it simmer for about five minutes.[20]

Although it lacked sophistication, Anglo-Indian cookery was the first truly pan-Indian cuisine. Mughlai cuisine never became an all-India phenomenon: the culinary styles of many Indian regions were not incorporated into the repertoire and its spread was limited. In contrast, the British adopted recipes, ingredients, techniques, and garnishes from all over the subcontinent and combined them in a coherent repertoire of dishes. Indeed, one of the distinguishing characteristics of Anglo-Indian cookery was its tendency to apply appealing aspects of particular regional dishes to all sorts of curry. In this way, mangoes, which were sometimes added to fish curries in parts of the southern coastal areas, found their way into Bengali prawn curries; coconut was added to Mughlai dishes, where it was an alien ingredient. In a similar fashion, Anglo-Indians applied the variety of relishes and garnishes that they discovered in India with indiscriminate enthusiasm to all their curries. Served alongside bowls of curry and rice would be little plates of the Persian garnish of chopped hard-boiled eggs, Punjabi lemon pickles, south Indian finely sliced raw onions, desiccated coconut, neat piles of poppadoms, as well as fried onions and shreds of crispy bacon.[21] The Anglo-Indian passion for garnishes was also applied to the simple rice and lentil dish khichari, the ordinary food of the majority of the population, and a favorite dish with the Mughal emperors on their fast days. Khichari was frequently served for breakfast in Anglo-Indian households. It went well with fish, which was another breakfast item, as "in the hot season, fish caught early in the morning would be much deteriorated before the dinner hour."[22] The favored garnishes were hard-boiled eggs and fried onions, and eventually all three (fish, eggs, and onions) came to be seen as essential to a good kedgeree.

Recipe for kedgeree from Edward Palmer's Indian Cookery

Cold cooked fish (flaky fish preferable)
Cooked Patna rice
Butter
Chopped onions
A finely sliced clove of garlic
Ground turmeric
Hard-boiled eggs
Pepper
Salt
Green or red chillies

Cook in sufficient butter for a few minutes (but do not brown) the onions and garlic. Then add a teaspoonful of ground turmeric, and cook this mixture for a few minutes longer.

The rice and flaked fish is now added and the whole very lightly tossed together until warmed through. Pepper and salt to taste.

Serve piled on a dish garnished with slices of hard-boiled eggs and green and red chillies cut lengthwise.[23]

One of the most popular Anglo-Indian dishes is said to have been invented in Madras. The British are supposed to have asked their cooks to prepare soup as a starter, a concept unfamiliar to Indians, who place all the dishes on the table at once and who pour liquid dishes over rice. The nearest thing to a soup that Madrassi cooks knew was a watery rasam (broth) made from black pepper or chillies, tamarind, and water, which in Tamil is called *molo tunny*, or pepper water. Ayurvedic physicians considered pepper water "one of the great blessings which God has bestowed upon the world" and prescribed it for intermittent fever, hemorrhoids, dyspepsia, and cholera. It is still served to people recovering from a stomach upset in south India today, and a rasam of this kind is often poured over rice as a digestive. The Madrassi cooks inventively added a little rice, a few vegetables, some meat, and transformed this broth into mulligatawny soup. Anglo-Indians in Madras were said to imbibe such large quantities of it that they were known as "Mulls."[24] Mulligatawny soup was one of the earliest dishes to emerge from the new hybrid cuisine that the British developed in India, combining British concepts of how food should be presented (as soups or stews, etc.) and Indian recipes. It quickly spread to the other British settlements dotted around the subcontinent and "very hot mulligatani soup" was invariably served at every Anglo-Indian dinner party and ball.[25]

Recipe for Chicken Mulligatawny Soup from Indian Cookery "Local" for Young Housekeepers

Cut a Chicken into 12 or 16 pieces, and boil it in two teacups of water. Take five or six corns of black pepper, ⅛ of an ounce each of turmeric, and fresh ginger, five or six slices of garlic and a desert-spoon of raw coriander, with one red chilly, and grind them all together to make a fine paste. Mix the ground paste with the chicken broth and let it boil. After boiling, strain the gravy through a piece of muslin; warm a heaped tea-spoon of ghee in a stewpan, and fry a sliced onion, put in the meat and gravy together, stir and allow the curry to boil. Put no acid in the curry, serve it with a sour Lime cut in slices in a separate plate.[26]

Just as the British in Madras discovered *molo tunny*, the British in Bombay developed a liking for their region's specialities. Bomelon were small fish that the residents of Bombay treated with asafetida and then hung up to dry in the sun. Fried until they were golden brown and crumbled over food they imparted a strong salty taste that the British adored. They christened this seasoning Bombay duck as these fish were known to swim close to the surface of the water. As early as the seventeenth century, the British living at Bombay were known as "Ducks" due to their fondness for this delicacy.[27] The residents of the Bombay area also ate *papads*. These were thin fried discs of a paste made from ground and roasted lentils. They were used like bread as a side dish with the meal. The British called them poppadoms.

In the seventh and eighth centuries, fire-worshipping Zoroastrians had fled the Arab invasion of Persia and settled along the west coast of India. The Parsees, as they were known, adapted to their new surroundings, adopting many Indian habits. When the Europeans began to arrive, they adapted again, learned English, moved into shipping, and grew wealthy from the China trade. The East India Company merchants in Bombay mixed with the Parsees during the early days of the company, and later, once their rule was established, they often employed Parsee butlers in their households. By these means the Parsee dish of dhansak became well known to the British. This is a dhal of four pulses, which is made with either chicken or mutton and vegetables. It is thick and very spicy, and is best eaten, Parsee-fashion, with caramelized brown rice and fried onions.[28] The use of tamarind and jaggery in the dish betrayed the influence of the Gujarati love of sweet and sour on Parsee cooking. Dhansak was one of the "curries" that regularly appeared on Anglo-Indian dining tables and that eventually became a standard item on British Indian restaurant menus.

Not only did the Anglo-Indians' eclectic approach to Indian cookery create a repertoire of dishes that brought together in one kitchen influences ranging from all over the subcontinent; they also transported this cuisine around India. By the middle of the nineteenth century, British influence could be felt from the southern tip of Ceylon, to the Northwest Frontier with Afghanistan, to the eastern Burmese jungles. Wherever they went the Anglo-Indians took curry.

The British in India were constantly on the move. Every two or three years company officials (both civil and military) were posted to new stations, which necessitated packing up and transporting their entire households over vast distances. Emma Roberts thought "a more unfixed, unsettled, floating community cannot be imagined."[29] After Frederick Shore finished his year of studies at Fort William College in Calcutta, he moved at least seven times in the course of his 19 years as a Bengal civil servant. His first posting was as assistant to the Board of Commissioners at Farrukhabad. He had two choices as to how to travel the 500 miles from Calcutta to Farrukhabad. The first was to dawdle upriver in a large, cumbersome flat-bottomed boat known as a budgerow. By this means the journey would have taken about four months. The alternative was to travel by dak (post), along the route taken by the postal runners who carried the mail. The dak passenger was transported in a palanquin, carried by six or eight bearers who were changed every few miles, like horses for stagecoaches in Europe. This would have cut the journey by half but it was by no means a comfortable means of transport, as one army officer warned:

> We cannot promise you much pleasure in the enjoyment of this celebrated Oriental luxury. Between your head and the glowing sun, there is scarcely half an inch of plank, covered with a thin mat, which ought to be, but never is watered. After a day or two you will hesitate which to hate the most, your bearers' monotonous, melancholy, grunting, groaning chant, when fresh, or their jolting, jerking, shambling, staggering gait, when tired. In a perpetual state of low fever you cannot eat, drink or sleep; your mouth burns, your head throbs, your back aches, and your temper borders upon the ferocious.[30]

It was necessary to make good arrangements for provisions on such a long journey. Early travelers in India had learned that it was best to travel well equipped, otherwise one could expect to live frugally. Given that the majority of the population was vegetarian, it was difficult to buy anything other than a few lentils, some rice, and a little butter and so the British took virtually everything they might need with them. In 1638, Albert de

Mandelslo journeyed with some British merchants carrying supplies of silver and trade goods to the factories that dotted the route from Surat to Agra. On the way they shot wild ducks and met "with so many Deer and wild Boars, that it was no hard matter for us to get a good supper." They even traveled with their own cooks to ensure the meat was prepared to their liking.[31] Lord Auckland did the same when he traveled from Calcutta to Simla in 1837. He took his French chef St. Cloup, who presided over a small army of cooks whipping up lavish breakfasts and good dinners for the governor-general's guests, including the nawab of Oudh. His entourage was the size of a small city. A train of 850 camels, 140 elephants, 250 horses, and 12,000 personnel stretched across the plain for ten miles, raising a cloud of dust that must have been visible for miles. This was travel in the style of the Mughal emperors, whose effect as they passed over the country was that of a plague of locusts. Besides the damage done to the farmers' fields, the Mughal camp would requisition all available food to supply the entourage and leave hunger and misery behind them. Lord Auckland's servants were instructed to pay for any food supplied by the peasantry but this did not make the farmers any less reluctant to relinquish their stores, especially as much of the area they passed through was already suffering from famine.[32]

Travelers who went by budgerow or dak caused less devastation. They would buy from the villagers "boiled and smoked milk in earthen pots, [and] very small eggs of doubtful age," but otherwise budgerow travelers were served by a cook-boat that would draw alongside at mealtimes to serve the passengers hot rolls for breakfast and meat curries in the evenings.[33] It was, however, always wise to keep some provisions on the main boat (as well as tea-making equipment) as the cook-boat was occasionally delayed and no dinner obtainable.[34] Traveling by dak was done at night in order to avoid the heat of the sun and the day was spent in camp where the cook rustled up meals over a small portable stove. In the 1840s a network of dak bungalows was built that provided the traveler with food and a place to rest. These soon became notorious for their cookery. "The [dak] bungalow khansaman, knowing that he has no other condiment whatever to offer to the hungry traveller, will, when asked, unblushingly profess to provide every delicacy of the season; but when he appears and uncovers his dishes, there is fowl, nothing but fowl, of every age, size, and degree of toughness."[35] Chicken was the only meat that could easily be made available at a moment's notice. Anglo-Indians often joked that as soon as he saw the dust of a traveler rising in the distance the bungalow cook would rush out to catch and kill one of the scrawny chickens scratching in the yard. The ubiquitous chicken was often presented to the traveler in the form of "country captain," one of the best-known Anglo-Indian curries. There are many different versions of this dish but it was basically a curry of freshly killed chicken, flavored with turmeric and chillies, both ingredients that kept well. Nobody knows how the curry acquired its name but some suggest that it was invented by the captain of a "country" (i.e., Indian) boat. It was certainly frequently served to the British when they were "up-country," traveling by budgerow or dak.[36] It was accompanied by "country" bread, which most Anglo-Indians hated. But despite all the complaints "chuppaties made of coarse flour like oatmeal, and deliciously hot, were an excellent substitute [for European bread] . . . Fresh goat's milk could also be had, and as travellers always carried their own tea, it was quite possible to get a hearty and satisfactory meal."[37]

Recipe for Country Captain from Thirty-Five Years' Resident,
The Indian Cookery Book

Cold meats and curries are sometimes converted into this dish, the condiments for which are as follows:—Two chittacks or four ounces of ghee, half a teaspoonful of ground chillies, one teaspoonful of salt, a quarter of a teaspoonful of ground turmeric, and twenty onions, cut up lengthways into fine slices.

Cut up in the usual way an ordinary curry chicken. Warm the ghee and fry the sliced onions, which when brown set aside; fry the ground turmeric and chillies, then throw in the chicken and salt, and continue to fry, stirring the whole until the chicken is tender. Serve it up, strewing over it the fried onions.[38]

Another set of curries belong under the heading of camp cookery. During the cold weather between October and May the civil servant traveled around his district "surveying the country, inspecting and forwarding the work of irrigation ... settling with the zemindars for their taxes," and administering justice. Life in camp was far more luxurious than dak or budgerow travel, and each campsite was transformed into a "large and handsome" village of tents, all of which were fitted out with glass doors and a stove. Emma Roberts was impressed that "Indian servants [in camp] never permit their masters to regret the want of regular kitchens." They would produce "fish of every kind, fresh, dried, pickled or preserved, or hermetically sealed in a tin; delicate fricassées, rissoles, croquettes, omelettes, and curries of all descriptions; cold meats and game of all sorts, jellies, and jams from London and Lucknow, fruits and sweetmeats; with cakes in endless variety, splendidly set out in china, cut glass, and silver."[39] Often a party of men and women would accompany the civil servant, spending their days indulging in the favorite Anglo-Indian pastime of shikari (hunting). This gave rise to an entire branch of Anglo-Indian curries, including braised quail, wild duck, and rabbit curry.[40] To accompany these, the cooks made up fiery shikari sauces of salt or fermented fish, chillies, cayenne pepper, asafetida, mushrooms, and wine that Roberts thought "assuredly the most piquant adjuncts to flesh and fowl which the genius of a gastronome has ever compounded."[41]

Like the Mughals and the Portuguese before them, the British refashioned Indian food according to their tastes, and created an independent branch of Indian cookery. This Anglo-Indian cuisine was even the first truly pan-Indian cuisine, in that it absorbed techniques and ingredients from every Indian region and was eaten throughout the entire length and breadth of the subcontinent. But Anglo-Indian cookery can never be described as a truly national Indian cuisine as the hybrid dishes that it produced were only consumed by the British in India. Unlike the Mughals and the Portuguese, the British failed to create a new branch of cookery that spread to the rest of the population.

Dhansak

بضع علمی کتابی دمحوسی دورة بجبی طهرشا ره مش منه خالف الشافعی رح فانة لاوصع
لمه منذا ه لکل سعنه کمانیادار رعون دز بمانی یا تذلی فی کله شبار لبعة دراتم

This is the Parsee dish that the British liked best. The Parsees brought a liking for mixtures of meat and vegetables or meat and fruit with them to the west coast of India, where they were influenced by the Gujarati love of sweet and sour and Indian spice mixtures. Traditionally, dhansak is made with four different sorts of lentils and eaten with caramelized brown rice and fried onions. Serves 6–8.

3 oz. red split lentils (masoor dhal)
3 oz. split mung beans (moong dhal)
3 oz. skinned toor dhal
3 oz. skinned split chickpeas (chana dhal)
2 large onions, finely sliced
½ teaspoon turmeric
1¼ lb. vegetables of your choice, chopped into bite-size pieces, such as pumpkin, aubergine, potatoes, peppers, spinach
⅜ in. piece of fresh ginger, chopped
2 whole garlic cloves
bunch of fresh coriander, chopped
4–6 tablespoons vegetable oil
¾ in. piece of fresh ginger, finely grated
6 cloves garlic, crushed
1 teaspoon cumin powder
1 teaspoon coriander powder
½ teaspoon chilli powder
2 brown cardamoms
⅜ in. cinnamon stick

1 teaspoon black mustard seeds
½ teaspoon fenugreek seeds
3 tomatoes, chopped
2 green chillies, chopped
2⅕ lb. chicken cut into pieces
1¼ cup chicken stock
1–2 teaspoons of jaggery or soft brown sugar
juice of 1 lemon or lime

Wash the lentils and peas and soak in salted water over night.

Drain the lentils and peas and place in a large pan with 3 cups water with the onions and the turmeric. Bring to the boil and simmer for about 20 minutes. Add the vegetables and the ⅜ in. piece of ginger, 2 whole garlic cloves and most of the fresh coriander, and simmer until the lentils and peas are soft. Remove from the heat and leave to cool. Then mash or purée the mixture with a potato masher or in a food processor.

Heat 4–6 tablespoons of oil in a pan and add the grated ginger, crushed garlic and fry for 5 minutes. Add the cumin, coriander, chilli powder, cardamoms, cinnamon, mustard seeds, and fenugreek seeds and continue frying. After a few seconds add the tomatoes and green chillies. Fry for another 2 minutes, stirring. Add the chicken and fry until all the pieces are browned.

Add the chicken and spice mix to the lentil mix and salt to taste. Add 1¼ cups chicken stock, the jaggery, and lemon or lime juice. Simmer and serve when the meat is thoroughly cooked. Garnish with chopped fresh green coriander.

The "Empress" Currie Powder is prepared from an old Indian recipe with condiments of the finest quality. *Sold in Bottles,* 4d., 6d., 1/-, 1/6, and 2/- *each.* Also in Tins, ¼ lb., ½ lb., 1 lb., 2 lb., 4 lb., & 7 lb., At 2/- per lb.

6

Curry Powder: Bringing India to Britain

O N 27 MARCH 1811, an advert appeared in the *Times* that announced
to the retired East India Company officials of London that
they would now be able to enjoy "Indian dishes in the highest
perfection" at the newly opened Hindostanee Coffee House. At the
corner of Charles Street and George Street, the coffee house was well
placed, as this area, around Portman Square had recently become
fashionable among returned Anglo-Indians. The old India hands could
sit in custom-made bamboo-cane chairs, surrounded by paintings of
Indian scenes, and reminisce about their former lives while savoring
curries "allowed by the greatest epicures to be unequalled to any . . . ever
made in England." In a separate smoking room, they could whiffle
away at their hookahs. One notorious patron, Charles Stewart, who was
rumored to have had 16 Indian wives and to have bathed in the Ganges
every morning when in Calcutta, referred to the establishment as the
"Hooka Club." The Indian proprietor, Sake Dean Mahomed, assured
his customers that the spices, oils, and herbs, both for the curries and for
the hookah tobacco, were all specially procured in India. This ensured an
"authentic" taste that allowed his customers to feel themselves transported
back to their old haunts.[1]

Sake Dean Mahomed designed the first curry house in Britain to appeal
to men like William Makepeace Thackeray, the first bearer of that name,
who made a fortune in India as the collector of Syhlet district. In this wild
and forested part of Bengal, he collected the East India Company's

revenue in the form of cowry shells for a salary of about £62 per annum. This was hardly a sum to make a man rich. However, elephants were plentiful in Syhlet and Thackeray rounded them up and sold them to the company at a rate that enabled him, after only ten years in India, to capture a pretty bride and retire aged a mere 27. On his return to Britain in 1776, he settled down to a peaceful life digging the garden of the small country estate at Hadley, in Middlesex, which he purchased with his riches.[2]

Retired East India Company officials were by now familiar figures on the London scene. They were known as nabobs, a British corruption of the word nawab, meaning a governor or ruler of a district. Like Thackeray, these men used their wealth to buy themselves country estates; often they also bought seats in Parliament, thus purchasing themselves a place in the British social elite. The established aristocracy, feeling their position of power was threatened, attacked the nabobs as social upstarts, and accused them of corrupting honest hardworking Britain with oriental luxury. An alternative school portrayed them as bumbling but likeable figures of fun. Nabobs popped up, often as minor figures, in many of the plays, books, and newspapers of the period. William Makepeace Thackeray's grandson and namesake often included a nabob as one of the characters in his novels. Jos Sedley in *Vanity Fair* is the collector of Boggley Wollah. He suffers from a "liver complaint . . . superabundant fat . . . indolence and a love of good living." A foolish, greedy figure, he is easily hoodwinked by the antiheroine, Becky Sharp. In Thackeray's *The Newcomes*, the "loose trousers, long mustachios and yellow face" of the kindly Colonel Newcome of the Bengal Cavalry reveal that he is a nabob. The colonel loses his fortune in the Bundelcund Bank crash.

Dean Mahomed's speculation in curries was as unsuccessful as Colonel Newcome's venture into Indian banking. Less than two years after he opened the Hindostanee Coffee House, he was forced to petition for bankruptcy. Although the food and ambience were favorably reviewed in the *Epicure's Almanack*, the Hindostanee was unable to compete with a number of other coffee houses that were better established and closer to the City of London. Norris Street Coffee House on the Haymarket had been serving curries since at least 1773 and the Jerusalem Coffee House in Cornhill was already established as the base for East India Company merchants and officials.[3] Mahomed's partner carried on the business, although it is unclear whether he maintained the Indian atmosphere. Mahomed, with more success this time, set up a vapor bath in Brighton where the Prince Regent enjoyed being "shampooed." This involved vigorously massaging the skin with a loofah-like glove.

It is likely that many of the nabobs who settled around Portman Square had no need of Mahomed's curries because they could afford to employ their own Indian cooks. Returning Anglo-Indians, unwilling to exchange the smooth subservience of their Indian servants for the truculence of British housemaids, routinely brought their ayahs (nannies), menservants, and cooks back to Britain with them.

Ringa Swamee bitterly regretted hiring himself to a sahib in Benares, who had "brought me to England fifteen years ago and then died and left me helpless." Ringa Swamee and his English wife and child had been reduced to begging. In *The Asiatic in England* Joseph Salter, a missionary who worked with stray Asiatics, described how the journey to Britain ended in disaster for many of these domestics. Newspapers were dotted with notices posted by Indian servants hoping to escape such a fate by finding work with a family returning to India.

Other notices asked for sightings of Indian absconders. Escaped domestics could disappear into the oriental underworld that the East India trade had created in London. A network of grubby boarding houses existed in Whitechapel, and in the "Oriental quarter" around the high street in Shadwell. Here, lascars (Indian sailors) stayed while they waited for their ships to sail. Joseph Salter visited one such house in the 1850s, kept by "Abdool Rhemon, a native of Surat, near Bombay... [who] thrives at his countrymen's expense." Rhemon was said to have begun his career sweeping a crossing at St. Paul's Churchyard, but after the Nepalese ambassador took an interest in him he was able to set up his own business. "He kept two houses in this vicinity... the first floors being set apart as opium smoking-rooms. When Lascars were in the docks, these houses were invaded... We might go upstairs... and see them reclining on beds, smoking the insidious opium."[4] Many of the boarding-house keepers were "assisted by an English mistress, some of whom have lived so long in this element, that they use the Oriental vernacular [and] bear names...

such as Mrs Mohammed . . . or Calcutta Louisa, and Lascar Sally." Many of the sailors jumped ship and made a living begging, thieving, or working as street sweepers and hawkers of cheap goods. Salter came across one who made ends meet by selling "curry powder to gentlefolks in the suburbs" and others must have found employment as cooks in the households of returning company merchants.[5]

If they were unable to afford the expense of bringing an Indian cook home with them, and could not find an Indian in Britain, old India hands employed women like Sarah Shade, who had learned to make curries in India. Sarah had led an adventurous life as a soldier's wife. In an account of her experiences, she claimed to have fought off a tiger by grasping the root of its tongue, and to have been laid out ready for burial perfectly sensible of what was happening to her, after a severe case of the flux had left her prostrate. Caught up in the Anglo-French wars in southern India, she was wounded in the face by shot and in the arm by a sabre, and then captured by the Sultan of Mysore's army. Sarah's knowledge of Indian cooking now came in useful as one of her captors was so impressed by her ability to speak his language and to prepare Indian food that he helped her, and her husband, to escape. Sarah undoubtedly picked up her culinary and linguistic skills among the Indian and Eurasian wives of the other soldiers. Many British soldiers married "pretty, half-caste girls," and in 1813 one army officer estimated that "a third of the people in this country are either married to this race or have children grown up by Hindoostanee women."[6] Sarah Shade left her husband in India to return to Britain in the 1780s. Here, her knowledge of Indian cookery again helped her to survive as she kept herself out of the workhouse "by making curry for different East Indian families."[7]

British households did not necessarily need an Indian cook for curries to be produced in their kitchens. Indian food found its way into British food culture by various channels. Family members at home were eager to learn about the exotic lives of sons and brothers in India and the young men often enclosed recipes in letters. Wilhelmina and Stephana Malcolm stranded, unmarried, at the family home of Burnfoot, Dumfriesshire, kept up a regular correspondence with their ten brothers, some of whom were seeking their fortunes in India. The sisters copied their brothers' instructions on how to make "mulgatawy" soup and Indian pickle into their kitchen notebooks alongside more traditional recipes for Brown Windsor soup and potato puffs.[8]

Equally eclectic recipe collections were put together by the women who accompanied their husbands to India, garnered from their Indian cooks. When they retired, or returned to Britain on leave, Anglo-Indians instructed their British cooks in the art of preparing a good curry. In Thackeray's *Vanity Fair*, Jos Sedley's mother mentions that she has ordered the cook to make him a curry for dinner that night just as he likes it. Having set her sights on Jos as a possible marriage prospect, Becky Sharp decides to gain his favor by tasting the dish. She suffers "tortures with the cayenne pepper" and Jos and his father mischievously add to her misfortune by offering her a chilli. Misled by the name that sounds like "something cool" she eats it with relief, only to discover that it is even hotter. Forced to throw dignity to the wind, Becky calls for water, to peals of laughter from Mr. Sedley and his son. Outside fiction, however, Anglo-Indians were often successful in introducing their relatives and friends at home to the delights of Indian food. Although Thackeray was born in India, he was sent home at the age of four, like most Anglo-Indian children, to receive a British education thus, leaving India before he could acquire a liking for Indian food. But he discovered a taste for curry at the dining tables of his various aunts and uncles who had lived there. Indeed, he was so enthusiastic that he is said to have written "A poem to curry."

> Three pounds of veal my darling girl prepares,
> And chops it nicely into little squares;
> Five onions next prures the little minx
> (The biggest are the best, her Samiwel thinks),
> And Epping butter nearly half a pound,
> And stews them in a pan until they're brown'd.

What's next my dextrous little girl will do?
She pops the meat into the savoury stew,
With curry-powder table-spoonfuls three,
And milk a pint (the richest that may be),
And, when the dish has stewed for half an hour,
A lemon's ready juice she'll o'er it pour.
Then, bless her! Then she gives the luscious pot
A very gentle boil—and serves quite hot.
PS—Beef, mutton, rabbit, if you wish,
Lobsters, or prawns, or any kind fish,
Are fit to make a CURRY. 'Tis when done,
A dish for Emperors to feed upon.[9]

Specialist recipe books began to appear, catering to the returned Anglo-Indian's desire to reproduce Indian food. In 1831, the Oriental Translation Committee published a pamphlet entitled "Indian Cookery" for the benefit of "that...considerable number of individuals and families in this country [who] have, from a long residence in the East, acquired a strong predilection for Indian modes of life."[10] It contained instructions on how to prepare the standard fare of Anglo-India— pilau, korma, dopiaza, khichari, kebabs, and mango preserve—although the recipes were much closer to the Indian originals than later British recipes.

Enthusiasm for curries was no doubt fueled by the bland nature of British cookery. Becky Sharp's response to the cayenne pepper and chilli in *Vanity Fair* reveals how unused to spicy foods the British were at this period. This seems strange, given that it was the hunger for pepper and spices that had taken the British to India in the first place. But spices had slowly fallen out of favor in the West. During the seventeenth century, Europeans were captivated by the grace and beauty of classical architecture and sculpture, and they developed a passion for the societies of ancient Greece and Rome. This led to an investigation of classical cookery. The Romans loved pepper, and did in fact enjoy spicy food, but what interested seventeenth- and eighteenth-century cooks was the salt/acid taste combination of classical cookery, based on olives, capers, and anchovies. This style of cookery accorded well with new scientific theories of digestion that envisaged the process as one of fermentation rather than combustion. Foods that had previously been shunned, such as mushrooms, anchovies, and oysters, were redefined as healthy because they fermented easily. Spices, which had been seen as useful fuel to stoke the fires of the stomach, were now less valued. In France and Italy the almond-based, spicy, and fragrant cookery of the High Middle Ages, which relished the combination of sweet and sour, was replaced by a nouvelle cuisine. This eliminated the sweet from savory dishes and relied on sauces based on butter and oils, which were thought to help bind the salts and chemicals that were the end result of fermentation. As a consequence, European cuisines became much blander.[11]

Britain took its culinary lead from France, and spices such as nutmeg, cloves, and cinnamon were banished to the realm of puddings and cakes. Boxes of cumin, coriander, cardamom, and saffron, which had once been regarded as precious luxuries, grew dusty on the pantry shelves. Hot spicy food was condemned as overly stimulating and likely to arouse dangerous passions and lusts.[12] These prejudices were combined with a distrust of vegetables. Onions, garlic, and leeks were regarded with suspicion because they tainted the breath and were thought to be difficult to digest. By the end of the eighteenth century, the range of "safe" vegetables was limited to old potatoes, cauliflowers, broccoli, French beans, and asparagus. Meat, roasted, boiled, and baked in pies, was still the staple food among the middle classes. Under these conditions, French nouvelle cuisine suffered in the hands of British cooks. A Swiss pastor complained in 1782 that the normal fare in a coffee house was "a piece of half boiled or half roasted meat; and a few cabbage-leaves, boiled in plain water; on which they pour a sauce made of flour and butter, the usual method for dressing vegetables in England."[13] Curries must have made a very welcome change.

Although the demand for spices had lessened, the British remained greedy for oriental goods. In the seventeenth century, tea drinking was introduced into polite society from China and this stimulated the demand for elegant tea bowls and fine Chinese porcelain. A number of small shops specializing in oriental wares sprung up in London. At Peter Motteaux's boutique in Leadenhall Street, the connoisseur of luxury goods could buy tall blue-and-white Chinese jars, rich brocades, and cabinets in burnished gold.[14] Ladies' fashions incorporated Eastern elements, and there was a craze for turbans, the soft pashmina shawls of Kashmir, and Indian muslins worked in silver and gold. Returning nabobs introduced Indian architecture into Britain. At Sezincote in the Cotswolds, Charles Cockerell built himself a house in the oriental style with domes and ornamental pillars. At each end of the house he constructed summerhouses with stars painted on the ceilings so that he could recapture the Indian experience of sleeping outside under the night sky. The Prince Regent followed suit with the Brighton Pavilion refashioned (1815–1823) into an oriental fantasy of domes and pillars. Alongside this enthusiasm for exotic wares, interest grew in the cookery of the East. Ordinary British ladies and gentlemen with no connection to India began to look with curiosity upon these newfangled curries.

By the 1840s a number of Indian products were for sale and their producers went to great lengths to persuade the British public that they should add curry to their diet. Edmund White, the maker of Selim's Curry products, presented curry as a health food. In accordance with the methods of Victorian advertising, he wrote a pamphlet pompously entitled "Curries: their Healthful and Medicinal Qualities; their Importance in a Domestic, Commercial, and National Point of View." In this, he argued that the consumption of fish curries made with Selim's True Indian Curry Paste would aid digestion by stimulating the stomach, which would in turn stimulate the circulation of the blood, resulting in a more vigorous mind.[15] He even claimed that curries could save lives and cited the preposterous case of a Mr. Harper of the Jerusalem Coffee House (the well-known haunt of East India merchants) who, having tried all medicines without relief, had fallen into despair, only to be saved by the aromatics administered to him by Mr. White in a curry paste.[16]

The Duke of Norfolk, perhaps irritated by these advertising strategies, suggested that if curry was so beneficial perhaps the Irish poor, then suffering under the effects of the potato famine, might use it to stave off their hunger pangs. This insensitive remark was deservedly lampooned in *Punch*, which claimed that he would soon be publishing a brochure entitled "How to live on a pinch of curry" containing a recipe for "A capital soup": "Take a saucepan, or, if you have not one, borrow one. Throw in about a gallon of good water, and let it warm over a fire till it boils. Now be ready with your curry, which you may keep in a snuff box if you like, and take a pinch of it. Pop the pinch of curry into the hot water, and serve it out, before going to bed, to your hungry children."[17]

Among the general populace there were stalwart believers in the health-giving properties of curries. One of the readers of *Queen* magazine reported in 1863 that her "Great Aunt always had a great idea of the advantage of adding a curry to her bill of fare in hot weather. It is good for the digestion, she would say, and that is why hot things are so relished in India. Excessive heat interferes with the vital functions, and the digestive powers require a stimulant when enervated by the heat. She was very proud of her home-made curry powder, the receipt for which had been given to her by some of her Eastern friends in her younger days."[18]

The first British cookbook to include Indian recipes was Hannah Glasse's *The Art of Cookery* published in 1747. In it she gave three different recipes for pilau. Later editions included recipes for fowl or rabbit curry and Indian pickle. An adventurous cook, Glasse also included recipes for potatoes and instructions on how "to dress Haddocks the Spanish Way," which included tomatoes.[19] Although these New World vegetables had been known to the British since Columbus's voyages to America, they were still confined to the experimental kitchens of the wealthy, whose servants Glasse's manual was designed to instruct.

Curries initially suffered from the fact that they were viewed as a form of stew that was regarded as a lower-class way of preparing meat.[20] It was not until the middle classes developed into a powerful social and economic force during the first half of the nineteenth century that curry really entered British kitchens.

The domestic ideology of the middle classes, which celebrated the virtuous housewife, transformed thrift into a mark of respectability. Cookery books and household manuals praised the middle-class woman who ran an efficient and economic household and who was able to stretch the food budget. Curries came into favor as an excellent way of using up cold meat. The British in India sometimes curried cold meat, and this is the origin of the jalfrezi that appears in Anglo-Indian cookery books as cold meat fried with lots of onions and some chillies.[21] In Mrs. Beeton's definitive middle-class recipe book, all the beef and chicken curries were labeled as suitable for "cold meat cookery." The irony of this state of affairs was unappreciated by most British consumers of curries who were unaware that the consumption of leftovers was taboo among the majority of Hindus.

Whether it was for its taste, its practicality, or its nutritional values, curry was firmly established as part of the British culinary landscape by the 1850s. The author of *Modern Domestic Cookery* (1852) commented that while curry was "formerly a dish almost exclusively for the tables of those who had made long residence in India, [it] is now so completely naturalised, that few dinners are thought complete unless one is on the table."[22] If the recipe books are to be believed, there was virtually nothing that the British would not stew in curry sauce, from ordinary cuts of meat to calf's feet, ox palates, sheep's heads, lobsters, and periwinkles. The middle classes were beginning to abandon the excess of the eighteenth century, when all the dishes were placed on the table at the same time in a display of profusion. Following the new French fashion, polite society dined *à la Russe*. This meant that the dishes and joints were placed on the sideboard and handed round, one by one, by the servants. The meal was divided into a number of courses, and a standard pattern of soup, fish, entrée, roast, followed by dessert, and sometimes a savory, was established. The emphasis shifted from the quantity of the food to its refinement. To the discerning consumer, the light and often fanciful entrées were the most important dishes. Curries provided the chef with another opportunity to display his finesse in "made" dishes, as opposed to simple joints of meat. The curry even shook off its reputation as a way of using up leftovers and began to appear at dinner parties. In the 1850s, a range of suggested menus for dinners of various sizes were published in a book entitled *What Shall We Have for Dinner?* The author was given as Lady Maria Clutterbuck but the real writer is believed to have been Charles Dickens's wife, Catherine, and Dickens himself may even have had a hand in the publication. Curried lobster, curried oysters, and mutton curry rice were all included in the menus alongside roast goose, stewed eels with oyster sauce, and cold pigeon pie.[23]

As the taste for curry spread to more and more people in Britain, it became a subject of discussion in the letter sections of women's periodicals. "Madame," wrote W. M. B. from Bath in the ladies' magazine *Queen*, "you supply me at times with such excellent recipes, I should be glad if you could favour me with a good one for dressing meats with Indian curry powder." Other readers sent in their favorite curry recipes and there were lengthy discussions about how the rice should be served (separately or with the curry sauce poured over it), which implements it should be eaten with (spoons were favored), and whether Patna was more suitable than Carolina rice. The correspondents frequently proudly emphasized the "authenticity" of their recipes, claiming they had been passed on to them by native cooks. One reader even claimed to have learned the secret for preparing "Genuine Madras Curry Powder" from the butler to one of the sons of the infamous Tipoo Sahib.[24] Even Richard Terry, chef de cuisine at the Oriental Club, felt the need to emphasize that the recipes in his *Indian Cookery* were "gathered, not only from my own knowledge of Cookery, but from Native Cooks."

Despite these protestations, Rakhal Haldar, professor of Sanskrit at University College London in the 1840s and 50s, found the curries his British hosts kindly ordered "in consideration of my being an Indian . . . as different from the genuine Indian curry as two things can possibly be."[25] And of course, the curries and pilaus produced in nineteenth-century British kitchens were even more Anglicized than those that were prepared in India for Anglo-Indian consumption.

British curries in India used a basic formula: first spices, onions, and garlic were ground and bound together by ghee, then this paste was added to some meat, and simmered. As Thackeray's poem to curry illustrates, in Britain a similar recipe was followed. Onions and meat were first fried in butter, then curry powder was added, followed by stock or milk, and the mixture was left to simmer. Just before serving, a dash of lemon juice was added. The curries to be found in British recipe books are all variations on this template. The same recipe could be transformed into "Bengal Chicken Curry" by adding to the sauce a spoonful of Bengal chutney, pickled limes and mangoes, or into "Melay Curry" by adding half a grated coconut.[26] What distinguished curries in Britain from their Anglo-Indian counterparts was their reliance on curry powder, something that no self-respecting Indian cook would have allowed in their kitchen. Indian kitchens were not properly equipped without a heavy flat grindstone on which the spices were laboriously crushed by a rolling-pin-shaped stone. The day's supply of spices was freshly ground each morning, and in wealthy households a special assistant, the masalchi, was employed to grind the spices.[27] The stones were also used to crush onions, garlic, chillies, and fresh herbs such as coriander, to produce cooking pastes and chutneys. Freshly ground spices impart a flavor incomparable to that given to food by preground spices that have been kept in a store cupboard.

Recipe for Bengal chicken curry from Richard Terry's
Indian Cookery

Cut into small dice 2 onions, and fry with 2 pats of butter: add your chicken cut into small joints, with one tablespoonful of curry paste, ½ of powder, ½ of Bengal chutnee, ½ pickled lime, and ½ pickled mango: stir the whole over a slow fire 10 minutes, cover the chicken with broth or water, and let simmer 1½ hours—by this time the curry will be almost dry—add 1 teaspoonful of cream, and serve with rice, separate.[28]

Even when they were cooking for their British masters, Indian cooks would have maintained the principle of adding freshly ground spices at different stages of the cooking process. When Anglo-Indians initially began to collect Indian recipes to bring home with them, they too followed this principle. In eighteenth-century Britain the nabobs purchased their coriander and cumin seeds, their cardamom pods and cinnamon sticks separately from their local chemist. When curry first appeared in a British cookery book, no mention was made of curry powder. Hannah Glasse in 1747 instructed her readers to "Brown some Coriander Seeds over the Fire in a clean Shovel" before beating them to a powder, much as an Indian masalchi would have done.[29] The Oriental Translation Committee's "Indian Cookery" of 1831 listed the specific spices for each recipe and followed the principle of adding them at separate stages in the cooking process.

But as the Anglo-Indians began to think of curries as variations on one theme, they began to collect recipes for spice mixtures that they simply labeled "Curry Powder." By the 1850s British cookery books called for a spoonful of curry powder in most of their dishes. Sometimes they supplied recipes for curry powders that the cook could make up in advance, but as the popularity of curries became widespread it became easy to buy curry mixes. As early as 1784, Sorlie's Perfumery Warehouse in Picadilly advertised that it was now selling ready-mixed curry powder.[30] Between 1820 and 1840 imports of turmeric, the main ingredient in British curry powder, increased threefold, from 8,678 lbs. to 26,468 lbs.[31] Nevertheless, the British preferred Indian-made products and a correspondent to one ladies' periodical complained that no British-manufactured curry powders or pickles (including Crosse & Blackwell's) could equal those of Manoekjee Poojajee's of Bombay.[32] In the 1860s, Payne's Oriental Warehouse in Regent and Mortimer Streets proudly advertised that all its curry powders and pastes, chutneys, pickled mangoes, tamarind fish, essences of chillies, and preserved ginger were made at the Belatee Bungalow in Calcutta. The Leicester Square Oriental Depot advertised that it was prepared to send goods out to country residences for those enjoying time away from London on their country estates. By the end of the century, even nonspecialist grocers normally stocked three types of curry powder: a yellow, a brown, and a fiery, chilli-flavored red one.[33] The condiments necessary to make curry were easy to procure but the delicate nuances of Indian cookery were lost.

Mr Arnott's Currie Powder from Eliza Acton's Modern Cookery

turmeric 8 oz.
coriander seed 4 oz.
cummin seed 2 oz.
foenugreek seed 2 oz.
cayenne ½ oz.

We recommend Mssrs Corbyn and Co., 300 High Holborn for the spices.[34]

Overreliance on curry powder meant that British curries had a tendency to degenerate into a kind of "hash."[35] In 1845, Edmund White derided British curries as "nothing more nor less than a bad stew, rendered the more abominably noxious from the quantity of yellowish green fat which must inevitably float in the dish. It would be ridiculous to call such dishes . . . True Indian Curries, or to talk about their healthful properties . . . they can only be referred to as a sample of the kind of dishes generally in use in England."[36]

Pre-prepared spice mixes, known as masalas in India, are used occasionally on the subcontinent but they are usually added to the dish at the end of the cooking process. In Kashmir the women still make *ver*, a mixture of mustard oil, garlic, and chillies ground together with a combination of spices that is made into a paste and shaped into doughnut-shaped discs. These are left to dry in the shade and then threaded on to strings and hung from the ceiling in the kitchen. A little *ver* is crumbled over dishes as they are placed on the table to impart a hot zing to the food. In Gujarat travelers carry balls of pounded garlic, red chillies, and salt bound together with oil that they sprinkle over meals made over the campfire.[37] There are good reasons why Indians rarely use pre-prepared masalas as the main flavoring for their dishes. Spices take different lengths of time to release their flavor. Thus it is better to add slow-releasing coriander to the cooking oil before adding turmeric, which is quick to impart its flavor, or cumin, which is apt to burn. Spices thrown into hot oil simultaneously tend to cook unevenly and the cook runs the risk of flavoring the dish with a slightly burnt or a slightly raw taste. The Christian communities of Bombay and Bassein get around this problem when they make curry powder by roasting each spice for the necessary amount of time before grinding it and mixing it with all the others. Their spice mixture is known as "bottled masala," as they store it in long green bottles.[38]

Another typically British habit was to add the curry powder at the same time as the stock or water. In fact, spices release their taste more effectively when they are first fried in hot oil. For this, pots in India are often rounded in order to allow the oil to collect at the bottom so that the spices can be fried first without using excessive quantities of fat.[39] The flavor of spices is also determined by the way in which it is treated before it is added to the dish. For example, roasted and crushed cumin tastes nutty, but fried whole in hot oil it imparts a gentler liquorice flavor.[40] Spices added to a wet sauce give a different, less aromatic flavor to the dish than when the spices are fried.

Thirdly, British cooks routinely thickened curries by making a roux of curry powder mixed with flour, a technique that was used to thicken stews and casseroles. Wheat flour is never used in this way in Indian dishes—they are given body with ground almonds, coconut cream, or a paste of onions.

One of the more authoritative British cookery writers, Eliza Acton, lamented "the great superiority of the oriental curries over those generally prepared in England," which she attributed to "many of the ingredients which in a *fresh* and *green state* add so much to their excellence, being here beyond our reach." She was also aware that Indian cooks varied their "dishes . . . with infinite ingenuity, blending in them very agreeably many condiments of different flavour, till the highest degree of piquancy and savour is produced . . . With us, turmeric and cayenne pepper prevail in them far too powerfully." But within the limitations of curry powder and British currying techniques, Acton recommended a number of measures that would save British curries from turning into spice-flavored casseroles. "A couple of ounces of sweet sound cocoa-nut lightly grated . . . in the gravy of a currie is . . . a great improvement to its flavour," she pronounced. This was an attempt to reproduce the flavor of coconut milk frequently used in south Indian dishes. Acton also pointed out that "tamarinds imported *in the shell*—not preserved" were available as a way of giving British curries an authentic taste. Most British cooks, however, had to rely on lemon juice (and sometimes sour gooseberries) as a substitute for unobtainable tamarinds. Lemon juice, added at the end of the cooking process, became a standard ingredient in British curry. Apples were often used to replace mangoes, cucumbers or marrows to replace bitter gourds, which were essential ingredients in Bengali cuisine. Sultanas, which were sometimes added to Mughlai pilaus, also found their way into curries. They added a touch of the exotic and perhaps it was thought that they complemented the apples. After time, these ingredients were no longer viewed as substitutes for more authentic ingredients but instead as *essential components* of a good curry. When Leon Petit ran the restaurant in Spence's Hotel in Calcutta in the 1950s he was "met with polite smiles of disbelief when [he] tried to explain to Indian cooks that apples [and sultanas] are essential to Western curries."[41]

Recipe for Curried Veal from Joseph Edmunds,
Curries and How to Prepare Them

The remains of cold roast veal, 4 onions, 2 apples (sliced), 2 tablespoonsful of "Empress" curry powder, 1 dessertspoonful of flour, ½ pint of broth or water, 1 tablespoonful of lemon juice.

  Slice the onions and apples, and fry them in a little butter; then take them out, cut the meat into neat slices, and fry these to a pale brown. Add the curry powder and flour, put in the onions, apples, add a little broth or water, and stew gently till quite tender; add the lemon juice and serve with an edging of boiled rice. The curry may be ornamented with pickles, capsicums, and gherkins arranged prettily on top.[42]

On arrival in Bombay in 1858 as the bride of a British army officer, Matty Robinson discovered that Anglo-Indian curries were quite unlike the British ones she was used to: "I can't touch the Indian fruits or the fish which they say is so delicious, and as to the curries it makes me sick to think of them; give me an English one!" she wrote.[43] When Eliza Acton included Mr. Arnott's authentically Anglo-Indian curry in her *Modern Cookery*, she warned that it "will be found somewhat too acid for English taste in general, and the proportion of onion and garlic by one half too much for any but well-seasoned Anglo-Indian palates." [44] The Anglo-Indians also liked their curries extremely hot. Curry-powder vendors spent a great deal of energy trying to persuade their British customers that it was not necessary to "experience the discomfort occasioned by excessive heat in order to enjoy the full delicacy of Eastern condiments."[45]

Once curries were firmly established in Victorian food culture, distinctively European herbs such as thyme and marjoram began to find their way into Indian recipes. Anglo-Indian dishes such as mulligatawny soup and kedgeree underwent further Anglicization in the hands of British cooks. Richard Terry of the Oriental Club not only added the by now standard apples to his mulligatawny but also bay leaves, ham, and turnips. Mrs. Beeton included bacon in hers, while Eliza Acton strove for authenticity with "part of a pickled mango" and grated coconut, but gave herself away by also suggesting the addition of the "pre-cooked flesh of part of a calf's head" and a sweetbread (bull's testicle) as well as "a large cupful of thick cream."[46] Meanwhile, the transformation of the ever-versatile khichari continued. The Anglo-Indians had already added fried onions, fish, and hard-boiled eggs to the rice and lentil dish. Now the aristocracy, who served kedgeree for breakfast during their country-house weekends, settled on smoked haddock as the definitive fish to add to the rice, and almost invariably abandoned the lentils.

Recipe for an Anglicized Mulligatawny Soup from Richard Terry's
Indian Cookery

Stock for the soup:
Cut into small pieces 1 fowl and 7 lbs of lean veal; place it in a stewpan with 1 oz. of lean ham, 2 carrots, 2 turnips, 4 cloves, 2 allspice, 1 blade of mace, and a small bunch of mixed herbs. Add one pint of water; place the stewpan over the fire, and let all the water reduce, then fill the stewpan up

with water, and then let boil gently for four hours, then strain it off into a pan. Have ready another stewpan 1 small carrot, 2 onions, 4 apples sliced, ½ a turnip sliced, 2 oz. of lean ham, 1 bay leaf, 1 celery, 2 sprigs thyme, 3 cloves, 1 blade of mace, 4 oz. of butter; stir the whole over a slow fire for ten minutes; add 5 tablespoonful of curry powder and 1 of paste; stir again over the fire for 2 minutes; add 4 tablespoonful of potato flour, 2 of Arrowroot and ¾ lb. of flour; stir all well together, then add the stock, and stir over the fire till boiling; add a small piece of garlic, the size of a pea, let all boil for 2 hours; if this should be too thick, add more stock; any kind will do. The soup should then be rubbed through a tammy and placed again in a stewpan; add a little more stock and stir till boiling, let boil gently at the corner of the stove fire for 1 hour, keeping well skimmed; season with a tablespoonful of salt and of ½ of sugar; if this soup should be too hot in flavour, add more potato flour; when finished this soup should not be too thick, and serve with small pieces of chicken in the soup, and rice in a separate dish.[47]

The British also took their curries to their other colonies. Australia's climate appealed to retiring Anglo-Indians, who took their Indian eating habits with them. British companies exported curry powders and pastes to the Australian cities, and the earliest cookery book published in Australia in 1864 "had a short essay on curry stuffs and the value of mixing one's own." It included recipes for the standard curries of Anglo-India— Madras, Bengal, and Bombay—and suggested the typically British trick of substituting apples for mangoes. It also used the British technique of thickening the sauce by mixing the curry powder with flour. Australians made their own contribution to the development of curry by adding wattlebird and kangaroo tail to the long list of meats that received the British curry treatment.[48]

European travelers to seventeenth-century India discovered that with their meals the Indians ate a wide range of achars, or pickles and chutneys. Many of these were freshly made each morning. While preparing the spices for the main dish, the masalchi might grind together fresh green coriander leaves, coconut, and green chillies to create a sharp, tangy, bright green paste, delicious with the soft and spongy south Indian rice breads known as idlis. Other pickles and chutneys were more like preserves and the Europeans found them very useful when they traveled across the vast subcontinent. Pietro della Valle, who had so much trouble finding anything to eat while traveling in India, equipped himself for his journey with "many Vessels of conserves of the Pulp of young Indian Cane, or *Bambu* (which is very good to eat after this manner) and of green Pepper, Cucumbers and other Fruits wont to be pickled by them."[49] European sailors used to buy up jars of achar to take with them on their sea voyages and these must have greatly improved their diet of dry, and usually wormy, biscuits and hard salt meat.[50]

When jars of these pickles and chutneys arrived back in Britain with East India Company merchants and sailors, British cooks eagerly tried to reproduce them, just as they had done with curry, with the result that they underwent a similar process of metamorphosis. Indians very rarely used vinegar, and their pickles were made by layering vegetables or fruits in jars with oil or water. The mixture was flavored with salt and spices and the jars were set in the hot sun where they were left to ferment. Lacking the intense heat of the Indian sun, British cooks resorted to vinegar to carry out the pickling process. Unable to lay their hands on mangoes or bamboo shoots, they tried out various substitutes such as marrows, apples, or tomatoes for mangoes, and elder shoots for bamboo. Sultanas, persistently associated in the British mind with anything spicy, were also added. To reproduce the piquant heat provided by chillies, they added European flavorings such as horseradish and mustard powder.[51] The bright yellow mixture of cauliflower, onions, and mustard, known as piccalilli, almost certainly evolved out of these recipes. While curries made few inroads into British working-class households, jars of pickle became standard in all British pantries, and in the 1920s and 30s, housewives would prepare tomato or marrow chutneys for Christmas as a way of livening up the cold remains of the turkey.

> ### *To make Indian pickle, from Hannah Glasse's*
> ### The Art of Cookery Made Plain and Easy
>
> To a gallon of vinegar one pound of garlick, and three quarters of a pound of long pepper, a pint of mustard seed, one pound of ginger, and two ounces of turmeric; the garlick must be laid in salt three days, then wip'd clean and dry'd in the sun; the long pepper broke, and the mustard seed bruised; mix all together in the vinegar, then take two large hard cabbages, and two cauliflowers, cut them in quarters, and salt them well; let them lie three days, and then dry them well in the sun.
>
> N.B. The ginger must lie twenty-four hours in salt and water, then cut small and laid in salt three days.[52]

In China, East India Company merchants discovered soy sauce, and a number of soy-based condiments known as catsups. They took these dipping sauces back to India with them and John Ovington, who ate pilau and dum poked chicken with the English East India Company merchants at Surat in 1689, noticed on the factory dining table "Bamboe and Mangoe Achar, and Souy, the choicest of Sawces, are always ready to whet the Appetite." These sauces had the virtue of keeping for an extraordinarily long time and sailors stocked up with barrels of soy sauce and catsup for the long sea voyages. Recipes for these useful seasonings began to circulate in Britain. Hannah Glasse gave a recipe directed to the "Captains of Ships" for a "Catchup to keep twenty Years." It combined stale beer, anchovies, mace, cloves, pepper, ginger, and mushrooms. She pointed out helpfully that "You may carry it to the Indies; a Spoonful of this to a Pound of fresh Butter melted, makes fine Fish-Sauce. Or in the room of Gravy-Sauce."[53]

The commonest catsup was made from mushrooms until tomatoes became popular in the nineteenth century. Tomatoes had been cultivated in Britain since the sixteenth century but many people thought them poisonous as they belonged to the Solanaceae family of plants that includes poisonous nightshades such as belladonna. It was known, however, that the Italians ate them with olive oil and by the eighteenth century the British had plucked up sufficient courage to include them in their diet.

Philip Miller, superintendent of the Chelsea Physic Garden, noted in 1752 that tomatoes were "much used in England for soups." It is possible that tomatoes were introduced into the British diet by Jewish families from Spain and Portugal who had strong trading links with the Caribbean and Americas, where tomatoes were routinely eaten. By the nineteenth century, British cooks had discovered how useful they were as a souring and thickening agent, in soups and broths, and they also adopted them as a base for catsups.[54] Today the oriental origins of tomato ketchup, surely one of the most widespread relishes in the world, are forgotten.

In India, catsups were the inspiration for the piquant shikari sauces that the Anglo-Indians enjoyed with their game and it was one of these sauces that eventually became one of the best-known British flavorings. Sometime in the 1830s, Lord Marcus Sandys, the former governor of Bengal, drove into Worcester from his nearby country estate to visit Lea & Perrins, his local chemist-cum-grocer. The shop on Broad Street sold foodstuffs, cosmetics, and all sorts of medicines and was known for its supply of spices and dried fruits specially imported from Asia and the Americas. Lord Sandys arrived with a recipe on a scrap of paper and requested Lea & Perrins to make up his favorite Indian sauce. The mixture that Messrs. Lea and Perrins duly concocted was so fiery that it made their eyes water. But as has already been mentioned, according to Emma Roberts these sauces were "assuredly the most piquant adjuncts to flesh and fowl which the genius of a gastronome has ever compounded." Sandys was delighted with the results. But the chemists were disgusted with the mixture. They put the extra barrels that they had made up for themselves in the cellar, where they were forgotten. During a spring clean, however, it was noticed that an appetizing aroma was rising out of the abandoned barrels and on tasting the contents Lea and Perrins discovered that the concoction had matured into a pleasing spicy sauce. The enterprising pair went into immediate production. By 1845 they had set up a factory in Worcester, and by 1855 were selling over 30,000 bottles a year. Worcestershire sauce was even exported back to India.[55]

In 1858, the East India Company was abolished and India was brought under the administration of the Crown. The previous year Indian troops had rebelled against their British officers and sparked a popular uprising against the British in parts of northern India. In the light of the Indian mutiny it seemed inappropriate for a vital part of the British Empire to be controlled by a trading company. In 1877, Queen Victoria was crowned Empress of India, as part of Prime Minister Disraeli's project to revive the popularity of the monarchy. Empire and monarchy, bound together, were symbols in a political and social strategy that encouraged patriotism in the working classes. Music-hall songs, popular plays, children's adventure stories, all celebrating Britain's empire, distracted the working man from the inequalities in British society by encouraging him to identify with a larger imperial project. The enthusiasm for empire that developed in Britain during the last quarter of the nineteenth century was expressed in the exotic names given to an array of commercial sauces and relishes, such as Nabob's, Mandarin, or Empress of India.[56]

Public interest in the empire was encouraged by a series of exhibitions that began with the Great Exhibition of 1851, housed in the specially constructed Crystal Palace. This combined the atmosphere of a fun fair with educational displays of art, science, natural history, and industry.[57] After the stunning success of the Great Exhibition many others followed in London and Paris, and in the provincial towns of Britain. They marked a change in the British attitude toward empire, from a source of magical luxuries—spices, pashmina shawls, porcelain jars—to a more industrial and blatantly commercial interest. The galleries of the exhibitions demonstrated the usefulness of the colonies to Britain's Industrial Revolution by displaying the various goods imported from the empire. The bales of hemp and jute and the sacks of tea contrasted with the cotton piece goods that Britain, in a reversal of fortunes, was now exporting to places like India. This impressed upon the spectator the importance of the empire as an export market for Britain's industries.

Even the Queen caught empire fever. She was particularly fascinated by India. In Osborne House, which she and Albert built on the Isle of Wight, she collected Indian furnishings, paintings, and objects in a specially designed wing. This included a durbar room with white and gold plasterwork in the shapes of flowers and peacocks. Here the Queen, bedecked in jewels and looking like a parody of a maharani, would entertain guests. Indian curries were prepared in the royal kitchens and Victoria employed Indian servants in gorgeous costumes to stand at her dining table. She was particularly fond of these servants, who attended to her every need with quiet efficiency, gliding in and out of rooms to assist the ageing and rather overweight Queen to stand up and walk about. One of these Indians, a handsome 24-year-old named Abdul Karim, gained a sinister level of influence over her. Known as the Munshi, the Indian title for clerk, he appointed himself to the position of personal secretary. He taught her to write and speak a little Hindustani and, unlike the other servants who communicated with the Queen in writing, he had personal access to her.[58] The resentment of her other servants and the concerns of government officials eventually reached such a pitch that the Queen was persuaded to demote her favorite Indian. But she never lost her powerful, if somewhat hazy, sense of affection for her Indian subjects in her distant empire.

If India featured prominently in the Queen's imagination, its place in the popular fantasy world was assured by the Empire of India Exhibition held at Earls Court in 1895 and 1896. As a commercial enterprise, its main purpose was entertainment rather than education. One of the main attractions was a replica of an Indian town. Wooden buildings, which had once stood in the town of Pune, were reconstructed to recreate what one of the organizers claimed was "a really typical and realistic Indian village." Nevertheless, a slight air of unreality must have been added by the mock-Indian jungle at its center, decorated with life-size model tigers, crocodiles, snakes, and elephants. The narrow streets were lined with shops populated by "eighty-five Indian craftsmen, including silk and carpet weavers" who were brought over from India. In addition, over 100 jugglers and dancers performed in the streets and animal keepers wandered about, leading behind them specially imported camels, elephants, and cattle.[59] Outside the Indian city, the visitor could sample a Mughal ornamental garden filled with Indian flowers and trees, while snake charmers, fakirs, and lion tamers provided entertainment.

The snake charmers' cobras kept on dying, and Indian sailors had to be bribed to smuggle replacement snakes on to their boats. Large quantities of ghee were also imported, to feed all the Indian craftsmen and entertainers working at the exhibition. Unfortunately, the Indians did not take to British mutton and all the goats within the vicinity of Earls Court were quickly consumed. Men had to be employed solely for the purpose of traveling ever further afield to buy goats.[60] While the organizers struggled to provide their workers with acceptable food, they fed their visitors Anglo-Indian curries. In the Curry House visitors could sample "Eastern dishes, prepared by a staff of Indian cooks, and placed before [them] by native servants."[61]

Indian cafés and restaurants were a theme at many of these exhibitions. One enterprising Indian waiter, who worked in the Ceylon Tea House at Liverpool's Royal Jubilee Exhibition in 1887 and at Glasgow's International Exhibition the following year, published a cookery book: *Curries and How to Make Them in England.*

Recipe for Economical Curry Paste from Daniel Santiagoe's
The Curry Cook's Assistant

1 lb. Coriander Seed	¼ lb. Saffron
¼ lb. Dry Chillies	¼ lb. Pepper
½ lb. Mustard Seed	2 oz. Dry Ginger
2 oz. Garlic	½ lb. Salt
½ lb. Dried Peas	½ lb. Brown Sugar
2 oz. Cumin Seed	½ pint Vinegar
½ pint Lucca Oil	

N.B. Few Bay Leaves in Ceylon and India. Use Carugapilbay or *Curry Leaves*, black.

Grind with vinegar. Put in jar. Cover with Lucca Oil. Use a large spoon for Madras Curries.[62]

Ironically, while Londoners enjoyed sampling the chaotic and exciting atmosphere of an Indian town at the Earls Court exhibition, the British who actually lived in India would not have dreamed of setting foot inside one. British cantonments were built at a safe distance away from the Indian townships. One member of the Raj remembered that as a little girl the Indian town was forbidden to her, even though she longed to ride her pony under the gates into that "mysterious and fascinating" world.[63]

The British Empire Exhibition at Wembley in 1924–1925 was one of the most successful of all the exhibitions. During its course, 27 million people traveled, as it were, from one end of the empire to another. The Indian section, housed in a pavilion modeled on the Taj Mahal, had the usual mock jungle, jugglers, and snake charmers, a display of shikar trophies, a model of the Khyber Pass, and a jumble of Indian goods, including carpets, silks, indigo, and tea. The café served curries and pilaus, and the visitor could enjoy a cup of Indian tea "under the trees on the north side of the grounds among typical Indian scenery."[64] It was run by Edward Palmer, the founder of E. P. Veeraswamy & Co., Indian Food Specialists, who imported spices, chutneys, and curry pastes from India and sold them under the label "Nizams." The company may have been named for Palmer's grandmother, one of the Indian wives of his grandfather, William Palmer, who founded the banking house of Palmer & Co. at Hyderabad in the late eighteenth century. Indeed, Edward Palmer came from a family of men who had served in India and married Indian women. His great-grandfather, also William, married the beautiful Muslim princess Begum Fyze Baksh, and a painting of the family by Johann Zoffany hangs in the Oriental and India Office Collections at the British Library today.

Palmer had an interest in producing authentic Indian food. In a cookery book that he published in 1936, he insisted that it was possible, using his curry powder, to make a "proper curry . . . equal to the very best made in India," as long as the cook fried or grilled the powder to rid it of its raw taste before adding it to the dish. He also specified that flour should "on no account" be used to thicken curries and that apples and sultanas did not belong in a curry.[65] When the Wembley exhibition closed Edward decided to establish the café in a permanent home at 101 Regent Street, and Veeraswamy's opened in 1926. The successor to Sake Dean Mahomed's Hindostanee Coffee House, it is the oldest surviving Indian restaurant in Britain today. Decorated with lights from the Maharaja of Mysore's palace, cane chairs, and potted palms, it retained the Raj atmosphere of the exhibition café. The waiters were specially imported from India, and wore the bearers' uniforms of British India. The food that the restaurant served was also firmly Raj: duck vindaloo and Madras curry. The restaurant was patronized by nostalgic Anglo-Indians and the rich and fashionable, including the Prince of Wales.

Green coriander chutney

اسننع جعلم كماني وكوسبي ووقئ ريم طلهرخشارة من هند خلاع الشافعي رحه فانذل الوضح
لمه خشناره ام لكلسعذ كماية دوالسعون ازربمارت باخذني لكم شهدار لعة دراهم

This is a fresh chutney that should be made just before it is required. It is difficult to give precise amounts for the ingredients in this sort of dish. It is best to keep tasting it and adjust the flavor as you make it. It tastes good with idlis (you can buy packet mixes from Indian grocers if making them from scratch seems intimidating). It is also good as a side dish with coconut-based curries and with grilled fish.

large bunch of fresh green coriander (the size you can buy at vegetable markets rather than the tiny packets you can buy in supermarkets)
½–¾ cup coconut milk, or fresh coconut, grated
1–6 fresh green chillies
⅜ in. piece of fresh ginger, chopped
2–3 cloves of garlic, chopped
a handful of raw peanuts (if you only have salted ones, add less salt)
salt to taste
sugar to taste
lemon or lime juice to taste

Wash the coriander and blend it in a food mixer with the other ingredients until it is smooth. Add more coconut milk or lemon juice if you need extra liquid. Keep tasting and when it is sharp, tangy, bright green, and smooth it is ready.

Our Cook Room

7

Cold Meat Cutlets: British Food in India

I N OCTOBER 1873, John William Laing arrived in Bombay to spend five
months on a sightseeing tour of India. He stayed with friends in
Malabar Hill, an exclusive area of Bombay, and in his diary he wrote
down the menu for the dinner he was served on 28 October:

Gravy soup
Fillets of fish Parsley Sauce
Entrées
Breast Mutton Compôte
Joint
Mutton Chicken Pie
Second Course
Italian Eggs
Pudding
Lemon Custard Baked[1]

Curry did not feature, neither in the form of the Mughlai food familiar to
the East India Company merchants, nor as bowls of Anglo-Indian curry
and rice.

Although he noted down what he ate, John Laing saw no reason to
comment on the food or the manner in which it was served. By the 1870s
"a person fresh from England" found nothing unusual in Anglo-Indian
dining habits. Just as it was in Britain, the dinner was served at seven or

eight in the evening; the men and women wore evening dress; the food was served on the best Wedgwood china, imported from Staffordshire, and eaten with elegant silverware; and the champagne or claret was drunk from fine crystal glasses. One or two attentive servants changed the dishes and removed the plates as each course was brought to the table. Despite the alien surroundings, the late-nineteenth-century Anglo-Indian dinner party faithfully reproduced the food and table etiquette of the urban bourgeoisie in Britain.

All the hallmarks of the *burra khana* had been eradicated. The crowds of servants, which had surprised Fanny Parks in the 1820s, had been greatly reduced. In the 1830s Anglo-Indians had begun printing "No hookahs" in the corner of their dinner invitations, and by the 1870s the pipes no longer bubbled quietly behind every chair. The airy white linen the gentlemen used to wear had been exchanged for respectable black evening dress. As early as 1838, a visitor to India was pleased to discover that "French cookery is generally patronised, and the beef and mutton oppressions of ten years since are exploded." The huge saddles of mutton, the hams, and the turkeys had been replaced with "made" dishes, served in separate courses. Moreover, curry and rice had been dropped from the menu. A review of a cookery book in a Calcutta periodical in 1879 noted with satisfaction that "the molten curries and florid oriental compositions of the olden time . . . have been gradually banished from our dinner tables."[2] As Victorian Britain was enthusiastically embracing the idea of empire, and curry was becoming a favored dish among the middle classes, Anglo-Indians were busily eradicating as many traces of India as possible from their culture.

This change in dining habits demonstrated a desire to keep up with fashions back at home. In the early nineteenth century it had been commonplace for visitors to India to refer to the uncouth nature of Anglo-Indian society. One handbook snootily asserted that to anyone who had "been accustomed to move in the good circles of England, the contrast must be striking, and we apprehend, unfavourable to the Anglo-Indian community."[3] The author went on to state that in India "in little appertaining to the table . . . is the *comme il faut* thoroughly understood."[4] But Anglo-India was changing. More women were beginning to arrive in the colony, and the introduction of steamships and an overland route to India via Egypt improved communications with Britain. Gradually, the rough and ready nabobs began to lose ground to a new group of Anglo-Indians—the sahibs and memsahibs—who resented the implication that they were nothing more than nouveau-riche parochials and concentrated their efforts on maintaining civilized standards, even in the remote wilds of India. Advocates of the new utilitarian and evangelical ideologies were also beginning to arrive. They argued that British officials were not in India to run the country for a money-grubbing trading company but to bring to its backward and impoverished people the benefits of civilization. The men to carry out this program needed to be fine upstanding representatives of Englishness. Nabobs who smoked the hookah, lazed about in cool white linen, and kept an Indian mistress in the purdah quarters of their bungalow began to give way to black-coated bureaucrats. After the abolition of the East India Company in 1858, the racial theories of the latter half of the century emphasized the need for both the civil servant and the military officer to demonstrate the superiority of the British race. The gentlemanly product of the public schools was promoted as the ideal colonial ruler. These were young men who were supposedly self-reliant, decisive, independent, and athletic, with a strong sense of their own authority. And, most importantly, they were thought to be capable of upholding British prestige at all times.

As part of the imperial project to maintain prestige, curry and rice were demoted: "A well considered curry, or mulligatawni—capital things in their way,—[were] still frequently given at breakfast or luncheon," and curry was the main dish out in camp, on long journeys, at dak bungalows, and in a variety of informal settings. But to serve a curry for the evening meal was now frowned upon. In Victorian Britain, dinner was the central meal of the day and it was therefore singled out by the Anglo-Indians as the most important meal, when they concentrated on demonstrating their Britishness. Many complained that it was absurd to don black evening dress in the stifling Indian heat and sit down to eat roast beef and suet puddings but this was precisely what the British did. Cookery books were published that instructed the memsahib "how best to produce, under the special circumstances of the country, the dishes approved by the taste of polite society at home."[5] The recipes inside *Wyvern's Indian Cookery Book* and *The Wife's Cookery Book being Recipes and Hints on Indian Cookery* were not for the curries and Indian pilaus that one might have expected, but for cheese crumb croquettes, thick kidney soup, sole au gratin, stewed beef with oysters, toad in the hole, Yorkshire pudding, and white sauce.[6] This was a selection of dishes that could have come from Mrs. Beeton. What the memsahibs tried to achieve was the same plain, wholesome British home cooking, mixed with the occasional dash of French sophistication that was current in Victorian Britain. The results, however, tended to be disappointing. On the whole Anglo-Indian British food was "monotonous, tasteless, and not nourishing." One missionary who lived in India in the 1930s referred to it as "pseudo-European."[7] What the memsahibs created was a second branch of Anglo-Indian cookery. The pseudo-Indian curries, mulligatawny soup, and kedgeree of the first half of the nineteenth century were now joined by an array of slightly orientalized British dishes.

A variety of circumstances conspired against the Anglo-Indians' attempts to produce palatable approximations of British food in India. Firstly, the Muslim cooks the British usually employed were hampered by their lack of personal experience of the food they were trying to produce. The Indian cook could not hold up the taste of his salmon mayonnaise or plum pudding against the memory of a meal eaten in Britain. This, combined with the fact that Indian and British cookery were very different, meant that it was extremely difficult for them to form an accurate concept of what they were aiming for. The result was a long line of cooks trained in a culinary style of which they had no personal understanding, each one passing down his own eccentric and peculiar interpretations of British dishes, until they eventually became engrained in the Indian understanding of British cookery. This could lead to some truly awful misunderstandings. One army officer was eventually forced to sack his cook because he insisted on indiscriminately adding vanilla to *every* single dish he cooked whether it was beef olives, grilled fish, or bread and butter pudding.[8] Divorced from culinary developments in Britain, Anglo-Indian cookery inevitably developed into an independent branch of cuisine.

A variety of British dishes underwent a process of orientalization. Meat casseroles, usually made with carrots and celery in a wine-based sauce, thickened with flour, were livened up with Indian spice mixtures (masalas). The results were neither curries nor casseroles but something in-between. Anglo-Indian cookery used the cuts of meat familiar to the British, and the same methods of roasting and grilling, but the treatment given to the meat was often distinctively Indian. Rather than stuffing chicken with breadcrumbs and herbs, the Anglo-Indians' cooks smothered the meat in coriander, cumin, and pepper and created masala roasts. In Britain, cooks would thriftily use up leftover cold meat by mincing it and then covering it in mashed potatoes. These "chops" or "cutlets" were then dipped in egg and coated in breadcrumbs and fried. In India, the memsahibs taught their kitchen staff this method for using up leftovers, but the cooks added their own distinctive masala mixtures to the mince or mashed potato to produce spicy Anglo-Indian "cutlets."

Recipe for cold meat Cutlets from
Indian Cookery "Local" for Young Housekeepers

Materials. One lb. of cold Beef or mutton minced fine and pounded on a board with the "Koitha" [a long knife used with a wooden board]. Moisten the mince with a little gravy or broth, add a minced onion, with its juice pressed out, some pounded spice and pepper, a few leaves of chopped mint, a green chilly, and a slice of bread soaked in water and well squeezed. Salt to taste. Put the meat pulp and the other ingredients together, mix well with a raw egg, form the mixture into balls, put a layer of bread crumbs on the board and lay on it a ball of meat, form it into the shape of a cutlet, sprinkle a thick layer of crumbs over, and fry the cutlets brown in ghee or dripping.[9]

The Indianization of French cuisine began with the names of the dishes that were frequently "strangely transmogrified." George Cunningham, an Indian civil servant in the 1920s sent home a menu for

Consumme Royal
Beef Filit Bianis
Roast Fowl
Girring Piece Souply
Putindiala Jumban
Dupundiala Promison

> What do you make of the enclosed menu, the joint result of one of Mugh cook's kitchen French and a Hindu Babu? The beef fillet bearnaise and the green pea soufflé are fairly easy, but "pouding a la jambou" (it was made to look like ham) is not so obvious, and the "Permesan" savoury beats me. It was little rounds of cheese pastry with cheesy eggs on top but I can't think what word he is driving at.[10]

The results were not always unpleasing. Bland, cream-based sauces were given some bite with a dash of Worcestershire sauce or a pinch of cayenne pepper. But the Indianization of French cuisine did produce some spectacularly unappetizing concoctions. Lady Minto, the wife of the viceroy (1905–1910), dutifully copied into her cookery notebook a recipe for Soufflé de Volaille Indiénne that required a mousse of chicken and curry sauce to be poured into a soufflé case. Once set, a circle of the mousse was removed and the hole filled with mulligatawny jelly mixed with rounds of chicken and tongue. This was served with a salad of rice and tomatoes mixed with mayonnaise and curry.[11]

Matters were not helped by the fact that many memsahibs had no idea how to cook themselves. They arrived in India with a clear idea of how British food should taste, but no real notion of how this was achieved. Many had left home when they were very young and had no experience of running a household. The problem of inexperience was made worse by the fact that their knowledge of Indian languages was often limited to a few words spoken in the imperative. Some cookbooks tried to solve this problem by printing the recipes in Indian languages. This was all very well if one was lucky enough to employ a literate cook but even then things could go awry. *What to Tell the Cook, or the Native Cook's Assistant*, which printed the names of the recipes in English and the rest in Tamil, cheerfully asserted that it would "save the house-keeper the trouble of describing the *modus-operandi.*" But the second edition followed the suggestions of several readers and printed the English text on the opposite page.[12] Obviously some housekeepers wished to try and locate the reason for the cook's failed attempts at buttered crab and Snowden pudding.

Indian conditions were unfavorable to British ways of preparing meat. In Britain, carcasses were normally hung for a few days after the animals were slaughtered. In the Indian climate this was out of the question, and the flesh had to be cooked the same day that it was killed. Roasting, grilling, or boiling did not help to make such tough meat any more palatable. Indian methods of stewing chicken in curries, or slowly tenderizing mutton in *dum pukht* dishes, or mincing and grinding beef or lamb into a fine paste before roasting it, were much more suitable for dealing with freshly killed meat. Some memsahibs acknowledged defeat and "gave up ordering roast chicken. The too recently killed victim tasted better if gently stewed or made into a curry."[13]

Indian kitchens were not really set up for the preparation of British dishes. The kitchen equipment was usually a grinding stone, a few large pots, a spit, a kettle, and a simple wood-fired oven. Even if the cook was provided with a table he would usually ignore it and conduct most of his tasks sitting or crouching on the floor. In the early nineteenth century, Thomas Williamson warned that only those with strong stomachs should investigate the cookroom. The sight of the cook basting the chicken with a bunch of its own feathers was likely to turn "delicate stomachs," and to catch the cook in the act of using the same implement to butter toast was quite off-putting. Similar warnings were still being issued in the 1880s and one handbook advised "either . . . visit the kitchen daily, and see that it has been properly cleaned out, or never go to it at all."[14] Many Anglo-Indians adopted the latter piece of advice and cheerfully followed Williamson's line of thought that if "the dinner, when brought to the table, looks well, and tastes well: appetite . . . prevents the imagination from travelling back to the kitchen."[15] Sometimes this suppression of the imagination was exercised even though the food was demonstrably unpleasant. One memsahib, very new to India, was horrified to discover that her breakfast of semolina porridge was full "of little cooked worms. It could almost be called worm porridge." In a small, frightened voice she commented on the worms. This brought the spoons of her breakfast companions to a halt, but she had the decided feeling that her "host felt he had been most unreasonably deprived of his breakfast." After some time in India she gave up trying to eradicate worms from flour and came to the conclusion that it is "Better to come to reasonable terms with Nature in the East."[16] For the more concerned memsahib, life turned into a constant struggle with the servants. She would spend her days doling out the supplies, watching to see that the milk and water were properly boiled, picking through the flour for worms, and worrying that the moment her back was turned the cook would revert to unhygienic habits.

India constantly conspired against the stuffy attempts of the British to impose a veneer of grandeur on their lives. In any Anglo-Indian house all one had to do to destroy the illusion of effortless elegance, so carefully created in the dining room, was to step on to the back verandah. Here one would discover a host of Indian servants: one pulling the punkah, some sleeping, others washing up or boiling a kettle for tea.[17] Indeed, it was the very servants who were essential to constructing this atmosphere of grandeur who so often introduced a false note or an atmosphere of tension. Bearers were in the habit of burping in the presence of their masters, butlers would demonstrate dissatisfaction by "snuffling . . . loudly and offensively" while serving dinner.[18] Even the respectful blank stare that many Indian servants adopted had the uneasy effect of making one feel negated. Besides, there was always the sneaking feeling that the smooth show of subservience concealed an attitude of contempt. Of course, many Anglo-Indians felt great affection for their servants, but even then this did not always mean that they were particularly competent. One family was blessed with "a disarmingly gentle" "Cookie" who would sit rocking their dog in his arms whenever it was ill. Naturally this meant that there was no supper, but this did not matter as much as it might have done, as he was an "abominable" cook.[19]

The British in India never really took to Indian fruit and vegetables. "I have often wished for a few good apples and pears in preference to all the different kinds of fruits that Bengal produces," wrote a homesick accountant from Calcutta in 1783.[20] The Anglo-Indians thought that aubergines and okra tasted slimy and unpleasant. Jean-Baptiste Tavernier described how the East India merchants at all the seventeenth-century European factories planted extensive kitchen gardens with vegetables familiar to them from home, such as "salads of several kinds, cabbages, asparagus, peas and principally beans, the seed of which comes from Japan."[21] The Europeans also brought with them newly discovered American vegetables, such as potatoes and tomatoes. It is hard now to imagine Indian food without these European and American vegetables, but in fact it took a long time for many of them to be integrated into Indian cookery.

How the potato came to India is unclear. The Portuguese or the Dutch may have brought the first specimens to the subcontinent, but they were unusual enough in 1780 for the governor-general Warren Hastings to invite his fellow council members to join him for dinner when he was given a basket of potatoes by the Dutch. Even in Britain at the time potatoes were a novelty, grown by wealthy farmers and professionals in their kitchen gardens, but not yet a part of the staple diet. One of the first things Lord Amherst did as governor-general in 1823 was to order that potatoes should be planted in the park at Barrackpore.[22] The Bengalis took to potatoes with enthusiasm. Their starchy softness contrasted perfectly with the sharp flavors of mustard seeds and cumin that were common in Bengali cookery. By the 1860s they had become an essential ingredient in the region's diet. From Bengal, potatoes spread inland. An army wife traveling through northern India between 1804–1814 reported that "the natives are all fond of it, and eat it without scruple."[23] In the south, potatoes took longer to become popular and James Kirkpatrick, resident at the Indian court of Hyderabad, missed them so much that he had a supply of them brought from Bombay with an armed guard through the wars raging in the Deccan. Even today, potatoes are regarded by some Indians with residual suspicion as a new and strange foodstuff, uncategorized by Ayurvedic medicine. The botanist George Watt noticed that the Indians thought they "cause[d] indigestion and flatulence," and orthodox Jains refuse potatoes on the grounds that as root vegetables they possess the ability to generate life and therefore cannot be consumed.[24]

The Bengali names of many European vegetables indicate that the Bengalis were introduced to them by the British. Tomatoes are referred to as *biliti begun* or English aubergine. It took longer for tomatoes to become popular, but George Watt noticed in 1880 that although they were still "chiefly cultivated for the European population . . . Bengalis and Burmans use [them] in their sour curries."[25] Nineteenth-century tomatoes were sourer than the ones we are accustomed to today and they were particularly well suited to the Bengali style of sweet-and-sour cookery. Other British introductions were pumpkins, known as *biliti kumro* or English gourd, cabbages, cauliflowers, and beans. But while the British changed the vegetables that Indians ate, they did not change the way that Indians cooked their vegetables. Just as Bengalis referred to European vegetables as an English form of an Indian vegetable, they prepared them in the same way as their Indian counterpart.[26] As Gandhi commented, "simply boiled vegetables are never eaten. I never saw a boiled potato in India."[27] The British had a tremendous impact on the Indian diet. The introduction of European vegetables into the subcontinent significantly widened the range of vegetables available to a largely vegetarian population. However, the British had very little impact on the style and techniques for preparing vegetables.

Orchards in the cool hill stations, and market gardens around the presidency towns, meant that the British were able to buy apples and pears and European vegetables during the cold season. In his "Kitchen Calendar" of available ingredients a "Thirty-Five Years' Resident" rejoiced in the long list including cauliflowers, potatoes, peas, and beans that were available in December and January, while in July he lamented that "the vegetable market is very indifferent . . . potatoes become poor and watery. Young lettuces, cucumbers, and sweet potatoes are now [virtually all that is] procurable."[28] For the rest of the year, and for a variety of other articles, they had to rely on imports from Britain. When Elizabeth Gwillim arrived in Madras in 1801, to start her new life as the wife of a judge, she brought with her two gammons of bacon, which made her luncheon parties popular. "Sir S Strange and Mr Sallivan . . . came every day whilst the first lasted," and the gammons were eaten "clean to the bone." Her stores also made her popular with her Indian servants, who particularly liked English pickles. Elizabeth described how "their passion for these pickles is so great that they condescend to eat them though made by us whom they account the lowest of all and class with the kamars or outcasts." These British versions of those bamboo and mango achars, which company sailors had taken home with them in the seventeenth century, had been transformed into strange and enticing delicacies for the Indian servants. Elizabeth was forced to keep the pickle jars locked away and when she required some she would dole out a little at a time on to a saucer and, even then, had to watch carefully that it appeared on the table.[29]

The process of hermetically sealing food in tins and jars was invented at the beginning of the nineteenth century and Anglo-Indians took full advantage of the new technology. At the European stores in the larger British settlements it was possible to buy hermetically sealed oysters, salmon, asparagus, and raspberry jam; even cheese came in tins. But these products were regarded as very expensive as they cost 30 to 40 percent more than they would have in Britain. The adventurous, who were willing to brave the "heat, fatigue and abominations which beset their path" in the native bazaar, could find "capital bargains."[30] At the foot of the hill station of Landour, Fanny Parks discovered a wonderful bazaar where all sorts of European articles could be procured: *"paté foie gras, bécasses trufflés,* sola hats covered with the skins of the pelican, champagne, bareilly couches, shoes, Chinese books, pickles...and various incongruous articles."[31] But many handbooks advised that it was cheaper to bring a large store of goods with you and then have a friend or relative send a box out at regular intervals containing

> Tart fruits in bottles; jams in patent jars; vinegar; salad oil; mustard; French mustard; pickles and sauces; white salt; caraway seeds; Zante currants and raisins in patent jars; dessert raisins and prunes in bottles; candied and brandy dessert fruits; flavouring essences; biscuits in tins; hams and bacon in tins ...; cheese in small tins; salmon, lobster, herrings, oysters, sardines, peas, parsnips, Bologna sausages, mushrooms, in tins, cocoa, and chocolate; oatmeal, vermicelli, macaroni; and tapioca; if near Christmas, a jar of mincemeat.[32]

The vogue for tinned foods began as a result of "the fashionable depreciation of things native"[33] but it soon grew into a fixed principle. Tinned foods became increasingly important in Anglo-Indian cookery, as they solved the problem of obtaining the necessary ingredients to create a properly British dinner-party menu. At least, they made it possible to create dishes that sounded and looked British. The drawback was that the food in the tins was often rather nasty. The tinning process was not really perfected until the Second World War and the metallic tang of tinned food could give it a "nauseous" flavor. But the British dinner was less about the taste of the food than its symbolism. The Anglo-Indians stuck to their hard bottled peas, tough roasts, and slightly metallic pâté de foie gras because it was a daily demonstration of their ability to remain civilized and to uphold British standards.

For Anglo-Indians living in remote stations, tinned foods and boxes from relatives were a rare luxury. Sometimes the closest store with a supply of European goods was at least a day's journey away. The only available fruit and vegetables were pumpkins, gourds—"green, attenuated things like desiccated cucumbers which had no flavour at all"—okra, bananas, and papayas. For meat there was "goat-mutton and skinny moorghi [chicken] day in day out," occasionally supplemented with game shot while out hunting. Understandably, many Anglo-Indians living in isolated areas thought a great deal about food, and placed great value on a good cook. A railway engineer and his wife were happy to overlook the fact that their cook Abraham had just come out of prison as he produced such tasty meals.[34] Although some misdemeanors could not be ignored. When one memsahib living in a distant outpost on the Northwest Frontier discovered that her cook was running a small brothel in one of her spare sheds she had to sack him.[35] Nevertheless, even under such difficult circumstances, the majority of Anglo-Indians adhered to the principle that curry was not acceptable for dinner and endured the tedium of tasteless approximations of British food.

One of the places where Anglo-Indian cookery really came into its own was on the railways. After the mutiny in 1857 the British constructed an efficient railway system across the subcontinent, which enabled them to transport troops around the country quickly. The standard of the food served at the station restaurant and in the dining car was similar to that provided at the dak bungalow. The train would "stop at a station right out in the country; just a long platform and no sign of civilisation. And there would be no sound, except for the hissing of steam and the occasional slamming of doors. Then a man would come along and say, 'Lunch, lunch!' and you'd detrain and walk along the platform to the dining car where you'd get in and sit down and you would be served lunch."[36] Lunch was usually curry or "last night's tepid roast, euphemistically called cold meat, with thin slices of tomato and beetroot called salad." Dinner was, of course, British: "thick or clear soup, fried fish or minced mutton cutlets with a bone stuck in, roast chicken or mutton, custard pudding or soufflé." The chicken was usually as tough and stringy as dak-bungalow fowls and one English visitor to India was "greatly touched when on his last meal in the Madras-Bombay Express he read 'Roast Foul' on the menu. He felt rewarded for all the indifferently cooked but correctly spelt fowl he had consumed on India's railway system."[37]

Of course, there were a number of highly skilled Indian cooks who could "put to shame the performances of an English one."[38] Goan cooks were especially sought after. It was "quite astonishing what [they could] . . . turn out on charcoal and a few bricks, one on top of each other."[39] These cooks introduced vindaloo into the repertoire of Anglo-Indian curries, and cookery books referred to it as a "Portuguese curry." For the British, the Goans applied the techniques of vindaloo to all sorts of meats, with duck being the favorite. By the 1920s a Goan cook had become a marker of status. One of the first things Viola Bayley did, after her husband's promotion, was to employ a Goan cook. "Florian [was] . . . an accomplished chef and pastry-cook. The sweets he made for dinner parties were memorable. There was a toffee basket filled with fresh fruit and cream, and a meringue trifle, and ice-cream castles of fabulous design."[40] The Goans had preserved the Portuguese talent for magical desserts and the British enthused over their chocolates, fondants, and sugar-coated fruits. A classic Anglo-Indian dish known as beveca, made from sugar, rice flour, coconut cream, and rose water, was a simplified version of the Goan layered coconut cake, *bebinca*.[41]

Recipe for Beevica (Portuguese Dish) from
The Art of Ceylon and Indian Cookery

INGREDIENTS:—1 measure of rice flour, 3 large cocoanuts, 8 eggs, 1½ lb. unshelled almonds, sugar to taste.

MODE: Broil the rice flour, add the *thick* milk of the cocoanuts, 8 eggs well beaten, ground almonds and sugar to taste. Mix well together and bake in a round shallow tin.[42]

When the viceroy, Lord Reading (1921–1925), visited the tiny princely state of Bahawalpur (sandwiched between the Punjab, Sind, and Baluchistan) to install the new nawab on his throne, arrangements were made for a splendid Anglo-Indian–style banquet in his honor. "Goan cooks and waiters, complete with the ingredients of the meal, were specially bought from Lahore, two hundred and fifty miles away." For the sake of the honored guests, "it had to be an English meal consisting of soup, tinned paté, salmon, also out of a tin, with white sauce, a variety of roast birds, caramel custard pudding, Kemp's bottled coffee and a savoury on toast." The Indian guests looked forward to this rare opportunity to taste the prestigious food of their rulers but they were "greatly disappointed." They thought the plain boiled fish, "unsalted and unseasoned roast meats," and the odd baked pudding were completely tasteless, while the unfamiliar knives and forks turned the meal into "quite an ordeal. They longed for the spicy, saffron-tinted cuisine of the palace cooks."[43]

For the British the symbolic weight of English food was more important than the fact that it was bland and uninteresting. Soup and roast meat, custard and pudding, were all essential elements in the maintenance of prestige. Those Indians who adopted the cuisine of their rulers did so for similar reasons. Nawab Sadaat Ali Khan of Lucknow (1798–1814) employed a French, an English, and an Indian cook, and the wife of a British army officer observed that "three distinct dinners" were served at his table. By the time Sadaat Ali Khan came to the throne he was well aware that the tide was turning in favor of the British. Before his accession he had spent many years in Calcutta, and when he returned to Lucknow he set about Anglicizing the court. Besides the French chef, he brought with him a suitcase packed with an English admiral's uniform, a parson's outfit, and some of the latest fashions in wigs. He redecorated the palace in English style with "gilt chairs, chaises longues, dining tables, swagged velvet curtains and a profusion of chandeliers and girandoles," and the various different dinners were all served in the best English china.[44]

Sadaat Ali Khan was one of the first in a long line of Indian princes who incorporated the dominant culture of the British into their courts. By the end of the nineteenth century many Indian princes had received English educations, either from an English tutor, or at a public school, in either Britain or India. A great many of them led semi-Indian, semi-European lives. Often their wives maintained the Indian side of things, continuing to live in separate quarters, furnished in Indian style, and wearing traditional dress, while in their kitchens they supervised the preparation of exquisite Indian dishes. In contrast, the public areas of the palace were a statement of the successful acquisition of British culture, in the furnishings, the food served on the dining tables, and the daily routine of the ruler himself. The gaekwar of Baroda is a good example. Just before the First World War he was visited by the tiresomely sycophantic Reverend Edward St. Clair Weeden, who wrote a book about his visit in which he described the gaekwar's daily routine: *chota haziri* (little breakfast), followed by a ride, breakfast, and a morning playing billiards and receiving visitors. After tiffen the maharaja worked while his son and his guest took a rest, played tennis or cricket, or went for a drive. Dinner was succeeded by billiards, bridge, and bed. The gaekwar employed a number of English servants, including a valet, "a capital fellow named Neale from the Army," a French cook, and an English maître d'hôtel who had been butler to Lord Ampthill when he was governor of Madras.

The gaekwar's dining habits established his status as a gentleman. His breakfasts, Weeden claimed, were "very much what you would get at a first class restaurant in London." At dinner there were "two menus, as the ladies [the maharani and her daughter] may prefer to have Indian dishes, which are served on large golden trays, placed before them on the table." The maharani insisted that he should taste some of these Indian dishes. Rather churlishly, Weeden complained that this "made the dinner rather long," although he did enthuse over her pilaus: "made of beautifully cooked dry rice, chicken, raisins, almonds and spicy stuffing, covered with gold or silver leaf which gives it a very gay look. It is served with a most delicious white sauce flavoured with orange or pineapple."[45] Weeden seems to have been unaware that his hostess was something of a gourmet. Her granddaughter remembered that the food from her kitchen was always superb, whether it was "the Indian chef who was presiding or . . . the cook for English food." "She spent endless time and trouble consulting with her cooks, planning menus to suit the different guests . . . Her kitchen was particularly well known for the marvellous pickles it produced and for the huge succulent prawns from the estuary."[46]

The maharani of Baroda passed this love of fine food on to her daughter, Princess Indira, who married into the princely family of Cooch Behar. This family employed three cooks: "one for English, one for Bengali and one for Maratha food." (Cooch Behar is in Bengal and Princess Indira was a Maratha princess.) Each had his own kitchen, scullery, and assistants. The Cooch Beharis were a very modern, westernized family. They moved in the best circles of British as well as Indian society and traveled widely in Europe. Princess Indira was thus exposed to a variety of cuisines. She encouraged her kitchen staff "to experiment and introduced them to all kinds of unfamiliar dishes." She is said to have taken one of her cooks to Alfredo's in Rome because she wanted him to understand what Alfredo's pasta tasted like. Thus, some princely households outdid the British on their own ground. The British food served at their tables was not the boarding-house level common in Anglo-Indian society but demonstrated a mastery of the various sophisticated cuisines of Europe.[47] Other princely families just went through the form of consuming European food, without caring for it. Prakash Tandon witnessed this phenomenon among a family of maharajas in Hyderabad in the 1930s. Invited to lunch by a prospective son-in-law of the family, Tandon was eager to escape "the eternal roast mutton and Anglo-Indian curry at the hotel" and went along expecting "a moghlai feast":

> To my astonishment the meal began with a watery soup and followed its course through indifferently-prepared English dishes—mince chops with bones stuck in, fried fish, roast mutton and a steamed pudding. Instead of the famed Hyderabadi moghlai cooking I faced a meal as dull as my daily hotel fare. I accepted my fate, but noticed that the family only picked at their food, which I attributed to their noble blaséness. My friend managed to whisper that the English meal was a touch of modern formality of which no one took notice; the real meal was yet to follow, and it did. As soon as the pudding was removed, there began an unbelievable succession of dishes served in beautiful Persian-style utensils: pullaos and biryanis, naans and farmaishes, rogan joshes and qormas, chickens, quails and partridges, upon which the family . . . fell to. Indifference gave way to healthy vocal appetites, and I followed suit with my second lunch.[48]

British attitudes to Indian attempts to assimilate European culture into their courts were often condescending. Central to the justification of British rule was the assertion that Indians were incapable of achieving civilization on their own. It therefore undermined British self-confidence to acknowledge that Indians did understand and suavely adopt their ways. The army wife who visited the court of Sadaat Ali Khan claimed that while she was in Lucknow a misunderstanding arose over chamber pots. A set of Worcestershire china had arrived from England and in celebration the nawab had invited the British inhabitants to a breakfast. The table looked splendid except for about 20 chamber pots placed at intervals in the center of the table, which the "servants had mistaken for milk bowls." Surprised by his guests' reluctance to drink the milk, "the *Nawaab* innocently remarked, 'I thought that the English were fond of milk.' Some of them had much difficulty to keep their countenances."[49] Such mistakes, or a weakness for garishness, were interpreted as a sign that the Britishness of Indians was always a thin and fragile veneer. Lady Reading's personal secretary regarded the gaudy palace of the Maharaja of Bikaner as a sign that his "Europeanism ... for all its show, [was nothing] more than skin deep." Unfortunately, a number of maharajas appeared to confirm this British conceit by displaying a weakness for foolish European things. The Maharaja of Scindia's palace was like a "pantomime palace and rather fun, I think. Vast chandeliers, glass fountains, glass banisters, glass furniture and lustre fringes everywhere. It is really amusing and comfortable." He also had a vulgar device for delivering after-dinner drinks and sweets: "Then he pressed a button—and the train started. It is a lovely silver train, every detail perfect, run by electricity and has seven trucks—Brandy— Port—cigars—cigarettes—sweets—nuts—and chocolates. If you lift the glass lining to the truck or a decanter the train stops automatically. It is the nicest toy—and perfect for a State Banquet!"[50]

Maharajas were not the only Indians to adopt British habits. The British introduced an English system of education into India in the hopes that this would foster a collaborative elite, in the now well-worn phrase of Thomas Macaulay, "Indian in blood and colour, but English in taste, in opinions, in morals, and in intellect."[51] In and around the presidency towns, and particularly in Calcutta, which was the seat of British government, new business opportunities created by British commerce, the reform of the Indian judicial system and eventually the creation of parliamentary institutions, created jobs for the Western-educated Indians. Alongside the Indian sepoys in the army, these clerks, lawyers, doctors, publishers, engineers, and teachers provided a raft that kept the British Raj afloat and they began to adopt aspects of the dominant British culture. As early as 1823, Bishop Heber noticed that among the wealthy Indians "their progress in the imitation of our habits is very apparent ... their houses are adorned with verandahs and Corinthian pillars; they have very handsome carriages often built in England; they speak tolerable English, and they shew a considerable liking for European society." The 1832 Select Committee, investigating the sale of British goods in India, found that

Indians had developed a taste for wines, brandy, beer, and champagne. Yet as Heber remarked, "few of them will . . . eat with us."[52]

European travelers to Mughal India were often disconcerted when their Indian hosts simply sat politely by and watched them eat, but would not touch any food in their presence. The East India Company surgeon, John Fryer, commented that "every cast in India refuses to eat with those of contrary tribe or Opinion, as well as Gentues, Moors, and Persian, as any other."[53] Anglo-Indians in the nineteenth century were surprised and shocked to discover that they were considered impure by the majority of their supposedly inferior subjects. This was forcibly demonstrated to Mrs. Deane, traveling upriver in the early nineteenth century. Every evening the boatmen would prepare their food on the river banks. First, they would carefully create a flat circle of mud, at the center of which they would place their stove. "A number of these plans had been formed on the ground near our boat, and being ignorant at that time of their customs, I unfortunately stepped into one of the magic circles in my attempt to reach the high land." Nothing was said, but when she reached the top of the river bank and turned to look at the view she observed the boatmen "emptying the contents of their cooking pots into the river, and afterwards breaking the earthen vessels in which their food had been dressed." By stepping inside the circles, she had polluted the food and made it impossible to eat. As there was no village nearby the boatmen had only parched grain to eat that evening.[54]

As the British became a powerful presence in India, the question of interdining became more pressing. For the British, sharing food was an important way of cementing bonds and creating friendships. Some Indian communities found it easier to compromise than others. The fact that the British tended to employ Muslim cooks and waiters meant that Muslims would often overlook their scruples, as long as no pork was served. The Parsee merchant community in Bombay was particularly enterprising and adaptable. By the end of the nineteenth century, a high proportion of Bombay's factories and businesses were owned by Parsee gentlemen, who dressed like the British, ate at dining tables and, if they were very wealthy, employed three cooks, to make Goan, British, and Parsee dishes.[55]

The group that most enthusiastically embraced Western education were the Bengali Hindus. Under the Mughals, Muslims had dominated in government positions, but as power was transferred to the British they were slow to adapt and reluctant to learn English (the language of government had been Persian). The Hindu community quickly stepped in and grasped the new opportunities offered by a Western education. And yet the Hindus were the community for whom westernization caused the most problems. Orthodox Brahmans were said to take a purifying bath after any contact with Europeans who "contaminated themselves by eating beef, by the employment of cooks of all castes, and by allowing themselves to be touched by men and women of even the lowest castes."[56]

Some members of the Indian middle classes firmly rejected the adoption of British dining habits, let alone eating with Englishmen. In fact, many Indians employed in the British administration increased their observance of Brahminical rituals of distinction as a way of demonstrating their newly elevated social status. But, as educational and employment opportunities increased, Indians wishing to take advantage of them became increasingly vocal in their criticism of caste taboos. The evidence of an evangelical vicar in the 1820s may have been wishful thinking, but he claimed that "in numerous instances, we find that groups of Hindoos, of different castes, actually meet in secret, to eat and smoke together, rejoicing in this opportunity of indulging their social feeling."[57] Influenced by Western philosophy, a number of Bengali intellectuals criticized Indian culture, arguing that the caste system was an anachronistic obstacle to social progress. When Bhudev Mukhopadhyay, a future member of the Hindu revivalist movement in Bengal, attended the Hindu College in Calcutta in the 1840s, he discovered that "open defiance of Hindu social conventions in matters of food and drink was then considered almost de rigeur by the avant garde students of the College. To be reckoned a civilised person, one had to eat beef and consume alcohol."[58]

Meat eating among educated Indians was a response to the British claim that vegetarianism was at the root of Indian weakness. By the end of the nineteenth century, the British were less enthusiastic about the creation of a westernized Indian elite. They found that they had placed their own weapons in their subjects' hands. Armed with an understanding of Western philosophy and politics, educated Indians were able to demonstrate the injustices of imperialism using the rhetoric of their rulers. They began to demand their right to participate in the government of their own country. In retaliation, the British denigrated educated Indians, arguing that they were too degenerate to govern themselves. In the early nineteenth century, the British had argued that the steamy climate and frugal vegetable diet made all Bengalis languid and feeble. Now, in an attempt to justify their racially discriminatory policies, the British specifically labeled educated Indians as weak and effeminate.[59]

British arrogance, the fact of their ability ruthlessly to subdue Indians and impose their rule over them, and the assertion that this overwhelming power was, at least in part, derived from their meat-based diet, all gnawed away at Indian self-confidence. Faced with the incontrovertible fact that they were a subject people, educated Indians worried that their diet had made them feeble. This idea occurred to Gandhi growing up in Gujarat: "It began to grow on me," he explained, "that meat-eating was good, that it would make me strong and daring, and that, if the whole country took to meat-eating, the English could be overcome."[60] He and a group of friends experimented by roasting a goat. But the meat was like leather and Gandhi suffered from a guilty conscience. That night he dreamed that the goat was bleating inside him. "If my mother and father came to know of my having become a meat-eater, they would be deeply shocked. This knowledge was gnawing at my heart."[61]

When Gandhi decided to travel to London to study law in 1888, he was faced with the problem that Indians who traveled to Britain to study or to take the entrance examination for the Indian Civil Service were deemed to have lost caste. Overseas travel was considered polluting, added to which, while traveling, it was necessary to eat food cooked by non-Brahmans, and possibly in the presence of Englishmen. In order to please his mother, he took a vow that he would abstain from wine, women, and meat during his stay in England. Nevertheless, the caste elders designated him outcaste and even a purification ceremony on his return did not redeem him in the eyes of the orthodox members of his community.[62] For Gandhi, like many of his fellow students, the alternative world that his education would open up to him made him indifferent to the loss of caste. In fact, Gandhi was determined to transform himself into an English gentleman. On arrival in London he took dancing, elocution, and violin lessons and spent too much money on clothes.[63] Nevertheless, he intended to remain a vegetarian. His one foray into the world of meat eating had put him off for good. Consequently, food in Britain became an enormous problem for him.

The family Gandhi initially lodged with in London were completely stumped by his vegetarianism. As a result, he lived on a stodgy and unhealthy diet of soup, potatoes, bread, butter, cheese, and jam with an occasional piece of cake. It was not until he discovered one of the few vegetarian restaurants in London at that time, and moved into lodgings where he could cook for himself, that his diet, and his spirits, improved.

Food was always on Gandhi's mind when he lived in Britain, and later he wrote a *Guide to London* for the benefit of Indian students like himself. Almost half of it was devoted to the problem of what to eat. On the ship out, he recommended gradually increasing the number of European dishes the student ate, in order to habituate himself to the British diet. One problem was that "there could have been no worse introduction to English cooking [than the food served on the steamships]. Boiled, floury potatoes, raw leaves of lettuce and tomatoes, cold grey and pink, spongy slices of mutton and thick boiled wads of watery cabbage, all unsalted and unflavoured."[64] Once in Britain, Gandhi observed that with time and money it was perfectly possible to observe all caste rules and cook your own food, but "for an ordinary Indian who is not overscrupulous in his religious views and who is not much of a believer in caste restrictions, it would be advisable to cook partly himself and get a part of his food ready made." He was particularly keen on porridge, and gave instructions on how to make it. In fact, apart from the meals he ate at the vegetarian café, Gandhi seems to have lived on porridge, to which he added sugar, milk, and stewed fruit.[65]

Indian students in Britain were pressured to eat meat. The British believed that the animal energy contained within meat was essential to sustain the body in a cold climate. Gandhi was told he would die without meat. Indeed, the British faith in its mythical power was quite equal to the

Indian faith in the purifying and polluting potential of food. Victorians were cautious about giving meat to women or sedentary scholars as it was believed to arouse passions that, finding no outlet, would lead to nervous introversion and illness. But it was regarded as the ultimate food for the strong, aggressive, and manly Englishman.[66] Like Gandhi, Behramji Malabari, an Indian tourist in Britain, was horrified by the carcasses of animals hanging in the shops. "The sight is invariably unpleasant and the smell is at times overpowering ... It is an exhibition of barbarism, not unlikely to develop the brute instincts in man."[67] But a great many Indian students quickly gave up the struggle to remain vegetarian. A diet of porridge was not very appealing, and the majority lacked Gandhi's qualities of stubborn perseverance. In fact, they reveled in "the sense of freedom [and] liberty from social restrictions."[68] A few even developed a liking for fish and chips, tripe and onions, and black pudding.[69]

Indian students in Britain were joined in their rebellion by "apparently orthodox Babus" in India who could be found "in convenient European hotels in Calcutta and elsewhere, [enjoying] a hearty meal of forbidden food, cooked and served up by Muhammadans." It is possible that they consumed British food in the hope that they might absorb some of the essences that made the British so powerful.[70] Besides, strict observance of caste restrictions had few benefits for a lowly office clerk. No matter how scrupulous he was in his eating habits, no Indian from the upper echelons of the caste or class system would deign to dine with him. Instead, he derived a certain satisfaction from the fact that "if he cannot eat with the Brahman, he can do so with the *Sahibs* who rule India."[71]

During the 1920s and 30s, Indianization of the services and political reform meant that pressure increased for both sides to find ways of working and socializing together. Wealthy Indians responded by installing in their houses English kitchens, staffed by Muslim cooks. This meant that they could provide for British guests without compromising their own vegetarian kitchen. Reforming British administrators counted it a triumph to be invited to eat with their Indian colleagues. When Henry Lawrence was invited to dine at the home of a Brahman friend of his, where he was served by the women of the family, he considered it "the greatest compliment he has ever received."[72] The British made allowances on their side and would often provide Indian food for their guests. When Lord and Lady Reading had the Shafi family for dinner, they provided "Persian Pilaw for dinner—so good. Pink and green rice with curry and Mangoe chutney." For less relaxed guests, special arrangements were made and at her purdah party Lady Reading provided the Hindu ladies with separate metal plates and mugs, and lemonade and fruits prepared by Brahman cooks.[73]

The British, however, were always most comfortable with less-educated Indians, where there was no pretence of equality. In the 1930s, Prakash Tandon worked as an advertising executive at the British firm Unilever. He described how the Indian agent for the firm at Amritsar, "old Lala Ramchand," would invite the sahibs and their wives to his home, where he would ply them with Indian sweets, spicy savories, sickly rose-and banana-flavored sodas, and milky sweet tea, "with cheerful unconcern for the gastronomic capabilities of the protesting sahib" who did his best to disguise his fear of "lifelong dysentery." But when the thoroughly westernized Tandon and his Swedish wife attempted to socialize with his British colleagues it was a failure. The British made it clear that they would find Indian food unacceptable, explaining that although they liked their curry and rice on Sundays, made to their taste by a Goan cook, they did not want to eat it more often. The Tandons compromised and served Swedish food but they could find no neutral topics of conversation and they never received a return invitation. "This lack of response soon stifled my good intentions, but left me a little sad."[74]

Meanwhile, educated and thoroughly westernized Indians were made to feel uncomfortable by the example of Gandhi. The same young man who had set off for London determined to transform himself into a proper English gentleman had, by the 1930s, metamorphosed into a dhoti-clad ascetic, who nibbled on the occasional fruit or nut, and had carefully eradicated Western influences from his daily life. Gandhi's bold celebration of the Indian body was a powerful challenge both to the British and to westernized Indians. Following his example, a number of Indian campaigners for independence flung away their "Savil Row suits" and donned homespun cotton, renounced their "roast lamb, two veg. and mint sauce," furtively consumed in British restaurants, and replaced them with vegetarian rice and dhal.[75] But even Gandhi seems not to have altogether abandoned British table etiquette. When he died, among his few possessions were a couple of forks.[76]

After the First World War the Britishness the Anglo-Indians so self-consciously preserved became increasingly out of date. Newcomers to India in the 1920s and 30s felt as though they had been transported back in time. One memsahib described how she "stepped into an almost Edwardian life . . . The bungalow was large and old-fashioned, tended by an army of servants . . . we rode every morning before breakfast . . . Life was very formal. Winifred and I would be driven out to the shops or to pay calls in the morning, for which . . . one wore hat and gloves . . . In the afternoon . . . one rested or wrote letters." Socializing consisted of race meetings, garden parties, polo meets, and formal dinner parties.[77]

Anglo-India had failed to keep pace with social change in the home country. The dinner parties seemed conventionbound and old-fashioned. In Britain it was becoming less common to dress for dinner, but Anglo-Indians continued to insist on it, and everyone still sat at the table, no matter how small the party, in order of precedence. This insistence on stiff formality struck many as pompous and slightly absurd. In the nineteenth century Anglo-Indian pseudo-British dishes had been recognizable approximations of those eaten at home. Post-1919, the food seemed odd. Savories had been relegated to formal dinners in Britain, but even on the most ordinary occasions Anglo-Indians still served what they referred to as "toast" after the dessert. Usually this was something like sardines, or mashed brain spiced with green chillies on toast.[78] The Victorians had delighted in *trompe l'oeil* jokery. The famous chef Alexis Soyer loved to surprise his guests by making a boar's head out of cake, or saddles of mutton out of different colored ice creams.[79] Like the nawab of Oudh's inventive cooks who were able to manufacture realistic biryanis and kebabs out of caramelized sugar, the Anglo-Indian's cooks had a penchant for food trickery. It was not unknown for them to cheer up the dull food by dying mashed potatoes bright red and boiled carrots purple. But this sort of thing was now hopelessly out of date. Curry was certainly never served for dinner and it was possible for a British person to live in India without ever trying a one.

Curry survived in a few niches of Anglo-Indian life. In Calcutta in the 1930s, the clubs would serve curries for lunch at the weekends. After a round of golf in the mornings, the men would meet up with their wives at the club, where prawn curry was usually on offer. Club curries reduced the subtleties of Indian food to three different bowls, labeled hot, medium, and mild. The Sunday ritual was completed by a siesta and the cinema. Some households included mulligatawny soup for breakfast in the ritual.[80] On the P&O boats that linked India to Britain, curry was served alongside the roast joints at dinner, and on the trains it survived in the guise of "railway curry," as it was referred to by the Maharani of Jaipur's family. "Designed to offend no palate [it contained] no beef, forbidden to Hindus; no pork, forbidden to Muslims; so, [it was] inevitably lamb or chicken curries and vegetables. Railway curry therefore pleased nobody."[81] Both the British and the Indian army messes kept up the tradition of curry lunches. In 1936 Edward Palmer, caterer to the Wembley exhibition of 1924–1925 and founder of Veeraswamy's Indian restaurant, was invited to lecture to the army cooks at Aldershot on curry making. During the Second World War trainee cooks in the army catering corps were taught how to make curries by adding curry powder to a roux of flour and army stock books show that cooks were allotted supplies of curry powder each month. Major Eric Warren, who served with the Royal Marines from 1945 to 1978, ate curry throughout his career in officers' messes from Hong Kong to Cyprus and the West Indies. A standard item on the Sunday lunch menu, they were always accompanied by an array of side dishes, including sliced bananas, pieces of pineapple, and poppadoms. Slightly sweet yellow curries, dotted with raisins and made with fantastical fruits, were still served in British army messes in the 1970s and 80s.[82] Indeed, the army and the merchant navy were two important routes by which Anglo-Indian curries found their way to Britain. It was on board ship and in messes, during the Second World War, that many British men who had never traveled before were introduced to curry.[83]

After Indian independence in 1947, the self-contained world of Anglo-India was maintained among the British businessmen who stayed on. Club life continued, cucumber sandwiches and sponge cake were served at tennis parties, and savories still appeared at dinner parties.[84] At Queen Mary's School, Bombay, run by Scottish missionaries, Camellia Panjabi and her fellow pupils were treated to "baked fish, baked mince (cottage pie), dhol (English and Anglo-Indian for dhal) and yellow rice, mutton curry and rice, coconut pancakes, and Malabar sago pudding." It was only when she went to university in Britain that it became clear to her that real British food "had none of the spices and seasonings that we had experienced as children in 'English food' in India. It was then that I realized that 'Indian English food' was a sort of hybrid cuisine in its own right."[85] On the railways and in dak bungalows stringy chicken and masala omelettes survived for a while. The Bengalis, fond of sweets, have adopted a few British desserts such as caramel custard and trifle.[86] And in guest houses in Calcutta minced meat and mashed potato cutlets or chops are still on the menu. Soggy chips and vegetable cutlets served with a sachet of tomato ketchup, some toast, and a cup of tea are standard breakfast fare on Indian trains.[87] The dislocated Anglo-Indian community of mixed British and Indian heritage still eat stew and apple crumble. At the Fairlawn Hotel on Sudder Street in Calcutta, the white-gloved waiters politely hand round roast buffalo. The meal is finished with a savory of sardines on toast.[88] And at the Bengal Club in Calcutta the *burra khana* lives on: with one attentive bearer to every dinner guest and mulligatawny soup, "chicken dopiaz," and orange soufflé on the menu.[89]

Despite the fact that remnants of Anglo-Indian cookery clung on in odd corners of the subcontinent, an English roast was surrounded by an aura of the exotic for the young author Manil Suri, growing up in Bombay in the 1970s. Inspired by the novels of Enid Blyton, which were filled with picnics, and by an English cookery book picked up at the local store, he longed to taste tongue sandwiches, scones, and a roast lamb. But it was impossible to find the ingredients and his mother's kitchen was not even equipped with an oven. After several attempts that produced "grey and flabby" boiled goat, and an utterly inedible Neapolitan soufflé, to his family's relief Suri gave up.[90]

Bengali potatoes

The British introduced the Bengalis to the potato but no self-respecting Indian cook would have eaten plain boiled vegetables. The Bengalis quickly incorporated European vegetables into their own recipes and this particular way of cooking potatoes results in an unusual sweet-sour flavor. Serves 4–6.

5–6 tablespoons vegetable oil
1¼ in. stick of cinnamon
4 cardamom pods
4 whole cloves
2 bay leaves
2 onions, very finely chopped
10 cloves garlic, crushed
½ –1 teaspoon chilli powder
1 teaspoon turmeric
1¼ lb. small new potatoes
1 tablespoon tamarind pulp mixed with 1 cup warm water
salt to taste
jaggery (or soft brown sugar) to taste

Heat the oil. When it is hot throw in the cinnamon stick, cardamom pods, cloves, and bay leaves, and fry for about 1 minute. Add the onions and fry until they brown. Add the garlic and fry for another 6 minutes. Then add the chilli powder, turmeric, and the potatoes. Fry, stirring constantly, until the potatoes are coated in the spice mixture. Add the tamarind pulp mixture, the salt and jaggery, and bring to the boil. Then turn the heat low and simmer until the potatoes are done. You may need to add more water to prevent the sauce from burning.

Pathan laborers of the frontier area enjoying their afternoon tea between work

8

Chai: The Great Tea Campaign

ONE MORNING IN 1936 a "special demonstration unit" arrived at the door of a wealthy Nagarathar family in the provincial town of Karaikudi (Tamil Nadu). The special unit, consisting of "an experienced and senior Sub-Inspector and an Attender," was ushered into the house where they set up their equipment: a small stove, a kettle, milk jug, sugar basin, china cups and saucers, and a teapot. The kettle was set to boil and the ladies of the family were shown how to pour the boiling water over a carefully measured amount of tea. Once it had brewed for the required period, the golden liquid was poured into the china cups and the process of adding milk and sugar was demonstrated. The tea was then handed round to the members of the family who had gathered round to watch. The special unit were working for the Indian Tea Association and the Nagarathars were a small but influential subcaste who had resisted earlier attempts by the Tea Association campaigners to persuade them to drink tea. They had been buying half-anna packets of tea, but had been giving them away to their servants. Apparently, the fact that previous tea demonstrations had used tea prepared in the homes of their lower-caste neighbors had proved offensive. Determined to change their ways, the special unit had abandoned the tea urns usually used to make demonstration tea and had set about wooing 240 Nagarathar families in Karaikudi with freshly boiled water and elegant china cups. The unit's efforts were successful and the tea demonstrations became an event in the households they visited. By the end of four months, 220 of the Nagarathar families had been converted to tea drinking.[1]

The Nagarathars' refusal to drink tea was by no means exceptional. At the beginning of the twentieth century, the majority of Indians did not know how to make a cup of tea and were reluctant to drink one.

Now that India is both the world's major producer and consumer of tea, this seems incredible. It confounds the myth that the British acquired their love of tea from their Indian subjects. In fact, it was the British who introduced tea to the Indians. Although they barely changed the *way* Indians eat, the British radically altered *what* they eat and drink. While the introduction of a wide variety of European and American vegetables to India was an inadvertent by-product of British rule, the conversion of the population to tea drinking was the result of what must have been the first major marketing campaign in India. The British-owned Indian Tea Association set itself the task of first creating a new habit among the Indian population, and then spreading it across the entire subcontinent.

Tea drinking began in China during the fourth century. From China, it spread to Japan sometime between the sixth and eighth centuries, where it became an important social ritual. It also spread into Tibet and the Himalayan regions north of India, where tea was drunk as a kind of soup mixed with butter. On the eastern fringes of India, in Assam and further east in Burma and Thailand, the hill tribes chewed steamed and fermented tea leaves.[2] Despite being bordered by tea-drinking (or -chewing) countries, India remained impervious to the charms of tea. When the interpreter for the Chinese Embassy of Cheng Ho visited Bengal in 1406, he was surprised to note that the Bengalis offered betel nuts to their guests rather than tea.[3] Coffee had been introduced into India by the Arabs, Persians, and central Asians who found employment under the Mughals. The young German traveler Albert Mandelslo, who passed through Surat in 1638, noticed that the Persians "drink their Kahwa which cools and abates the natural heat." Coffee houses could be found on Chandni Chowk, Delhi's main thoroughfare. "An innovation from Persia, these were places where amirs [Mughal noblemen] gathered to listen to poetry, engage in conversation, and watch the passing scene."[4] Moplah Arab traders had introduced coffee to the west coast, and the southwestern hills were dotted with tiny coffee gardens.[5] For the most part, however, the coffee-drinking habit was confined to wealthy Muslims and did not spread to the rest of the population.[6] As the chaplain Edward Terry noticed, Indians preferred water: "That most antient and innocent Drink of the World, *Water*, is the common drink of East-India; it is far more pleasant and sweet than our water; and must needs be so, because in all hot Countries it is more rarified, better digested, and freed from its rawness by the heat of the *Sun*, and therefore in those parts it is more desired of all that come thither." In northern India the villagers also drank buttermilk, a by-product of the Indian way of making ghee, by churning yogurt (as opposed to the European method of churning cream). If they wanted something stronger, they drank arrack or toddy.[7]

European East India merchants brought tea with them to India from China. Indian textiles could be exchanged there for Bohea (black) and green tea as well as for silks, hams, Chinese jars, quicksilver, and vermilion.[8] Mandelslo, who noticed the Persians drinking coffee, observed that "at our ordinary meetings" the English at Surat "used only Thé, which is commonly used all over the Indies, not only among those of the Country, but also among the Dutch and English."[9] Indeed, the Dutch were said to be so fond of the brew that among them the teapot was "seldom off the fire, or unimploy'd." Under the influence of the East India merchants, the Banians at Surat learned to drink "liberal Draughts of Tea and Coffee, to revive their wasted Spirits, any part of the Day."[10] But Mandelslo was mistaken in his assumption that tea was used as a refreshing drink by the entire Indian population. Even in the nineteenth century Indians stubbornly regarded tea as a medicine. An Englishwoman living in Lucknow in the 1830s observed that "china tea sets are very rarely found in the zeenahnah; ... The ladies ... must have a severe cold to induce them to partake of the beverage even as a remedy, but by no means as a luxury."[11] Prakash Tandon's great-uncle, who was a pandit in the law courts of Punjab in the 1860s and 70s, would take a glass of milk, almond, or fruit juice at four o'clock but "tea was unknown in those days except as a remedy for chest troubles."[12]

Tea was initially used by monks in China (and later in Japan) as a herbal remedy for headaches and pains in the joints, as well as an aid to meditation. But it fairly rapidly became a favorite everyday drink with the majority of the population. Similarly, among the other nationalities who took up tea, it was first adopted as a medicine. The Dutch in India, who constantly had the teapot boiling, would mix it with spices and add sugar or conserved lemons, and even sometimes a slosh of arrack, to mix up a pleasant cure for headaches, gravel, "Griping in the Guts," and "Twistings of the Bowel."[13] Mandelslo attributed his recovery from burning fever and bloody flux to the tea that he drank on an English ship sailing across the Persian Gulf to Surat.[14] In Britain, Mrs. Pepys famously tried drinking tea in 1667 as a cure for "cold and defluxions."[15] Among all these nationalities tea quickly escaped from the medicine cabinet and found itself a secure home in the kitchen cupboard. In India, however, it remained firmly in the category of herbal remedy (even today Bengalis regard tea mixed with ginger juice as a cure for colds),[16] and the tea-loving British were forced to carry their own supplies of tea leaves when they traveled into the Indian countryside, as it was impossible to buy tea there.[17] But the British-run Indian Tea Association was to change all this.

In 1823 Robert Bruce, stationed as a British agent in Assam, noticed the Singpho people drinking an infusion of the dried leaves of a plant that looked suspiciously like *Camellia sinensis*, in other words tea. He wrote to his brother Charles, who later reminded the government that "I was the first European who ever penetrated the forests and visited the tea tracts in British Sadiya, and brought away specimens of earth, fruit and flowers, and the first to discover numerous other tracts."[18] Charles Bruce's injured tone arose from the fact that the British government paid absolutely no attention to his discovery. Then, in 1834, Lt. Andrew Charlton of the

Assam Light Infantry, also stationed in Sadiya, persuaded the authorities in Calcutta to investigate the possibility of growing tea in India. Charlton later received a medal for discovering tea in India, much to Bruce's chagrin. But Charlton's timing was better. At the end of the 1820s the British East India Company became concerned that they might lose their monopoly of the China trade, which they did in 1833. Given that tea was their main import from China, accounting for £70,426,244 of the £72,168,541 made from the China trade between 1811 and 1819, they had an interest in finding an alternative source of tea.[19] In addition, the Chinese reliance on small householders, who grew tea on their tiny plots of land, was a haphazard, labor-intensive, and unreliable way of producing a commodity that had become vital to the British. The company was required to keep a year's supply in stock at all times, to protect the British public from supply shortages.[20]

By the end of the eighteenth century, tea had become *the* British drink. At first a herbal remedy for the wealthy elite, it soon became a fashionable beverage. It provided a good replacement for the glass of sweet wine that aristocratic ladies used to take with a biscuit in the afternoons, and it allowed them to show off their collections of delicate porcelain tea bowls. In the 1730s, a direct clipper link with China and a reduction in taxes on tea meant that it became affordable for nearly everyone. In 1717, Tom Twining had two adjoining houses in London, one selling coffee and the other tea. By 1734, the consumption of tea had taken off to such an extent that he sublet the coffee house and concentrated on selling tea.[21] Tea suited the new middle-class lifestyle perfectly. Served with bread and butter and cake, it tided middle-class ladies over until dinner, which was now eaten much later, as the gentleman of the house did not come home from his office until after five o'clock. It was also popular among the laboring classes. With the addition of sugar it made an energizing drink and in 1767 road menders were observed pooling their money to buy tea-making equipment. Haymakers developed a preference for cups of tea rather than glasses of beer.[22] Henry Mayhew's *London Labour and the London Poor* noted that tea and coffee had replaced saloop (the powder of an orchid imported from India) and sugary rice milk.[23] By the early 1830s, the East India Company was importing approximately 30 million pounds per annum, which translated into each person in the country drinking about a pound of tea a year. This provided the Exchequer with £3,300,000 in duty, or one-tenth of its total revenue.[24] It therefore made perfect sense when Governor-General William Bentinck appointed a tea committee in February 1834 to look into the idea that India might be a good place to set up the company's own tea production under the latest efficient means of agricultural production.[25]

Initial British attempts to cultivate tea in India were something of a shambles. The committee decided that the Assamese climate would be suitable for an experiment in tea cultivation but they did not believe that the indigenous plant that Bruce and Charlton had seen growing there was suitable for tea production. G. J. Gordon was therefore dispatched to China to collect seedlings and to recruit Chinese who knew how to make tea. Although Europeans had been eagerly buying tea from the Chinese for over two centuries, they were still uncertain as to the precise production methods. These were secrets that the Chinese guarded jealously. It was extremely difficult to gain access to the tea manufactories and the Chinese would chase, and attempt to capture, any ship they suspected of smuggling out plants or seeds.[26] Gordon must have been a resourceful man as he duly sent back 80,000 tea plants in 1835, and two Chinese tea producers a couple of years later.[27] Their advice was much needed as the motley crew of Chinese carpenters and shoemakers living in the bazaars of Calcutta who had been sent to Assam as advisers "had never seen a tea plant in their lifetime" and had no idea how to pluck or treat the leaves. The Assamese, whose land had been requisitioned to create tea gardens, refused to work in tea cultivation, and to make matters worse, the Chinese tea plants failed to thrive. By the time the British had decided that the indigenous Assamese tea plants were in fact perfectly good for making tea, they had interbred with the Chinese plants, resulting in an inferior hybrid.[28]

Despite all these problems, the tea growers of Assam managed to produce 12 chests of tea in 1838. These were auctioned in London the following year to very little acclaim.[29] Old, hard leaves that had been overplucked, and then transported long distances before being processed, made poor-quality tea. Initially, Assam tea was so inferior it could barely compete with even the worst grades from China. Nevertheless the company handed over its plantations to the newly founded Assam Tea Company in 1840, though it was not until 1853 that Assam tea paid its first dividend.[30] In 1861, tea mania struck and retired army officers, doctors, engineers, steamer captains, shopkeepers, policemen, clerks, even civil servants with stable positions, scrambled to buy tea plantations or to get work as planters. These enthusiastic novices bought up and cleared unsuitable land and planted it out with tea. In 1865, they realized they would never make a profit, and the tea-mania businessmen sold in a panic and prices crashed. Unsurprisingly, the quality of the tea produced the next year was so abysmal that prices fell again and more tea gardens failed. It was not until the 1870s that the tea industry in India stabilized and finally began producing good-quality tea for a profit.[31]

Among the Indian population, a comparable rush brought even greater misery to India's poor. Contractors, who became known as "Coolie Catchers," hired desperate peasants as labor for the tea plantations. The first stage of the journey to the gardens on packed and insanitary boats resulted in the deaths of many of the laborers before they reached their destination. Once the survivors arrived, their living conditions were basic, disease was rife, and many of them suffered from enlargement of the spleen, which is a side effect of malaria. This meant that when their employers kicked or beat them (which happened lamentably often) they frequently died from a ruptured spleen. The only medical treatment available came from a few doctors and their medically incompetent employers. Life on the tea plantations was terrible for the workers.[32]

In 1870, over 90 percent of the tea drunk in Britain came from China, and the proportion was even higher in most other tea-drinking countries. But the producers of Indian tea were at last ready to challenge the Chinese and, in the 1880s, they began a vigorous global marketing campaign at the various colonial exhibitions. In Britain, the public enthusiastically accepted free samples of cups of Indian tea as well as the teaspoons, which disappeared inside their pockets at an alarming rate. Teapots also had a low survival rate, with only ten out of 180 surviving the London Health Exhibition of 1888. Indian *khidmutgars*, in colorful uniforms, were employed at the Paris exhibition of 1889 to create an exotic atmosphere, and in America they traveled the country selling tea at state fairs. At the Garden

Palace Exhibition in Melbourne in 1880 Indian teas carried off most of the prizes.[33] In Australia, the campaign was carried on virtually single-handedly by James Inglis, whose brother was a Calcutta tea merchant. Continental Europeans and Americans were fairly unresponsive, but the British and Australians began to develop a preference for the fermented black teas of India rather than the unfermented green of China.

In Britain and Australia, the working class's passion for strong black Indian tea was encouraged by inventive wholesalers who found ways of selling Indian tea at cheaper rates than Chinese teas. Thomas Lipton innovatively purchased his tea leaves in bulk, directly from India (and Ceylon where the tea plantations were first established in the 1880s). At his 100 shops around Britain, he was able to sell tea for about a quarter of the price charged by ordinary grocers. By 1909, tea was associated in British minds with India to such an extent that it was worth Lipton's while to employ an Indian to stand in front of one of his London cafés as an advertisement. The Indian in question was "an undergraduate," driven through poverty to find whatever employment he could. By 1900, only 10 percent (and falling) of the tea consumed in Britain came from China while 50 percent came from India and 33 from Ceylon.[34]

Although tea was strongly associated with India in British and Australian minds, Indians still did not drink it themselves. In the cities, to be sure, "gentlemen as have frequent intercourse with the 'Sahib Logue' (English gentry) ... [had] acquire[d] a taste for this delightful beverage" and Gandhi acknowledged that a few westernized Indians now drank a cup or two of tea for breakfast. But, he continued, "the drinking of tea and coffee by the so-called educated Indians, chiefly due to British rule, may be passed over with the briefest notice."[35] For the majority of the Indian population, tea was far too expensive a foreign habit. All the paraphernalia of tea drinking—teapots, china cups and saucers, sugar bowls, and milk jugs—were too costly for most people. Even in Assam, families working in the tea industry would not have drunk tea at home.[36] In his survey of the economic products of India, George Watt observed in 1889 that "while India has not only challenged but beaten China, during the past 30 years, no progress has been made in teaching the native population of India the value of tea."[37] In 1901, the Indian Tea Association woke up to the fact that their largest market was sitting right on their doorstep and they extended their marketing campaign to the subcontinent. This extraordinary venture, one of the first of its kind in India, used methods that were new to the region, and to advertising in general.

The Tea Association began by employing a superintendent and two "smart European travellers" to visit grocers. Their task was to persuade them to stock more tea on their shelves. Just before the outbreak of the First World War, at a dinner party given by the Maharaja of Udaipur, the Reverend St. Clair Weeden was surprised to find himself sitting next to one such "traveller," "an amusing Irishman, who had been going about India for the last five years, selling cheap packets of Lipton's teas, to which the natives are taking very kindly."[38] These salesmen also arranged for the delivery of liquid tea to offices, and in 1903 the committee in charge of tea propaganda in the south noted that they received complaints "should there be any failure in the daily supply at the various Government and mercantile offices."[39] Nevertheless, marketing tea in India was a dispiriting project. In 1904, it was reported that even after three years of hard work there was little to indicate "the existence of a proper tea market in India," and every year from 1901 to 1914, there were complaints that "increasing the consumption of tea in India is undoubtedly the most difficult branch of the work."[40]

During the First World War the campaign began to gain momentum. Tea stalls had been set up at factories, coal mines, and cotton mills where thirsty laborers provided a captive market. The war made factory and mill owners more conscious of the need to keep their workers happy, and they were persuaded to allow time off for tea breaks. The Tea Association hoped that "having learnt to drink tea at his work [the employee] will take the habit with him to his home, and so accustom his family and friends to tea." By 1919, the tea canteen was firmly established as "an important element in an industrial concern."[41] Thus, tea entered Indian life as an integral part of the modern industrial world that began to encroach on India in the twentieth century.

The railways were another example of the arrival of the industrial world in India, and the Tea Association transformed them into vehicles for global capitalism. They equipped small contractors with kettles and cups and packets of tea and set them to work at the major railway junctions in the Punjab, the Northwest Provinces, and Bengal. The cry of "Chai! Gurram, gurram chai!" ("Tea! Hot, hot tea!") mingled with the shouts of the *pani* (water) carriers calling out "Hindu pani!" "Muslim pani!"[42] Muslim rail passengers were less bothered by the caste restrictions that hindered Hindus from accepting food or even water from anyone of a lower caste, and they took to tea with enthusiasm. Although the European instructors took great care to guide the tea vendors in the correct way of making a cup of tea, they often ignored this advice and made tea their own way, with plenty of milk and lots of sugar. This milky, intensely sweet mixture appealed to north Indians who like buttermilk and yogurt drinks (lassis). It was affordable and went well with the chapattis, spicy dry potatoes, and biscuits sold by other station vendors, running alongside the carriage windows as the trains pulled into the station. Eventually, tea stalls at the railway stations catered to communal sensibilities and were divided into Muslim and Hindu sections.[43]

In the south, the tea marketers had to compete with coffee. Arab traders had begun cultivating small plots of coffee in the western hills by the seventeenth century, and coffee plantations were established in Ceylon in the 1830s. Thus, coffee had a head start on tea. Even today the coffee wallahs begin to outnumber the chai wallahs as trains pass south. But in the 1930s the Tea Association proudly pronounced the railway campaign a success. They congratulated themselves on the fact that "a better cup of tea could in general be had at the platform tea stalls than in the first class restaurant cars on the trains."[44] The chai wallah is still the first thing a passenger hears on waking up in a train in northern India as he marches through the carriages, a metal kettle swinging in one hand and glasses in the other, calling out "chai-chai-chai."

Another branch of the campaign set up tea shops in India's large towns and ports. These tea shops had a satisfactory snowball effect. "Immediately the tea shop was established on a selling basis, shops in the neighbourhood—which did not normally sell tea—commenced to do so, and the areas surrounding the tea shops were infested with tea hawkers who undersold our shops to such an extent that finally they had to be closed down." This was seen as progress. The only matter for concern was that the tea hawkers tended to flavor the tea with spices. The Indians demonstrated their characteristic tendency to take a new foodstuff and transform it by applying Indian methods of preparation. This was not a problem in itself, but in spiced tea they tended to use fewer tea leaves. For a campaign that counted every cup of tea and every ounce of tea leaf sold this was a move in the wrong direction. "Steps are now being taken to have this remedied" reported one campaigner. "It is in the Cawnpore Mill area where we have found this so-called spiced tea . . . and we are now employing our own hawkers in that district who sell well-made liquid tea in direct competition to the unsavoury and badly prepared decoction known as 'spiced tea.' "[45]

Tea shops only reached a certain type of clientele. A series of campaigns therefore set about taking tea directly into the Indian home, particularly to women who would not have visited tea shops. An army of tea demonstrators was employed to march on the large towns and cities. An area of each town was chosen, and for four months the tea campaigners visited every house, street by street, every day at the same time, except on Sundays. "As far as possible we aim at brewing the tea inside the house so as to teach the householder the correct method of preparation," one demonstrator explained. The campaigners expected to face hostility. Certain Muslim quarters in Lahore remained impervious, but they were surprised to find that "even in the more orthodox and conservative places quite a number of households will allow our staff to demonstrate right inside the house." The ladies would peek from behind purdah screens at the brewing demonstration, held in the courtyard. In very high-class purdah areas, the committee employed lady demonstrators. In rigidly orthodox Hindu towns, the Brahmans "quite definitely refused to accept tea from our demonstrators, in spite of their protestations that they and the Sub-Inspectors were just as good Brahmans as themselves." In Trichonopoly the demonstrators circumvented this problem by persuading the priests at the Srirangam temple to allow them to distribute cups of tea in the temple precincts.

Having established a habit of making tea at the same time every day in many households in the cities, the demonstrators moved out into smaller provincial towns and this is when they met the Nagarathars of Karaikudi, who started this chapter.[46] The special unit's triumph with the Nagarathars is an indication of the extent to which tea drinking was beginning to penetrate urban India. In the Punjab, the older generation began to complain about young people drinking tea rather than the milk or buttermilk that they thought much healthier.[47]

Syed Rasul left the town of Mirpur (now in Pakistan) in 1930 or 1932: "The first time I had a cup of tea was when I came to Bombay. In the village we used to drink only milk, and water. Only if somebody was ill they would give . . . something like a cup of tea—it was like a medicine."[48] Despite the money and effort channeled into the tea marketing campaigns, some corners of the country were still untouched. To address this the "packing factory scheme" was started in 1931. Lorries, and in Bengal houseboats, were sent to the local markets where "thousands of villagers . . . congregate" where they distributed cups of tea. The demonstrators reported that "at first we had to use much persuasion to induce the ryot to accept a cup of tea." But the cinema performances that accompanied the tea distribution helped to make it more popular. The women, who were provided with a special enclosure, particularly liked the films. They were observed "sharing [their] tea with children of all ages, even infants in arms." By the end of 1936, Indian villagers had become so accustomed to tea that in one year the demonstrators were able to give away 26 million cups of it with ease.[49]

During the Second World War, the marketing campaign was temporarily closed down and the Indian Tea Association concentrated their efforts on the army. Special tea vans were set up to supply the troops. Several of these were even sent overseas with Indian troops fighting in the European arena. The vans were equipped with radio sets, gramophone records of Indian songs, and letter writers so that the soldiers could keep in touch with their families at home while simultaneously acquiring the tea-drinking habit. An enthusiastic army officer, who had been a tea planter before the war, wrote to the Tea Association to commend their efforts: "During a 3 days march, under trying climatic conditions, [your tea] van served over 10,000 cups of good tea to Officers and other ranks of this Unit. Quite apart from the value of the drink on that and other occasions, which was much appreciated, the propaganda value must be incalculable.

Our sepoys are now definitely 'tea conscious' and in post-war days this tea-drinking habit will be carried into many villages throughout India."

Once the Japanese had brought the war close to India, tea vans serviced air-raid protection workers in the cities of Calcutta, Howrah, and Madras, and traumatized survivors of the Malayan and Burmese rout were supplied with hot, comforting cups of tea. In Bombay, the tea car dealing with embarking and disembarking troops was able to proselytize tea among the Americans. They "regarded tea with considerable suspicion at first, ... [but] on persuasion [they] were induced to take it without milk."[50] Indeed, tea became the British panacea for all ills during the war. The author of a handbook on canteens explained in 1941 that "Psychologically tea breeds contentment. It is so bound up with fellowship and the home and pleasant memories that its results are also magic."[51]

By 1945, even the homeless living on the streets of Calcutta were drinking tea, and the milkman would stop on his rounds to supply them with a drop of milk to add to their tea.[52] Nevertheless, the Tea Association was not entirely satisfied. In 1955, the per capita consumption in India was still only about half a pound, compared with nearly ten pounds in Britain. The marketing machine was restarted.[53] But it is in the nature of a marketing campaign to argue that people can always drink, or eat, more of its product. In fact, the relentless campaigning of the tea demonstrators, tea shops, railway stalls, and military tea vans had already significantly changed Indian drinking habits. They were so successful at introducing tea into India that at the end of the twentieth century, the Indian population, which had barely touched a drop of tea in 1900, were drinking almost 70 percent of their huge crop of 715,000 tons per year.[54]

Tea is now a normal part of everyday life in India. The tea shop is a feature of every city, town, and village. Often they are nothing more than "a tarpaulin or piece of bamboo matting stretched over four posts ... [with] a table, a couple of rickety benches and a portable stove with the kettle permanently on."[55] Men gather round, standing or squatting on their haunches, sipping the hot tea. The tiny earthenware cups, in which the drink is served, lie smashed around the stalls. Everybody drinks tea in India nowadays, even the sadhus (holy men), the most orthodox of Brahmans and the very poor, who use it as a way of staving off hunger.[56]

Admittedly, much of the tea that is sold in India would not be approved of by the Tea Association inspectors. It is invariably milky and sweet. This makes it popular with the calorie-starved laborer. A wizened, but sinewy, bicycle-rickshaw driver from Cochin once informed me that tea was the basis of his strength. This surprised me at the time, but one cup of this milky sweet tea can contain as many as 40 calories, enough to give a tired rickshaw driver a quick burst of energy.[57] Indian tea-stall owners flavor their tea in a variety of thoroughly un-British ways. In Calcutta, the speciality of one stall is lemon tea flavored with sugar "and a pinch of bitnoon, a dark, pungent salt."[58] The poor in villages also flavor their tea with salt as it is easier to ask for a pinch of salt from a neighbor than it is to ask for more expensive sugar.[59]

The tea stalls also sell that "unsavoury and badly prepared decoction known as 'spiced tea'" that the Tea Association inspector discovered being served in the Cawnpore mill district in the 1930s.[60] The tea leaves are mixed with water, milk, sugar, a handful of cardamoms, some sticks of cinnamon, sometimes black pepper, and simmered for hours. The result is faintly smoky, bittersweet and thick, with an aroma reminiscent of Christmas puddings. Indians have been flavoring milky drinks with spices for centuries. Ancient Ayurvedic medical texts recommend boiling water mixed together with sour curds, sugar, honey, ghee, black pepper, and cardamoms, for fevers, catarrh, and colds. In the Punjab, buttermilk is often mixed together with cumin, pepper, or chilli, and khir, a sweet milk-rice that uses dried fruits and aromatic spices such as cardamom, is a favorite dish throughout India.[61] Spiced tea is simply a variation on these drinks. Sold as chai, spiced tea is now becoming fashionable in American and British coffee shops. It is marketed as an exotic oriental drink and yet it is in many ways the product of a British campaign to persuade Indians to drink tea.

The spread of tea drinking in India has had a surprising impact on Indian society. In British hands the practices surrounding the sale of tea appear to have had a rather negative effect. The British are often accused of worsening relations between Hindus, Muslims, and Sikhs, due to the Raj policy of divide and rule. The rise of communalism in India during the nineteenth century is a complex and divisive subject. The British certainly worsened the situation, often inadvertently. When the British were responsible for providing food for their Indian subjects, they were usually scrupulous about respecting the caste and communal restrictions surrounding food preparation. At railway stations throughout India, Hindu and Muslim passengers were supplied with water by separate water carriers.[62] The same principle was applied to tea at the railway stations, and tea stalls were often divided into Muslim and Hindu sections. The tea vans that accompanied the troops abroad served Muslims from one window, Hindus from another. The overall effect of these apparently benign acts of cultural accommodation was to reinforce the divisions between the different communities, thus creating the conditions in which communalism could thrive.

While tea in British hands could become an instrument of communal separation, in Indian hands it has often improved intercommunal relations. For many Indians tea, as a foreign foodstuff, lies outside Ayurvedic classifications and is therefore free from the burden of purity associations. The neutrality of tea makes it easier to share with impunity with members of a caste normally rejected as eating or drinking partners.

Prakash Tandon observed the breakdown of caste restrictions within his own Punjabi Khatri family as British goods began to infiltrate the household. Tandon's father was a member of the educated Indian middle classes. Having graduated as a civil engineer he "joined the irrigation department of the Punjab government" in 1898. Tandon's mother came from an orthodox Hindu family. She was a strict vegetarian all her life, "consequently her food was cooked separately from ours, and while she did not mind onions entering the kitchen, meat and fish had to be kept and prepared outside. On nights when we children wanted to snuggle into her bed and be kissed by her, we would share her food. She did not say no, but we knew she did not like us smelling of meat." His mother was strict about intercommunal dining and when she accepted a glass of water from a Muslim household it was always with the assurance that both the glass and the water had been fetched from a nearby Hindu family.

In contrast to his wife, Tandon's father was uninterested in the preservation of caste and community divisions and he would bring his Muslim colleagues home from work to eat at their house. This posed his mother with a problem. She was reluctant to serve the guests on the metal plates and mugs that the family used as these would be indelibly polluted. "Interestingly, this problem was solved in our home, as in many other homes where a similar change was at work, by the introduction of chinaware. Our women . . . willingly shared china plates, cups and saucers. These were somehow considered uncontaminable. Their gleaming white, smooth surface, from which grease slipped so easily, somehow immunised them from contamination. My mother would not at first use the china-ware herself and reserved it for the menfolk and for Muslim, Christian and English guests, but she soon began to weaken." Once she had made these concessions his mother was prepared to accept unpeeled fruit from non-Hindus. "Then followed the acceptance of tea and manufactured biscuits and the English bottled lime cordial." These British packaged goods appeared neutral foods that were less contaminating. However, his mother never relaxed her guard to the point where she was prepared actually to eat with her husband's Muslim and English colleagues.[63] In general, women were far less prepared to abandon caste restrictions than men. For them, being made outcaste meant the probable loss of kin and friendship networks. Men had much to gain from free and easy social exchanges with their colleagues; women had everything to lose. Tea, and its associated products such as cordials and biscuits, as well as chinaware, all assisted them in accommodating to the breakdown of traditional social divisions.

Tea has also played a role in encouraging intercaste and community socializing in less westernized circles. In the 1950s, an anthropologist came across old men in a Rajasthani village lamenting the fact that caste rules were regularly broken without consequences. "A visible sign of the demoralised state of society was the willingness of young Brahmans, Rajputs and Banias to sit with their social inferiors, drinking tea in public tea-shops." Shri Shankar Lal, a Brahman from the village, freely admitted that he often took tea with men from all castes. If one village group manages to raise its status, the standing of another inevitably declines. This knock-on effect in village hierarchies means that there is a strong tendency toward inertia in the system.[64] But tea shops provide the men with a separate, compartmentalized space where they can form intercaste and intercommunal friendships and alliances without necessarily affecting their traditional standing in the village.

There are, of course, limits to the willingness of villagers to bend caste rules. Although Shri Shankar Lal was happy to drink tea with men from all castes he did not extend this accommodation to the "lowest sudras." All the men in his village admitted that they would suffer immense "internal distress ... at the thought of having to sit and eat and drink with members of the lowest 'untouchable' castes."[65] Although the legal position of the untouchable castes has improved since independence, old prejudices are difficult to overcome.[66] As one Punjabi villager remarked, "if throughout your life you have been taught to regard someone as filthy, a mere statute is not going to make you want to sit down and eat with him all of a sudden."[67] Tea in India is often served in small earthenware cups that are smashed on the floor once they have been used. This ensures that no one is polluted by drinking from a vessel made impure by the saliva of another person. Earthenware cups are standard in urban areas where the caste status of the customers is unknown to the stall owner. But in the villages these earthenware cups are often reserved for the untouchables, while the other customers are given their tea in glasses. In one village in northern India an anthropologist came across untouchables asserting their modern rights over the way they were served a modern drink. He was told that these days the untouchables throw away tea given to them in a clay vessel, demand a glass, and threaten the owner with litigation.[68]

The spread of tea by means of modern marketing and advertising techniques was just one of the ways in which technology and industrialization were beginning to change Indians' eating habits. The Muslims of India have always had a strong tradition of eating out, or buying food from bazaar cooks, while high-caste Hindus have traditionally avoided anything other than home-cooked food. But the changing political and economic circumstances of the nineteenth and twentieth centuries meant that increasing numbers of Hindus were confronted with the need to eat outside their own homes. More and more Indians traveled around the country on business. Single men left the villages to seek work in the urban areas. Crammed together on buses and trains it was hard to maintain the principle of separate dining arrangements, although stations did provide separate Hindu and Muslim restaurants. In 1939, a group of educated merchants told an American visitor to India that "trains and motors have put an end to all this affair of special food and separate meals."[69] At the Victoria rail terminus in Bombay there were three restaurants: Divadkar's for vegetarian Hindus, Karim's for the nonvegetarian Muslims, and Brandon's, for the British. For inquisitive young Hindus Divadkar's was dull and predictable. One Brahman from an orthodox Bombay family remembered his nonconformist uncle taking him to the Muslim restaurant to try out the mutton biryani.[70]

Many Indian businessmen seem to have compartmentalized their working lives in the cities and towns from their home lives in the villages. While they might have rigidly observed rituals of purity at home many businessmen tended to abandon them while traveling, even though restaurants and hotels in the cities employed Brahman chefs that provided careful Brahmans with a pure and safe place to eat.[71] One anthropologist was "asked by informants not to disclose in the village how they eat when in town." The further away from home they traveled, and the more anonymous the place, the less fastidious they became. A Brahman from a small village might not have eaten food cooked by a Muslim in the closest town, "but in Delhi he might."[72] Some even sought out these opportunities, and used the railway restaurants and hotel dining rooms as clandestine spaces for experimentation. While he was staying in Nagpur (in Maharashtra) in the 1930s, Prakash Tandon observed "dhoti-clad, vegetarian-looking small business men" shuffling into the railway station restaurant. He discovered they had come "to indulge in secret vices. Some drank beer and whisky but most came to eat savoury omelettes with potato wafers, or even mutton chops. The darkened verandah of the station restaurant provided a safe place for indulging these newly acquired tastes that would have horrified their women at home."

Single men looking for work in the new industrial and commercial spaces, such as the mills, factories, and offices, arrived in the cities in their droves. At first, special eating houses were set up that catered for men from a particular village or from a particular caste. But the new pressures and conditions of life created by capitalist enterprise made it increasingly difficult to observe the rules regulating food consumption. As one Punjabi villager commented, in Delhi "I never used to bother much about caste, in fact in the town it is not always even possible to know for sure what caste a man really comes from."[73] Gradually, a new civic culture developed in India's cities that inhibited the open expression of caste prejudice.[74] Changes in eating habits and the growth of eating houses was particularly pronounced in Bombay, which at the beginning of the twentieth century was the center of India's textile and iron and steel industry.

In the 1890s, the working men of Bombay were provided with tea and snacks by Parsee immigrants from Iran who set up small tea stalls on street corners, selling soda water, cups of tea and biscuits, fried eggs, omelettes, and small daily necessities such as toothpaste, soap, and loose cigarettes. When Bombay's Improvement Trust embarked on a program of urban renewal after the plague epidemic of 1896, new roads were cut through the most congested areas of the city. The Iranian tea-stall owners moved into the shops that were created as a result and "Irani" cafés became a Bombay institution. They had a particular interior aesthetic and were usually furnished with white marble-topped tables, spindly legged wooden chairs, and full-length mirrors. They were often plastered with officious and habitually ignored little notices, instructing the customers not to comb their hair in front of the mirrors or forbidding them from discussing gambling. Laborers and office workers of all castes and communities came to the Iranis to drink tea and snack on English buns, cream cakes and biscuits, and potato omelettes. They also included on their menus Parsee specialities such as dhansak, green chutney and patra fish, and a hard Iranian bread known as *brun-maska*, so crusty that it needed to be dunked in tea before it could be eaten. Newspapers were provided, divided up into separate pages so that as many customers as possible could simultaneously read the same paper. At first the café owners respected communal sensibilities and Hindu customers were served their tea in green cups, Muslims in pink, Parsees and Christians in other colors. But this practice gradually died away.[75]

During the 1920s and 30s the number of eating houses catering to middle-class office workers increased. These were functional places where the principle was to eat as quickly as possible. At the Madhavashram near the Girgaum Police Court, the customers had to bolt their food, as the next line of diners stood impatiently behind their chairs.[76] Most cafés, eating houses, street stalls, and bazaar cooks provided food for hungry working people and travelers. Very few Indians went to a restaurant simply to eat good food in a pleasant atmosphere. This was reflected in the simple decor of the majority of Indian eating houses. There are still many such places in Bombay where the food is eaten from plain metal thalis at smeary Formica-topped tables, and the kitchens beyond the swing doors look as though they could do with a thorough scrub. Indeed, it was partly the unhygienic reputation of eating houses that prevented the spread of restaurant going among India's population. Other hindrances included the reluctance of women to dine out in public, although some Irani cafés encouraged families to patronize them by providing special family cabins that meant that the women felt less exposed. Dietary preferences, rules, and restrictions also meant that most Indians would have visited a restaurant that served the sort of food they ate at home. And given that home-cooked meals, even today, are still generally tastier than anything served in a restaurant, the idea of a meal as a leisure experience did not catch on.

Today, office workers in Bombay can have a home-cooked lunch delivered to their workplace. This service is supposed to have been started by an Englishman who arranged for his bearer to bring lunch to the office. The idea caught on and developed into a lunch-delivery pool that now employs about 2,000 *dabba* wallahs, or tiffin carriers, to deliver over 100,000 lunches every day. Early in the morning housewives all over Bombay city and its suburbs start preparing their husband's lunch. Bachelors and working women rely on contracted cooks who supply home-style lunches. By ten o'clock the meals have been dished into three separate aluminium containers: one for rice, one for a meat or a vegetable dish, and the other for chutneys or bread. The three containers are then clasped together and loaded into a tin outer case that keeps the food warm and prevents it from spilling. This is the *dabba* or tiffin box. This is handed over to the *dabba* wallah, who calls at each private house at the same time every day and then hurries to pass his tiffin boxes on to the next *dabba* wallah in a long relay chain of carriers until each box reaches its designated office worker in time for lunch. Every box has a series of symbols painted on it that tell the wallahs where it needs to go at each stage of its journey. A yellow stroke signifies Victoria terminus, a black circle the *Times of India* offices, and so forth. After lunch the wallah returns to collect up the cases and they return along the same route in reverse until they are delivered to the housewife to wash up in preparation for the next day.

The *dabba* wallah's job is a hard one. The trays, which they carry on their heads, can weigh as much as 50 kilograms when crammed with tiffin boxes. They have to struggle on and off the overcrowded suburban trains and bicycle through the heavy traffic of the Bombay streets, and they are always in a hurry to get the *dabbas* to their destination on time. It is an amazingly complex system yet it is very rare for the vegetarian Hindu to open up his tiffin box to discover a meat curry. The only real threat to the proper delivery of the lunch are the *dabba* thieves who occasionally make off with a selection of assorted lunches. Although a Muslim nonvegetarian meal may be transported alongside a vegetarian Hindu one, the system ensures that clerical workers need risk neither their health nor their caste purity, at the reasonable price of about US $3 a month.[77]

Thirsty office workers in Bombay can choose from a range of drinks. These days many people will drink a bottle of soda with their lunch. This was another British introduction to India. The British began manufacturing soda water at a factory in Farrukhabad in the 1830s and the Indian population soon grew to like it. As a child growing up in the small Punjabi town of Gujrat, Prakash Tandon was impressed by the rows of "coloured aerated drinks" for sale in the soda-water shop. This particular shopkeeper offered 50 different flavors, in a variety of garish colours, including a mix of beer and pink-rose sherbet, which he made up specially for "a local barrister who had been to England."[78] Many of the Iranians in Bombay started off by selling sodas, as well as tea, on the street corners. But new drinks have not entirely ousted more traditional Indian fruit juices. Bombay street corners are dotted with fruit-juice sellers offering freshly squeezed orange and pineapple juice, and the Bombay chain of Badshah Cold Drink Houses sells grape and watermelon juices. Every café and eating house supplies the refreshing and rehydrating *nimbu pani* (lime water), made with sweet lime juice mixed with salt, pepper, and sugar. And Indians still retain their taste for milky drinks such as Persian faloodas and lassis of yogurt whipped together with iced water and flavored with either sugar or salt. Nevertheless, virtually every office worker in Bombay will finish off his or her lunch with a cup of tea: a symbol of the way eating and drinking habits have changed in an ever more industrial and modern India.

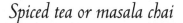

Spiced tea or masala chai

These are two ways to make that "unsavoury . . . decoction" spiced tea, which the tea hawkers sold in the Cawnpore Mill area in the 1930s to the disapproval of the Tea Association campaigners.

4 tablespoons ground ginger
2 tablespoons whole black peppercorns
2 tablespoons green cardamom seeds
1 tablespoon whole cloves
pot of tea
milk and sugar to taste

Grind the spices in a clean coffee grinder. Store the powder in an air-tight container and add ½ teaspoon to a pot of tea. Serve with milk and sugar.

Rebecca's masala chai

4 cups water
16 whole cardamoms, slightly crushed
2 cinnamon sticks
½ cup milk
3 oz. strong black tea leaves
honey or sugar to taste

Bring the water to a boil in a large pan and add the cardamoms and cinnamon sticks. Simmer for 15–20 minutes.

In a separate pan bring the milk to just below boiling point and set aside.

Add the tea leaves to the simmering water and then remove from the heat. Steep for 3–5 minutes.

Strain the leaves and spices and add the milk and honey or sugar to sweeten. Serve immediately. Serves 6.

Lassi

These days lassis are made with yogurt. Bombay lassis are often made with buffalo-milk yogurt, which is very good for this purpose. Serves 2.

¾ cup yogurt
¼ cup iced water (or chips of ice)
sugar or honey to taste (about 2 tablespoons)

Optional additions
⅛ teaspoon cardamom powder
2 teaspoons ground almonds or pistachios
salt and ½ teaspoon of garam masala to make a sour lassi

Put the ingredients in a blender and blend until the contents become foamy.

Mango buttermilk lassi

Originally, Punjabis made their lassis with buttermilk, which is a by-product of manufacturing ghee.

1 cup mango purée (or use any other fruit purée that takes your fancy)
1¾ cups buttermilk (if you prefer you can use yogurt)
1 teaspoon lemon juice
½ teaspoon salt
1 tablespoon honey
pinch of nutmeg
10 crushed ice cubes

Put the ingredients in a blender and blend until the contents become foamy. Serves 3–4.

Nimbu pani

وضع علم کنائی وموسی ووخ ناجی طهر عناره من فیه خلاف الشافعی رح فانه لایجوز
ملمة غتدام کله سعینه کمایه دوارعون ازرعمان یاخذ فی کله شهرار بعه دراهم

This refreshing drink is served all over India and is a very good way to rehydrate the body after a day in the heat.

juice of 3–4 limes
2 teaspoons of sugar
pinch of salt
a little freshly ground black pepper
¾ cup chilled water

Mix the lime juice, sugar, salt, and pepper with the water and pour over ice cubes in a chilled glass. Serves 1.

Indian employees at Veeraswamy's in the 1920s

9

Curry and Chips: Syhleti Sailors and
Indian Takeaways

T HE FIRST INDIAN restaurants in Britain and America were set up by
Syhletis and to this day Syhletis remain a dominant force in the
restaurant trade in both countries. Most of these men came from
the Seaman's Zone at the center of the small district—a predominantly
Muslim, jungly, tea-growing area situated on the northeastern border
with Assam of what is now Bangladesh. During the Mughal period the
Emperor Jahangir noticed that "in the province of Syhlet, which is a
dependency of Bengal, it was the custom for the people of those parts to
make eunuchs of some of their sons and give them to the governor in place
of revenue."[1] It was where Thackeray's grandfather made his fortune by
capturing elephants to sell to the East India Company. During the British
Raj the district was known for the sweet oranges that grew there, but it is
not an area famous for culinary achievements. The most distinctive
speciality from Syhlet is rotten punti fish. The fish, which abounds in the
lakes that cover the region, is put into earthenware pots and covered with
mustard oil, and then the pots are sealed and buried in the ground. By the
time they are dug up again, the fish has fermented into an oily paste that
the Syhletis fry with chillies and eat as a pickle, or add to fish curries to
give them a "cheesy flavour."[2]

During the Raj, Syhlet was strategically important due to a series of
waterways flowing through the district that provided a shortcut between

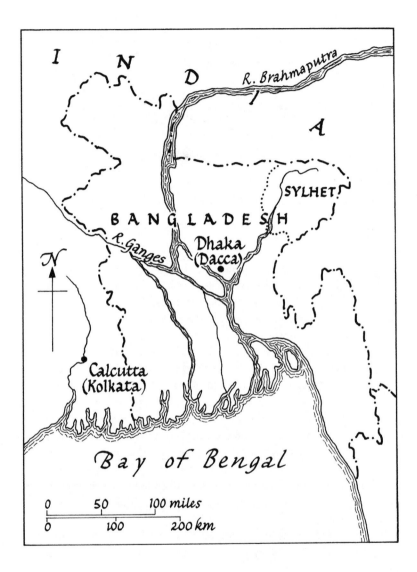

the Assam tea plantations and the port of Calcutta. In the 1840s, the British introduced steamships into these byways and rivers. The Syhleti boatmen, who until now had made a living paddling serenely along the peaceful waterways, found themselves stoking the fires down in the engine rooms of the steamships. Many set off for Calcutta in search of work. A change in the shipping regulations in 1849 meant that the demand for cheap and hardworking lascars, as Indian sailors are known, had increased enormously.[3] Syhlet's surplus boatmen found employment on the ocean-going steamships. Their lack of education meant that they were unable to get the more desirable deck work that required a knowledge of English because the deckhands needed to be able to communicate with the British officers. Instead, Syhletis were employed in the engine rooms where it was nerve-grindingly noisy. The job of stoking the huge boilers with coal was unbearably hot and on occasion men would die of heatstroke. Worse still, the boilers were prone to exploding, maiming and killing the firemen. Such appalling work was not well rewarded. In 1937, a Syhleti fireman earned £2.1.0 a month, one-fifth of the wages of a white fireman. Even during the Second World War, when lascars were risking their lives on the boats, they were paid a war bonus of only £2 compared to £10 for white sailors.[4] Given the conditions and the poor wages it is unsurprising that these Syhleti firemen were notorious for jumping ship. They could be found eking out a living in all the major ports from Rangoon and Singapore to Southampton and New York.[5]

A network of grubby boarding houses for lascars, run by ex-sailors and their wives, had existed in London's East End since the nineteenth century. These were the places where the missionary, Joseph Salter, discovered sailors smoking opium and gambling away their earnings. By the beginning of the twentieth century, these boarding houses were a little more respectable. One of the most famous was run by Mr. Ali, a Bengali, who had set it up with the help of his shipping company on the Victoria Dock Road, Canning Town. Nearby, he ran a small coffee shop, where the seamen could buy curry and rice. During the 1920s and 30s, a number of others followed Mr. Ali's example and by the beginning of the 1940s there were boarding houses and cafés catering for the Syhleti seamen at Sandy Row, Brick Lane, New Road, and Commercial Road. These seamen's cafés were the roots from which Indian restaurants in Britain were to grow.[6] They were meant to cater for ordinary seamen waiting for their ships to sail, but they also provided a support network for the steady trickle of deserters. Razaur Rahman Jagirdar, for example, jumped ship during a bombing raid on London in the 1940s. He spent a terrifying night out on the streets with the bombs dropping around him. In the morning he was relieved to find the Syhleti café on Commercial Road. From there he was directed to the basement Gathor Café at 36 Percy Street, in the West End. Here he discovered what was in effect "a Community centre for the Syhletis." Through the café he found somewhere to live: a terraced four-bedroom house that he shared with between 35 and 40 other Syhletis.[7] Overcrowded and poor accommodation was the norm for deserting seamen. Nawab Ali, who jumped ship in Cardiff during the war, ended up sleeping on a fold-out bed in the kitchen of a house on Commercial Road. It was also difficult to find work. One Syhleti seaman, who lived in London in the 1930s, recalled that his fellow boarders made their money by raffling chocolate in pubs, peddling clothes, or selling toffee on the streets.[8] Most jobs were in catering. Nearly all of the 150 Syhletis known to Razaur Rahman Jagirdar in the West End worked as kitchen porters, cleaners, or washers-up, in restaurants, clubs, and hotels.[9]

For those Syhletis who jumped ship in America life was much more difficult. They tended to work as peddlers as this allowed them to make a living while keeping on the move, thus escaping the attention of immigration officers. A few were able to gain American citizenship by marrying black women but strict immigration laws hindered the establishment of a settled community with a network of cafés acting as ad hoc community centers. Restrictive immigration laws had been put in place in 1917 in response to a tiny number of Punjabi immigrants who had begun arriving on the West Coast of America in the late 1890s. It was through these Punjabis, in a small pocket of agricultural California during the 1910s and

'20s, that Indian food originally found its way into North American food culture. Outlandishly, chicken curry probably first appeared on an American restaurant menu at either the El Ranchero in Yuba City or at Pancho's in Selma where curry and rotis were served alongside Mexican enchiladas.[10]

The Punjabis were often second sons who had been sent abroad to help pay off their family's debts or finance a struggling farm. They were nearly all poorly educated and young (16 to 35) and had heard tales of the incredibly high wages paid to farm laborers in America (two dollars a day in comparison to ten or fifteen cents in India). They intended to make their fortunes and return home as soon as possible. Many of them left behind wives and children. Moola Singh arrived in California in 1911 aged 15, leaving behind him a young and embittered bride. He had only been married for three months when he told his wife that he was going to America. " 'You're leaving me here?' she asked. 'Yes,' he replied, 'my mother is here.' 'What do I need a mother for? You started love; I need you.'" Moola promised to return in six years. His wife told him she would give him three.[11]

The men found jobs building and repairing railway tracks, in lumber mills, and working on fruit and vegetable farms. Although the wages had sounded high they were quickly gobbled up by the cost of living. The Indians lived in miserable conditions, and slept in shacks and outbuildings on the farms where they worked. Moola Singh did eventually save up enough money to bring his young bride over from the Punjab. But by then the immigration laws had changed to prevent wives joining their husbands. White workers, fearing their jobs were under threat, subjected them to a torrent of racial abuse and violence.[12] The level of hostility caused Canada to close down Indian immigration altogether in 1909. The United States followed suit in 1917. Despite all the fuss, only 6,400 Indians had come to America. Nevertheless, the atmosphere remained unwelcoming. In 1924, the citizenship was revoked of those Indians who had become naturalized Americans, and Indians were denied the right to own land or marry into the white population. This had the desired effect of persuading about 3,000 to return home.

Many of those who stayed on found consolation among their fellow agricultural laborers and married Mexican women. Marriage had the added advantage in that it enabled the men to buy small farms through their wives, who were legally entitled to own land.[13] During the 1930s in California a tiny community formed of about 3,000 Mexican Hindus, as they were called. (Although most of the men were Sikhs, the Americans referred to them as Hindus.) Moola Singh married his Mexican wife Maria La Tocharia in 1932. By then his Indian wife, worn down by the life of a daughter-in-law without her husband, had died.[14]

The Mexican-Punjabi marriages were characterized by a disproportionately high divorce rate.[15] But one area where these couples seem to have been compatible was in their kitchens, where they developed a harmoniously blended "Mexican Hindu" cuisine.[16] When they worked on the farms the men would cook together every evening, attempting to replicate the food that they would have eaten at home. Their diet consisted of a little chicken or lamb (which they would kill themselves), chapattis, a few vegetables, and as much milk and butter as they could lay their hands on. In northern India ghee (rather than meat) is regarded as the source of physical strength and "the daughter of a Korean farmer in California recalled how much the Sikh labourers enjoyed their butter: 'They would sit around a large pot of melted butter and garlic, dipping tortillas made with flour and water into it.'"[17]

Mexicans and Punjabis share a preference for fresh food, flavored with freshly ground spices. The fried chicken or lamb of the Mexican women was not that dissimilar to the chicken curries of the Punjabi men. The chillies the latter were used to in India were easily interchangeable with Mexican jalapeno peppers. Punjabi lemon pickle went just as well with corn-based tortillas as it did with wheat-flour rotis. The men would prepare lassis made from buttermilk for the children and, if anyone fell sick, they would make special curative dishes, according to their Ayurvedic knowledge of hot and cold foods.

However, the tiny numbers of the Mexican Hindu community and the strict United States immigration policy ensured that this combination of tortillas and chicken curry remained confined to California. It was not until 1946 when immigration laws eased slightly. Indians already living in America were at last granted the right to naturalization and a small immigrant quota for India was introduced that allowed some of the Punjabis to finally bring over their wives. For Syhletis jumping ship this made life a little easier. Nevertheless the numbers of Indians living in America remained insignificant at only 2,398 in 1950.

Meanwhile, in London, the growing number of Syhletis were beginning to carve out a niche for themselves in the restaurant business. Like the majority of his fellow Syhletis there, Nawab Ali began his career in catering—cleaning, washing up, and peeling potatoes—working in an Egyptian coffee shop on Cannon Street Road. Through a friend he moved on to the Savoy, where he kept the kitchen clean, and then on to Veeraswamy's, where he was given the task of putting rice on the plates. He was instructed to put one cupful on each plate, but the customers rarely ate all of it. "The rice that came back used to fill two dustbins, and I didn't like the rice to go in the dustbin." Rice is the most important ingredient in any Bangladeshi meal, and Bangladeshis hate to waste it. To throw away rice is like throwing away money.[18] Nawab Ali therefore reduced the amount he put on each plate and compensated by spreading the rice around the plate instead. On a visit to the kitchens the owner noticed what he was doing and was pleased to discover such economizing initiative among his staff. He left Ali a generous tip and gave him a raise. Unfortunately, this made him unpopular with the rest of the staff, and, as he did not like quarreling, he left the job.[19]

Veeraswamy's was one of a handful of Indian restaurants in London in the 1940s. An offshoot from the British Empire Exhibition at Wembley, it served Anglo-Indian curries to rich and fashionable Londoners and retired civil servants who felt nostalgic for their old home. A one-time general secretary of the Pakistan Caterers Association can also remember a restaurant known as Abdullah's, somewhere around Old Compton Street in the 1920s. This was run by "an expert cook . . . from Bombay," and Buckingham Palace was even said to have placed orders with Abdullah, who had been recommended to them by the Indian secretary of state.[20] Two other restaurants catered to London's population of Indian students.

Shafi's on Gerard Street might as well have been the London Indian Student Center. The middle-class equivalent of the Gathor Café on Percy Street, it was a comforting home from home for lonely students. The young author Atia Hosain, who had stayed on in London after 1947 as she was reluctant to return to a partitioned India, spent a lot of time at Shafi's "because it was a rendezvous for Indians." She came from a Muslim family for whom "food and companionship went naturally together; Shafi's was like being back home. The owner was host, friend and confidant to all who came, whether to eat or just to relax and talk. Never in India had I found myself alone at a meal. It would have been unthinkable not to share food with friends and relatives."[21] Shafi's was set up in 1920 by the Mohammed brothers from northern India. They came to Britain to study but, having discovered that Indian food was hard to find, they saw a good market opportunity and went into business. Bir Bahadur was another Indian student from Delhi, who opened up the Kohinoor on Roper Street in the West End. His restaurant was so successful that he brought his brothers Sordar and Shomsar over from India to help him establish a chain. By 1948, there was a Bahadur Taj Mahal in Brighton, Oxford, Cambridge, Manchester, and Northampton.[22] These pioneering Indian restaurants all employed ex-seamen in their kitchens and an extremely high proportion of the Syhletis living in Britain in the 1940s and 50s worked in them at one time or another. It was the ambition of many of the seamen to set up restaurants of their own and "The Kohinoor ... was the main training centre for many Bangladeshis for [a] long time. All the Bahadur brothers were kind hearted, they never took advantage of the poverty of their employees and always treated them well. Nearly all the first generation of Bangladeshis who owned Indian restaurants in the UK in the earlier days, learnt their trade from the Bahadur brothers. They learnt the skill of cooking and serving, also management, step by step. Even those who worked for Veeraswamy's restaurant or other Indian restaurants also came to Bahadur at last to have their final training."[23]

By the end of the war there were plenty of bombed-out cafés in need of renovation. The Syhleti seamen used their hard-earned savings to buy up these derelict cafés and small, down-at-heel fish-and-chip shops. Britain's ethnic minorities were already well established in the fish-and-chip trade. The earliest fish fryers had been Jewish immigrants to London's East End, and virtually all the fish-and-chip shops in Scotland and Ireland were owned by Italian immigrants. In the 1950s and 60s, Chinese and Greek Cypriot immigrants, as well as Syhletis, began buying them up.[24] The Syhletis would often spot a good location by looking out for a Chinese takeaway. They knew that "if they opened a restaurant where there was a successful Chinese it would do well."[25] When fish and chips were first sold in the nineteenth century, they were seen as slum food, the sort of thing prostitutes ate as they came off the beat. But they were gradually taken up by the working classes and by the 1950s they made a welcome change for many families from the monotony of roast on Sunday, hash on Monday, cottage pie on Tuesday, hotpot on Thursday, and stewed steak and chips on Friday. In working-class towns there would be a rush on the fish-and-chip shop after eleven o'clock as the men made their way home from the pub, and at the weekends they would be full of men buying a quick lunch on their way to the football game.[26]

The fish-and-chip shops' new Syhleti owners gave them a fresh lick of paint, bought new tables and chairs, and set about building up custom. After he left Veeraswamy's Nawab Ali followed this path. In 1943, after a spell of work in the factories in Coventry, he had saved enough money to buy a small coffee shop at 11 Settles Street. It was a good spot as it was near the Labour Exchange and "all kinds of different people" would drop in— "English, Indians, Arabs, Africans." He redecorated but did not change its name, or the menu, as he did not want to put off the old customers. "We sold tea, coffee, rice and curry, fish and chips—all the usual things."[27] Many Syhleti restaurant owners started out this way, and the names they gave their establishments—the Anglo-Asia or the Anglo-Pakistan— reflected the cultural mix of Syhleti owner and predominantly white customers. The Syhletis continued to provide their customers with the traditional fish and chips and hot pies, and simply tacked curry on to the old menu. They also continued the pattern of staying open after 11 PM to catch the trade as the pubs were closing. Unfortunately, this meant that they attracted plenty of drunken, bad-mannered, and violent customers. Gradually, the white customers became more adventurous and started to try the curries. In this way the British working classes discovered that a good hot vindaloo went down particularly well on a stomach full of beer, and the tradition developed of eating a curry after a night out in the pub. As the customers became increasingly fond of curry, these small cafés and old chip shops jettisoned the British dishes from their menus and turned into Indian takeaways and inexpensive Indian restaurants.

Nawab Ali's next venture was a Maltese café in Cardiff that he bought for £350, a price he negotiated with the help of a prostitute. Rather than trying to keep the old menu and the old style, he changed the name straight away, to the Calcutta restaurant, and offered an entirely Indian menu.[28] A number of such ventures sprung up around Britain in the 40s and 50s, usually with exotic-sounding names, like the Shah-Jalal and Khayam. Syhletis dominated the restaurant trade. Nawab Ali commented, "I will tell you why there were too many Syhletis. It was because we all helped each other: I brought twenty men myself, [before the war] . . . and I must have brought two hundred from the ship in the war, so if each of them helped twenty more . . . you see how it happened. Of course in those days we never imagined there would be so many people—we just wanted to help our brothers."[29] Engine-room crews were "close knit . . . all the men coming from neighbouring villages, and often related to one another," This pattern of emigration had a profound impact on particular Syhleti villages. The first group of emigrants never intended to stay in Britain and many sailors and restaurant owners returned to their villages comparatively wealthy men. Known as "Londonis" in Syhlet, they built themselves stone Londoni houses with indoor bathrooms and painted verandahs while the rest of the villagers continued to live in thatched mud huts. Land prices soared in the migrant districts and the women sang a song with the lines, "How can I accept that my husband has gone to London? . . . The land will be empty—what will I do?"[30]

By the time South Asian immigration into Britain began to increase in the 1960s, the Syhletis already dominated the Indian food business in Britain. They had, of course, acquired a new nationality by then. When India was partitioned at independence in 1947, East Bengalis, including Syhletis, became East Pakistanis overnight. After the Indo-Pakistan war in 1971 the Syhletis found their nationality had changed again: now they were

Bangladeshis. Some Bangladeshi and Pakistani restaurant owners find it irritating to be labeled "Indian" but many encourage the misunderstanding, as India conjures up romantic images in the mind of the British public. Syhletis have ensured that the restaurant business stays in their hands by training up their children. One restaurant owner lamented that, as soon as they were able, the children found themselves co-opted into their parents' or some other relative or friend's restaurant. Rather than spending their evenings doing their homework, "the poor Bangladeshi boys were kept awake until the late hours of night, cooking food or serving curry and rice to the customers." Consequently, while they might have dreamed of becoming engineers or film stars, they have all become cooks, waiters, and restaurant owners instead, and close to 90 percent of Indian restaurants remain in Syhleti hands.[31]

In the 1950s and 60s the early restaurants were frequented by "English people who had been in the civil Service and all that." One restaurant owner remembered that "they used to like sometimes if we called them 'Sahib,' you know . . . they used to be very happy . . . so we wanted to have a little more tip, so why not? They used to call 'Bearer! . . . Bearer!' Nowadays these fellows if anybody called them 'Bearer,' they wouldn't serve him —they would say 'Go out of this restaurant!'" Indian restaurants also became very popular among the student population. The "cheap, tasty, and plentiful" food suited undergraduate needs perfectly. The anthropologist Jack Goody recalled that before the war "under graduates [in Cambridge] could sign out from a meal in college and use the savings to buy a restaurant meal." They would go to the Chinese or Indian restaurants. Many of today's Indian restaurant regulars discovered the food during the 50s, when they were students. The food writer Michael Boddy remembered how he and his friends "would congregate at Indian restaurants . . . I remember Madras curries, the chicken pillaus, chappatties like large grey elephant's ears, saffron rice and pickles . . . the food was not very good. In fact, looking back on it, it was awful, the greasy-spoon side of Indian cooking." But then "the cooks were generally off ships and cooking curries was a way of making a living until something better came along."[32]

It was not unknown for the early restaurants to simply buy in catering-size jars of curry paste that the cooks then used as a basis for all the different dishes. The menus were copied from Veeraswamy's, Shafi's, and the Bahadur brothers' chain of restaurants, where the first Syhleti restaurant owners had learned their trade. Veeraswamy's served the curries beloved by Anglo-Indians: colored pilau rice; sour vindaloos, hot with chillies; creamy chicken kormas, thickened with almonds; hot Madras curries, spiked with lemon juice; dopiazas, thick with fried onions and sweet yellow Parsee dhansaks. The various owners of Shafi's, and the Bahadur brothers, from northern India, followed the lead of the few restaurants that existed there, serving a version of Anglo-Indian, Punjabi, and Mughlai cuisine, which included chicken biryanis, rogan joshes, mushroom curries, and spinach and potato side dishes. This ensured that while in India Mughlai cookery never became a national cuisine, outside India Mughlai dishes were regarded as the national food of all Indians.

Indian restaurants appealed to their customers as inexpensive places where the food was served promptly. These were not the ideal conditions under which to cook Indian food. In perfect circumstances, all the spices used should be freshly ground on a grinding stone, the dish should be cooked slowly and carefully, in a number of stages, allowing the flavors of the spices to be fully absorbed before the next step in the cooking process is begun. Sophisticated dishes such as biryanis or *dum pukht* recipes, which aim to produce meat so tender that it slips from the bone, require very slow cooking, preferably in a bed of hot ashes with hot coals placed on the lid of the cooking pot. Under pressure from their impatient customers, Indian cooks invented a number of short cuts that enabled them to serve cheap, quick, and tasty meals. Rather than using a paste of freshly ground onions, they used "boiled onion paste." This is made from puréed onions cooked in their own moisture without oil. It gives a good thick base for a curry sauce but imparts a slightly raw onion flavor that is one of the distinctive tastes of Indian restaurant food.[33] The curry sauces were prepared well in advance, using preground packaged spices, and a variety of flavor enhancers—asafetida, fenugreek seeds, tomato purée or ketchup, sugar, puréed mango chutney, and monosodium glutamate—to compensate for the lack of fresh ingredients.[34] When the meals were being prepared in the kitchen, precooked lamb or chicken, rice, onions, and the sauce were assembled to create a biryani; a dash of cream and some chicken created a korma; varying quantities of chilli powder were added to produce jalfrezis and vindaloos. A good dash of food coloring gave the dishes their appealing bright red or yellow appearance. Brightly colored food has become so much a part of the British experience of Indian food that when the cooks attempt to reduce the food coloring or leave it out, they find the customers send the food back with indignant complaints that it has not been prepared "properly."[35]

A code developed that assigned new meanings to traditional titles for Indian dishes. Thus korma came to signify a mild creamy dish, dhansak meant a slightly sweet lentil curry, and vindaloo simply indicated that the food would be very hot. The customers have come to expect a standardized menu, whichever Indian restaurant or takeaway they visit. Predictability is part of the appeal. Many regulars stick to one or two dishes that they always eat whenever they go "out for an Indian."

It was in British restaurants such as these that many Americans first discovered Indian food. In 1967 Cliff Earle, a visiting mathematician, and his wife, Liza, used to go down to London from Warwick University. They would eat spaghetti at Italian trattorias or rogan josh at Indian restaurants, preferring the tasty and inexpensive food at these establishments to the bland British food served in ordinary restaurants. On his first trip to Britain in the 1970s, a Californian remembered being introduced to the strange spicy food at an Indian restaurant, suggested by a fellow holiday maker as they were said to serve tasty food in plentiful quantities. He was struck by the solemn, rather formal atmosphere created by starched white napkins and tablecloths and the stiff waiters, whose air of deference was tempered by a hint of disdain.[36]

In the 1960s, global capitalism created the conditions for the spread of Indian food throughout the British population. On one side of the equation the poverty of many people in the newly formed Asian nations, and their willingness to take on menial and unpleasant jobs at unsociable hours, combined with British industrial expansion to encourage increased immigration. Between 1956 and 1958 British immigration laws were changed. Bangladeshis were now able to apply for British passports, and the immigrants already established in the UK brought their families over to join them. There was plenty of work. Pakistanis from the Punjab arrived in the northern towns of Manchester and Bradford to take on night-shift work in the textile factories. It was illegal for women to work at night and white men regarded textile work as women's work. Similar prejudices meant that the rapidly expanding food-processing, plastics, man-made textiles, and rubber industries in west London could not find enough workers. The firms advertised in newspapers in India for labor and by the mid-60s Asians from the subcontinent made up 12 percent of Southall's population. In Tower Hamlets, Bangladeshis took on work in the rag trade that white workers also scorned.[37] Metal works and car-production factories in Birmingham similarly absorbed Asian labor. Punjabi Muslims and Sikhs, Gujaratis and Pakistanis added to the swelling community of Bangladeshi Syhletis. Brutal Africanization programs in the early 70s resulted in the arrival of many "twice-migrant" Indian families from Kenya and Uganda.[38]

The growing Asian immigrant community in London stimulated the growth of a Little India around Drummond Street, near Euston station. Here, Asian grocers supplied the Bangladeshis with bitter gourds, and fresh hilsa fish to make jhol, their favorite dish. This is a watery stew made with hilsa, aubergines, and potatoes. Eating food produced in their home country was very important to Bangladeshis. It enabled them to absorb the essences of Bangladeshi soil and maintain a sustaining link with home.[39] Ambala Sweets sold a range of fudgy barfis made from milk boiled down until it forms a thick paste, powdery laddus made from chickpea flour or nuts and sugar, and crispy gulab jamans coated in a delicate rose-water syrup with a soft and melting milky filling. It was on Drummond Street that the twice-migrant Pathak family (now a household name as Patak's) set up their first British shop, selling vegetables, spices, samosas, and jars of pastes and pickles. This Gujarati family had moved to Kenya where they ran a sweet shop before they moved on to Britain. The Diwani

Bhelpuri House, with its Formica-topped tables and stainless-steel plates, bowls, and cups, recreated the atmosphere of a Bombay office workers' eating house in London. It won awards and helped to popularize Indian vegetarian food in Britain.[40] Not far from Portman Square, the old site of the Hindoostanee Coffee House, Drummond Street in the late 1960s was a small piece of the Indian subcontinent transported to London.

Indian immigration into the United States was of a different nature. The 1965 Immigration Act allowed Indians entry in to America in significant numbers.[41] But rather than poverty-stricken workers these migrants were young, well-educated, highly qualified middle-class professionals who looked for work as doctors, engineers, and scientists. In their wake followed enterprising Syhletis, hoping to emulate the success of their fellow countrymen who had jumped ship in Britain. Most Syhletis arriving in America in the 1970s headed for New York, where they set up restaurants that mirrored those already doing so well in Britain. Madhur Jaffrey recalled that on her first visit to New York in 1958 "it seemed as if menus from the flock-wallpapered restaurants in England had been xeroxed and sent to proprietors here."[42] Beside the restaurants, grocery stores, clothes, and jewelry businesses sprang up, all serving the growing Indian community. A number of thriving "Little Indias" were established around East 6th Street and 1st Avenue and around Lexington Avenue and the 20s in Manhattan, and in Queens. South Asians living throughout the city would visit at the weekends to buy gold jewelry, saris, spices, pickles, and to eat an Indian meal. Just as in Britain, Syhletis came to dominate the Indian restaurant business in New York. On Second Avenue at East 82nd Street there is a block between First and Second Avenue that includes 27 Indian businesses. All of these are owned, managed, and staffed by Bangladeshis. "'I'd say 95 percent of New York's Indian restaurants belong to Bangladeshis,' said Akbar Chowdhury, a daytime manager of Great India." And almost all of them come from Syhlet.[43]

The other side of the equation that enabled the growth in popularity of Indian food on both sides of the Atlantic was a shift in tastes. From the late nineteenth century until well after the Second World War the British diet was dominated by an emphasis on red meat, accompanied by plain boiled potatoes, carrots, or cabbage. Behramji Malabari, who visited in the 1890s, remarked that the British were exceptionally "slow of imagination and wanting in taste" when it came to food. "As a rule the Englishman's dinner is plain and monotonous to a degree. The cook knows nothing of proportion in seasoning his food; knows little of variety, and has a rough slovenly touch."[44] For a large section of the British population a good and "proper" meal consisted of a hearty meat soup or meat and two "veg."[45] Olive oil was regarded as a medicine, not a cooking ingredient. It was bought at the chemist's and kept in the medicine cabinet. It was rubbed onto sore skin or swallowed by the teaspoonful like cod liver oil. Similarly, middle America was prejudiced against anything containing garlic or chillies, and against dishes that could be classed as "mixed" or spicy. Heavily flavored soups and stews were regarded with suspicion as they were reminiscent of the peasant origins of many Americans. Home economics classes in American schools in the 1930s encouraged the children of immigrants to replace pasta with potatoes, parmesan and garlic with butter, plain cheese, and salt. The preferred American meal was white bread, meat, and potatoes, accompanied by thoroughly cooked vegetables, all served separately on the plate.[46]

After curry's heyday in Victorian Britain, a prejudice had developed against curry as "spicy and disagreeable to respectable middle-class English stomachs." Curries were also thought of as smelly dishes to cook, which was a consideration in the 1950s when middle-class kitchens moved up from the basement into the main living area of the house. In the 50s and 60s, the closest many ever came to eating Indian food was the "touch of curry powder in the weekly stew." Those curries that were produced were extremely British: "made with Vencatachellum [curry] powder with swollen sultanas in it and ground minced beef."[47] The curry was either served in the middle of a ring of white rice, or spooned round a pile of white rice in the center of the plate, although in many homes curry was eaten with potatoes and vegetables rather than with rice. For many housewives at the time rice was something they would "never have dreamed of serving except as a pudding." Curry was also eaten with chips, probably due to the fact that many working-class people first encountered curry in Syhleti-run fish-and-chip shops, and initially ate their curries as a sauce on their chips, rather than with rice.[48] The most distinctive thing about British curries of the 60s and 70s was that they were almost invariably flavored with dollops of chutney and fruit. When the comedian Jeremy Hardy joked that, apart from pineapples, apples, and sultanas, "white mothers" even add jam to their curries, he was not entirely wrong. In 1916, the *Australian Household Guide* recommended that a curry could be improved by adding rhubarb, bananas, and "a spoonful of jam as a substitute for apple."[49] Apricot jam also appeared in vaguely oriental concoctions such as coronation chicken, served at Queen Elizabeth II's coronation lunch in 1953. This mixture of cold chicken, mayonnaise, curry powder, apricot jam or mango chutney, and sometimes cream, grated carrot, and pineapple, was reminiscent of Anglo-Indian dishes such as Lady Minto's Soufflé de Volaille Indiénne. These inventive variations on curry as an exotic casserole were often preferred to "proper Indian food."

A 1970s curry

1 lb. topside steak cut into strips (or can use minced steak)
2 large stalks celery sliced
1 tablespoon soy sauce
1 tablespoon white vinegar
1 tablespoon oil
1 tablespoon brown sugar
1 cup water
2 whole cloves
2 heaped teaspoons curry powder
¼ teaspoon each of ground ginger, cinnamon, and mixed herbs
3 heaped teaspoons fruit chutney
½ cup sultanas
¾ cup tomato juice

salt
8 whole black peppercorns
1 or 2 rings fresh or canned pineapple (diced)

Heat the oil in a large saucepan. Sauté the celery and the meat until well browned. Add the curry powder, stir, and cook for 3 minutes. Add spices, tomato juice, chutney, soy sauce, vinegar, and sugar. Stir well. Add remaining ingredients, stir well. Cover and simmer for 50 minutes. Serve with hot rice. Serves 4–6.

All this was to change in the 1960s and 70s: sex, drugs, and rock and roll were accompanied by a revolution in eating habits. In 1958 over two million Britains went abroad for their holidays. Travel expanded people's horizons and made them open to new foods. "Little" Italian restaurants became fashionable. Inside, a spurious "Italian" atmosphere was created with dim lighting, red tablecloths, and empty Chianti bottles used as candlesticks. The Italians dishing up spaghetti in these trattorias cautiously introduced olive oil and garlic into their cooking. Although Americans did not holiday abroad as much as the British, there were plenty of well-traveled American journalists, officials, soldiers, and sailors returning with taste buds tantalized by foreign flavors from reporting on, and administering, the United States' expanding informal empire. On both sides of the Atlantic, food reemerged from the austerity of the post-war years as a middle-class status symbol. Now that middle-class women were working in the kitchens themselves, they relished the chance to show off by whipping up sophisticated and "authentic" dishes for their dinner-party guests.[50] In Britain, Elizabeth David began her campaign to improve British eating habits and, in her bossy tone, persuaded the middle classes that the "authentic" flavors of fresh basil and mozzarella were far better than tired dried mixed herbs and cheddar cheese.[51] In America, restaurant critics expanded their horizons and began to advertise the pleasures of "Northern Italian" and Chinese cookery alongside the more standard

French cuisine. As the definition of high-class food expanded more people ventured into ethnic food stores, following in the footsteps of health-food enthusiasts. These turned into delicatessens and gourmet stores, while ordinary grocers increased their range, to provide for the demand for the new authentic ingredients necessary to make good Italian and French food. Polish and Italian had dominated the ethnic restaurant scene until the 1970s, but now the middle classes looking for an affordable and interesting evening out began to explore the Indian restaurants. Cliff Earle, the mathematician, and his wife Liza, back from their visit to Warwick University, began to frequent the Kashmir and the Karachi in New York. Although the atmosphere was not high class, and the décor utilitarian, an Indian meal was an adventure. In contrast, French restaurants in the same price bracket were less interesting as they offered something that the Earles might have cooked for themselves at home. In Britain, one writer's 1960s diet of "mince and potatoes, haddock and chips ... cheese omelettes ... mutton pies ... lagers and lime," had by 1974 changed to "chicken bhunas ... sweet and sour porks ... lamb kebabs and ... bottles of retsina."[52]

In Britain the Syhletis responded by opening new restaurants and improving the quality of their cooking. Nawab Ali gave his Calcutta restaurant in Cardiff to a friend—who gambled it away—but he had soon set up another in Plymouth called the Bengal. Haji Shirajul Islam returned to the restaurant business by opening the Karachi in Russell Square and then another, larger version in Marchmont Street, so that his customers would no longer have to queue. This he sold, only to buy the Moti Mahal in Glendower Place and another in Chelsea.[53] By 1970 there were 2,000 Indian restaurants in Britain. Asian immigration, combined with British wealth, and an interest in the foods of other cultures, came together to make Indian restaurants part of the landscape of every British town, and curries part of the diet of virtually every British person. Although curry did not take off to the same extent in America it gradually became established as an interesting ethnic alternative alongside the many other ethnic cuisines such as Chinese, Japanese, Greek, and Italian.

The majority of the population living in the South Asian subcontinent would not have recognized the food served in these restaurants as Indian, Pakistani, or Bangladeshi. In the early 1960s Margaret Orr Deas took an Indian friend to a restaurant in London. He politely remarked that "we have very different food in India" and in the following days worked his way along all the Indian restaurants on Westbourne Grove trying to find something that approximated the food he was used to at home.[54] Besides the inexperience of the cooks, and the need to take short cuts, there was also the problem of unadventurous British palates. "In those days garlic was not liked at all; even coriander was frowned on."[55] The cooks produced milder, creamier dishes with far less chilli and black pepper than would have been used in India. In America the chefs adapted to popular tastes by cutting down on the amount of cumin, turmeric, chillies, and mustard seeds. Haji Shirajul Islam commented, "Of course the food is not like in Syhlet—there we use all fresh things, fresh spices, that makes a lot of difference, and the meat and fish and everything, all fresh." He never ate the curries prepared in his own restaurants, preferring to cook for himself at home. On the other hand, for a generation of Indians growing up outside India, this food was as authentically Indian as the food they ate in their homes. Haji Shirajul Islam's son even preferred his father's restaurant curries. "When he goes to the restaurant he eats Madras—hot one . . . Me I always eat in the house. When I offer him food he eats it, but he says it's not tasty like restaurant food, because he's the other way round now."[56] For generations of customers, and even second-generation Indians, the vindaloos and dhansaks, tarka dhals and Bombay potatoes, *are* Indian food. In comparison, food cooked in an Indian home can seem disappointingly unfamiliar and lacking in restaurant tastes.

Shamsher Wadud arrived in Fairfield, Connecticut in the late 1960s as an American Field Service exchange student. His American host family took him to New York and, wanting to make him feel at home, to a Bangladeshi-run restaurant in the city called the Kashmir. Shamsher was disgusted. He thought the food unrecognizable as Indian and the service abysmal. Within a few years he was back in America having given up his technical education and determined to open a good Indian restaurant in New York City. His stylish restaurant, the Nirvana, on Lexington Avenue and 82nd Street, became one of the classier Indian eating places in the city, patronized by Ravi Shankar and the Beatles.[57]

A distinctively Anglo-Saxon way of eating Indian food has developed in Indian restaurants. Poppadoms and pickles would normally be eaten with the food in India. In restaurants they are served as a starter as a way of fulfilling the Western expectation that a meal should be divided into courses. Drinking beer with a curry is a very British practice. The idea is supposed to have originated at Veeraswamy's with the King of Denmark, who is said to have sent a barrel of Carlsberg to the restaurant every Christmas, in order to ensure that he would always have lager to drink with his duck vindaloo. But the British in India had been drinking pale ale with their roast meat and curries since the late eighteenth century. Already in 1810 Thomas Williamson was of the opinion that "nothing can be more gratifying . . . after eating curry."[58] The men who discovered curry on the way home from the pub in the 1940s and 50s were also accustomed to the combination, and once Indian restaurants acquired licenses they stocked beer and lager for their customers who had developed a liking for a few beers, a hot vindaloo, and chips.

A new range of dishes have been invented in British Indian restaurants. The Gaylord restaurant in Mortimer Street, London, was probably the first restaurant to acquire a tandoor oven. In 1968, *The Good Food Guide* reported that they were using a "proper mud oven" to produce "tandoori chicken masal" and "authentic puddingy 'nan'" for one shilling and sixpence.[59] The tandoor is a dome-shaped clay or brick oven that is heated by a wood fire at the bottom. Marinated meat is cooked on skewers inside the tandoor, and nan breads are baked by pressing the dough on to its sides. This was a traditional Punjabi way of cooking and imparted a smoky rich taste to the food. Few Punjabis would have had a tandoor at home but the people used to take their food to a public tandoor where it was cooked for them.[60] Other restaurants followed Gaylord's lead and installed a tandoor that enabled them to liven up their menus with smoky roast chicken tikka. This led to the invention of chicken tikka masala, as described in the first chapter, when tandoori chicken was served in a tomato and cream sauce. Gaylord is said to have introduced the tandoor to New York in 1974.[61]

In the 1980s, Pakistani restaurateurs in Birmingham invented the balti. People love to joke that balti means bucket but those who take their baltis seriously insist that this is the name of the dome-shaped wok in which the curry is cooked. Although the dish is said to have originated in Kashmir, the restaurant balti unashamedly makes a virtue out of restaurant short cuts.[62] It is made up of marinated and precooked meat, added to a pre-prepared balti sauce, which is a version of Indian restaurant curry sauce made from puréed onions, ginger, garlic, tomatoes, a few ground spices, and, most importantly, fresh coriander. Each balti is made distinctive by the way it is assembled. During the first stage of the cooking process a variety of different spices might be fried in oil before the sauce is added. Once the precooked meat has been mixed with the sauce a range of different ingredients—fenugreek, slices of pineapple, lentils—are mixed in to create different baltis.[63]

While the food in Indian restaurants took on a life of its own, independent from the food of the Indian subcontinent, the decor projected a romanticized idea of India, teeming with elephants and maharajas. "All the restaurants had an exotic look about them," commented one of the pioneering restaurateurs, and Haji Shirajul Islam thought his new Karachi restaurant in Marchmont Street "one of the nicest restaurants" at the time: "It was all canopies and things."[64] Many of the early restaurants took their lead from Veeraswamy's. With its high ceilings and beautiful lights from the Maharaja of Mysore's palace, Edward Palmer's creation had an air of 1920s elegance. But in 1933 it was sold to another Englishman, who added more Raj touches, including three elephant stools of gold plated wood. By the 1950s an Indian visitor to Britain thought it created "a stereotyped image of India." "A tall Indian wearing a turban stood at the door. The interior was Oriental with embossed wallpaper and ornate brass vases ... There seemed nothing authentic about the food. I thought it was specially prepared for the British palate. My host explained that the restaurant catered for people like him who felt nostalgic about India from time to time."[65] In many ways images of India had changed little from the days when Sake Dean Mahomed decorated the first Indian restaurant in Britain with specially made cane chairs, prints of Indian scenes, and provided a separate hookah-smoking room. The hallmarks of Indian restaurants became red-and-gold-flocked wallpaper, heavy carved and inlaid wooden furniture, colored tablecloths, little Indian statues, and tinny Indian music playing in the background. The badly paid waiters served the customers, in true British Raj style, with subservience mixed with an air of subtle defiance.

Meanwhile, Madhur Jaffrey had arrived in London, to study at the Royal Academy of Dramatic Art. She was allowed the use of the kitchen at her lodgings but she did not know how to cook. At her home in Delhi "food—good food—just appeared miraculously from somewhere at the back of our house," announced by "a bearer, turbaned, sashed and barefooted." Jaffrey sent imploring letters to her mother asking for help, and her mother obliged by sending detailed recipes and instructions back through the post. Like the nineteenth-century cooks before her, Jaffrey learned to adapt her mother's recipes to the limitations of the ingredients available in London. She substituted lemon juice for tamarind, parsley for fresh coriander, and eventually became sufficiently accomplished to invite her friends round for her own versions of Mughlai cuisine.[66] The fact that Jaffrey had to learn to adapt her recipes to the limitations of British grocers meant that when she began publishing her cookbooks her non-Indian readers found them particularly easy to use. But it was not until she went to New York that she became a cookery writer. In search of a supplementary income to help pay her children's school fees she began writing food articles. This spiraled into a television cookery series for the BBC. *Indian Cooking* was broadcast several times in the early 1980s and, through Jaffrey's books and programs, the British public learned to cook Indian food at home. Looking back on this series she wrote: "The day after I made my Lemony Chicken with green Coriander, I was told that all green coriander in Manchester had sold out. People had more leisure and more money in their pockets. I was cooking real Indian food and the British yearned for it."[67]

Like Madhur Jaffrey, Yousuf Choudhury found it was difficult to buy all the ingredients for Indian food in 1960s Britain. When he arrived in

Birmingham from Syhlet in 1957, he used to buy his spices from "a chemist off the Coventry Road by Birmingham city football ground." He and his uncle, and the nine other occupants of their three-bedroom house, retained a preference for freshly killed chickens, as opposed to the long-dead specimens available in British butchers. Live chickens were supplied by a group of dubious traders who hung out along the Varna Road, along with the prostitutes, on Sunday mornings. Thus it was possible to indulge in a little sexual dalliance while procuring dinner. But whoever had to carry the chickens home drew the short straw. "When we were on the bus, the chickens used to jump about, so whoever bought the chickens had to walk home." Eventually Noor Ali of Babon-Gaon opened up an Indian grocery store on Wright Street, with others soon following, so that it was possible to buy betel leaf and the favorite Syhleti fruit, satkora, in the Bangladeshi-run grocers.[68] As curries became more and more popular with the British, many Indian ingredients—fresh coriander, okra, and a range of spices—began appearing in British supermarkets.[69]

The earliest convenience foods also included curries. Vesta packet foods produced a dehydrated curry meal made with minced beef and the ubiquitous sultanas. A respondent to a survey on eating habits remembered how in 1953, aged 14, he "took a shine to Vesta packet meals, the first range of such dishes I recall. It must have seemed tres risqué to my mother, brought up on tripe, cow heel, ribs and M[eat] & 2 V[eg] ... my mother was prepared to indulge my culinary whims, so on high days and holidays it was vesta curry and rice dishes." These curries must have tasted similar to the unappetizing dehydrated lightweight meals walkers take with them on long hikes.[70] As convenience foods progressed from packets to frozen ready-made meals, curries kept pace. The spices and plentiful onions and garlic of Indian food made the processed meats and frozen vegetables much tastier. Frozen Indian meals were versions of Anglo-Indian pilaus and curries: rice, pieces of chicken, and chunks of apple and pineapple flavored with a sweet yellow curry powder; meat, fruit, and sultanas "churned together in a bland curry sauce." Indian food entrepreneurs responded to these terrible concoctions by producing their own. G. K. Noon had come to Britain in 1970 to make sweets for the Indian community in Southall. In 1988 he moved into frozen and chilled ready meals. He now supplies Sainsbury's and Waitrose, and as a result is the thirty-fifth richest Asian in Britain. Shehzad Husain rang up Marks & Spencer's to tell them how horrible their Indian ready meals were, only to find herself appointed consultant on their Indian food range, while the Pathak family expanded their pastes and pickle business, which had begun on Drummond Street.[71] By the end of the 1980s, Indian food was available in a huge variety of forms to every British supermarket shopper. In the unstable boom and bust of Mrs. Thatcher's Britain, curry appealed to a British public that was hungry for stability and tradition. Indian food could not perhaps be classed as traditionally English, but it carried with it echoes of empire and Britain's period of lost glory, and in 1984 a wave of Raj nostalgia swept over Britain with the screening of *The Jewel in the Crown*.

More than any other ethnic food, the British have made curry their own. These days it is considered an integral part of British culture. Going out for an Indian is such a British activity that Asian comedians were able to poke fun at the British with a sketch on going out for an "English." Each year the British spend at least £2 billion in Indian restaurants, while homesick British ex-patriots living in the South of France meet up for curry evenings. Marketing researchers for supermarkets no longer include standard curry paste in the ethnic foods category but treat it as a "mainstream British flavour." In 1997 the British spent £7.7 million on mango chutney.[72] When he was at Manchester United, David Beckham used to celebrate scoring a goal with chicken korma at the city's Shimla Pinks Indian restaurant.[73] Even that profoundly British institution, the pub, serves curry lunches. In 2002, the *Observer* newspaper made the point that curry is now a "British institution" with a mock cover for a "Nation Forward Party" magazine. A brutish-looking man in leather jacket and Union Jack T-shirt is pictured sitting down to an Indian meal while the slogans around him declaim: "Keep Curry British" and "Bhuna! Nan! Pilau! Curry is your birthright."[74]

As the *Observer* advert hinted, although the British eat vast amounts of curry, they are not always welcoming toward the Asians who make it for them. The lager-loutish tradition of rolling, uproariously drunk, into an Indian restaurant and proving one's machismo by ordering the hottest vindaloo or phal possible, is one of the disturbing sides of the British relationship with Indian food.[75] The consumption of large quantities of curry has not necessarily made the British any less racist. As the food writer Dorothy Hartley wrote in 1956, the British have an unfortunate habit of "naturalising" any foreign dish that enters the culture. They have thoroughly Anglicized Indian food, first with curry powder, apples, and sultanas, and now with chicken tikka sandwiches and curry sauce on chips. In a strange creolization of Russian and Indian, it is even possible to buy chicken Kiev filled with curry sauce. It can be argued that the prevalence of curry in the British diet is not a sign of a new multicultural sensitivity but rather is symptomatic of British insularity. The creolization of ethnic foods can be read as a sign that they are only capable of being cosmopolitan in their tastes, as long as they are able to integrate the ethnic dish into their thoroughly British food habits.[76]

Americans have not embraced curry as wholeheartedly as the British. The lack of a colonial connection between the two countries, the much lower level of immigration combined with the fact that the majority of Indian immigrants were professionals, and that most twice-migrants from countries such as Uganda chose the motel over the restaurant business, as well as the wide range of competing cuisines from American hamburgers to Chinese and Mexican fast food, have made it harder for Indian food to infiltrate American tastes. However, the last decade has seen a steady rise in the popularity of curries and "Little Indias" can now be found outside New York, dotted about in cities across the United States, from Chicago, where there are three blocks of Indian stores and restaurants near Devon Street, to the Bay Area where in one block of shops customers can watch an Indian movie, buy Indian music and movies, choose a salwar kameez, and pick up spices, pickles, and vegetables to make a meal at home, or eat a range of Indian foods from north Indian tandoori chicken to south Indian dosas.[77] Many restaurant owners are still cautious, and advertise their menus with the obliging message that all the dishes can be made extremely mild, but enthusiastic customer reviews of restaurants suggest that Americans palates are becoming ever more accustomed to spicy food.

A peculiarly American phenomenon is the rise of the kosher Indian restaurant. Syhletis have been joined in New York by a rising number of south Indians, offering their regional specialities—thalis, dosas, idlis, and chutney. Five of the south Indian establishments around Lexington Avenue and 28th Street are now certified as kosher. The Madras Mahal, which employs a chef from Kerala and another from Madras, was the first to gain a kosher certificate. Their original aim was to demonstrate that Indian food is not just tandoori chicken and heavy curries, but the vegetarian nature of much south Indian food meant that it also appealed to Jewish customers. One of these suggested that they ask a Rabbi to certify the food and now 30 percent of the restaurant's revenue comes from customers ordering kosher meals.[78] It is even possible to order an Ayurvedic meal in Manhattan at the Ayurveda café, where all the meals include the six *rasas* or tastes (pungent, acidic, salty, sweet, astringent, and bitter) in order to maintain a harmonious balance within the body.

Western attitudes toward India have also begun to change. The old images of poverty and fading Raj grandeur have been replaced by images of computer technicians and modern call centers. The wealthy Indian middle class have begun to appear on our cinema screens in films like *Monsoon Wedding*. Bollywood has become fashionable and these days the British rulers are cast as the bad guys in films such as *Lagaan*. As a result, the British have begun to look with new eyes at the Indian food that they have been consuming unthinkingly. The fact that Indian restaurant curries would be unrecognizable to many inhabitants of the subcontinent as Indian food has begun to stimulate interest in authenticity, despite the fact that British restaurant food is simply another variation within a food world characterized by variety. The focus on authenticity fails to acknowledge that the mixture of different culinary styles is the prime characteristic of Indian cookery and that this fusion has produced a plethora of versions of Indian food from Mughlai to Anglo-Indian, from Goan to British Indian.

Restaurants have responded to the new interest by including "authentic" dishes on their menus, and the change is reflected in the new-style restaurant. "Why do Indian restaurants have to be dark and dingy?" asked Nav Kandola, manager of Five Rivers in Leamington Spa. His restaurant is bright and open with chic waiters and a modern menu dotted with authentic dishes such as Goan-style mussels. He sees his restaurant as a reflection of the new India, which is a "fast, modern place." Just around the corner, Abdul Hamid has given in to the pressure for change and redecorated his restaurant, Kismet, with pale yellow walls that give the place a light and airy feel. Nevertheless, he regrets the demise of the red-and-gold flocked wallpaper, Indian music, and waiters in costume. He is proud of his Syhleti background and felt that it was accurately represented by the atmosphere of exotic glamour. He is saddened by the disappearance of what he sees as traditional India and can see nothing wrong with providing his customers with an oriental setting in which to eat their meal. For him this is not shallow multiculturalism, but a way of keeping his own culture alive within Britain.

The recent changes in Indian restaurants reflect the changes in patterns of Asian immigration. The gaudy but cheerful red-and-gold restaurants run by Syhleti sailors are gradually being replaced by a new-style restaurant, run by the second generation. A more recent wave of professional immigrants have begun to open high-class Indian restaurants where, with small portions of beautifully presented food, they have endeavored to place Indian cookery in the same bracket as cordon bleu French cuisine. They have been successful. Two Indian restaurants in London now have Michelin stars: Tamarind and Zaika. In Zaika, modern trendy India is combined with a nostalgia for the Raj. The food is served by waiters in chocolate-brown Nehru jackets and the simple but immensely versatile peasant dish, khichari, has been reinvented as "Indian risotto" made with red onions and coriander and topped with crispy prawns.[79] There is a surprising level of hostility across the Indian restaurant divide with some of the expensive rebranders of Indian food dismissing the old-style restaurant owners as "Pakis and Banglis who are just junglee peasants with rough habits." The traditional restaurateurs hit back with the retort that "These people are all rubbish. They are half castes, the bastard children who don't know their own fatherlands, think they know better than us because they speak English. Real food is here and it is cheap."[80]

These debates have crossed the Atlantic. Although Laxman Sharma, owner of three upscale Indian restaurants in Connecticut, is at pains not to be rude about the Bangladeshi and Pakistani owners of old-style restaurants, he worries about their impact on the reputation of Indian food. Sharma's concern is that customers might dislike the watery sauces characteristic of Bengali food, or the hot chilli flavors of Pakistani food and be wary of Indian restaurants in the future. In his opinion, in order to prevent any potential muddle in customers minds, it would be far better for Indian food's reputation as a whole if Bangladeshi- and Pakistani-run restaurants did not call their food Indian. According to Sharma the key to success in America lies in reducing the amount of oil in the dishes, placing a greater emphasis on steamed and healthy food, and educating the public in the authentic flavors of the different regional culinary styles of the subcontinent. Indeed, an increasing number of fancy Indian restaurants already exist in America, following the general trend in Britain.[81] The Bombay Club in Washington plays on the old-fashioned image of Raj India with pale green shutters at the windows and an ornamental carpet, brass and glass chandeliers, and a white grand piano in the dining room, all designed to evoke the atmosphere of a private club. But rather than offering British-Bangladeshi, old-style curries, the menu promises a culinary trip through regional Indian cooking.

September 11 has certainly made life more difficult for the old-style Bangladeshi-run restaurant. In the new atmosphere of hostility toward Muslim immigrants many Bangladeshis already in the United States gave up hope of gaining legal status and returned home. The stream of new immigrants, who would have replenished the depleted numbers, has dried up. Restaurant owners who used to train up this unskilled labor as cooks, waiters, and general kitchen staff now struggle to find employees. In response, Laxman Sharma has begun producing a bottled curry sauce to sell in 10- to 15-gallon jars to hard-pressed restaurants lacking in sufficient chefs to make fresh bases for their curry sauces. In the long run, however, a decline in unskilled chefs may force restaurants to employ properly trained staff, thus giving overall standards a boost. It may also give high-class restaurants that pay attention to the careful preparation of regional dishes the leading edge.

The Taste of India restaurant in Tonga's capital, Nuku'alofa

10

Curry Travels the World

WHEN INDIANS TRAVEL they take their food culture with them. Syhletis returning to Britain after a visit to Bangladesh carry back suitcases stuffed with jars of chutney, pickled mangoes, and dried punti fish.[1] Indian merchants in the sixteenth- and seventeenth-century spice trade took Gujarati and south Indian food to Malaysia. There, Indian spice mixtures were leavened with star anise, which Chinese traders had brought with them to the peninsula. This combined well with the Malayasian flavoring of lemongrass and coconut milk as a base for sauces. From Malaysia, south Indians traveled to the spice islands of Indonesia, where curries are now made with Sumatran spices such as kaffir leaves and galangal.[2] But Indian food has been spread around the globe most effectively by indentured laborers.

In 1836, the Liverpool merchant John Gladstone (father of the prime minister William) suggested that the shortfall of labor predicted by West Indian sugar planters, as a result of the abolition of slavery, might be made up by Indian laborers. Under the resulting system of virtual slavery, poverty-stricken (usually Hindu) peasants entered into binding contracts under which they agreed to give their labor for either five or seven years. In return they were given housing, food, medicine, clothing, minimal wages, and a free passage to the country where they were to work.[3] The first shipment of indentured laborers sailed for Demerara in 1838, and by the time the Indian National Congress successfully campaigned to bring the system to an end in 1919, 1.5 million had left India and, at the most, only one-third had returned home.[4] Indentured labor took Indians and their food culture around the globe to Mauritius from 1843, British Guyana, Trinidad, and Jamaica from 1845, South Africa and Fiji from the 1870s. All these countries now demonstrate a strong Indian influence in their cookery.

The majority of indentured laborers lost all contact with their home country from the moment they climbed on board the ship. On the voyage many of the caste restrictions that shaped their social lives broke down. It was impossible to eat in their caste groups, as everyone was served their food out of the same pot and water was distributed to all from the same container irrespective of caste or religion. Once the principle preventing interdining between men of different castes and communities had broken down on the ship, it was not reinstated in the new country. Nevertheless, Indian food remained central to their sense of identity.

This is still the case in Fiji. Indo-Fijians with northern and southern Indian roots express their sense of difference from each other through comments about their eating habits. Thus Indo-Fijians originally from northern India refer to their compatriots with a south Indian heritage as *kata panis* (sour waters). This is a mocking reference to the southerners' love of tamarind as a souring agent in their food. In retaliation, the southerners refer to the northerners as *kuri*. This implies weakness and stinginess. Here it refers to the lack of spices in northern food compared to southern sauces, which are thick with whole spices. The indentured laborers were often reluctant to eat the food of their new countries and continued to cook the dishes familiar from home. In Guyana and Trinidad, the Indian community have preserved the cooking traditions of their home region Uttar Pradesh, producing dark curries colored by preroasted spices. In Malaysia, where many of the laborers on the rubber plantations were Tamil, the Indians eat the sambars and lentil preparations that characterize south Indian food.[5] Even today, Indo-Fijians make few concessions to their new culinary environment. They occasionally buy the Fijian vegetables, breadfruit or taro, but usually only if there is a shortage of potatoes. Ironically, many of the ingredients such as potatoes, tomatoes, and chillies, which are now seen as Indian ingredients by Indian emigrants, are in fact alien foodstuffs introduced to the South Asian subcontinent from the New World by Europeans.

An Indo-Fijian taxi driver I spoke to in 2001 laughed aloud when I asked him if he ate Fijian food. "I'd rather starve," he cried. "I'd rather eat grass."[6] George Speight, the radical nationalist leader of the last political coup in Fiji in 2000, argued that the Indo-Fijians who make up 48 percent of Fiji's population should be denied political representation because they refuse to assimilate. He denounced them for wearing Indian clothes and eating Indian food. However, journalists claim to have observed George Speight and his political allies tucking into a curry. While Indians tend to preserve their eating habits wherever they end up living, their hosts, no matter how hostile, frequently cannot resist their cooking.

Indian food has become a popular fast food in many of the countries to which it traveled. In South Africa, Indians (known as bunnys from the mispronunciation of the word Banian) set up small eating houses selling curry and rice. Black South Africans developed a taste for these spicy dishes, but under apartheid it was illegal for them to be served in an Indian establishment. The problem was solved by serving the curries in hollowed-out loaves of bread that could be quickly passed to the customer at the back door and eaten without cutlery. These fast-food loaves filled with curry were known as bunny chow (Indian food).[7] In Fiji and the Caribbean, Indian food has become *the* fast food.[8] On the street corners, food stalls sell roti wraps to passersby of every ethnic origin. These are soft thin rounds of bread, filled with a rich, oily, and satisfying filling of chicken in a tomato sauce spiked with cumin.[9]

Rotis are the Punjabi version of chapattis, made from unrefined wholemeal wheat flour mixed with water, kneaded into a dough, and rolled out into thin circles and baked on a hot griddle. Fijians working as domestics in the homes of wealthy Indo-Fijians, or in the kitchens of restaurants and hospitals, learned how to make this simple Indian bread and took the skill back to their villages. Salote Sauvou grew up in a remote village on the island of Vanua Levu in the 1970s, and for breakfast, she and the other village children would eat a rolled-up roti and drink a cup of tea. The Fijians have made some adjustments to Indian rotis, however. Salote's mother, like most Fijian women, made her rotis with refined flour and, to soften it, she would dip the dough into coconut milk (one of the most important foods in Fiji).

The indentured laborers were often hampered by the lack of Indian ingredients in their new countries. Frequently they had to make do with a few lentils, rice, wheat flour, and a little turmeric. This forced them to adapt their cookery to the ingredients available in their new homelands —in South Africa, for example, cornmeal often replaced lentils. But wherever freed indentured laborers have formed communities of rural laborers, they have been followed by Gujarati traders and businessmen, who supply them with Indian clothes, jewelry, and foodstuffs. In Fiji, the Gujarati firm of Punja & Sons has been supplying the Indo-Fijian community with a huge variety of separate spices and masala mixes since 1958. In the last ten years, however, the Fijians have also begun to buy curry powders and dried chillies. Growing up on her island, Salote Sauvou had never encountered curry, but when she came to the capital city of Suva she learned how to make chicken curry. Indian dishes are now beginning to spread into the Fijian villages. The children of Lovoni on the tiny island of Ovalau, a day's journey from Suva, eat school lunches of dhal on Monday, curry on Friday, and Fijian-style soup and tinned fish on the other days.[10] Part of curry's popularity among the Fijian adult population stems from the fact that it goes well with the local intoxicating drink kava, which numbs and thickens the tongue.

From Fiji, Indian food has spread to other Pacific islands. The University of the South Pacific has contributed to this process. When the university opened in 1968 the students' canteen was divided into an Indian section offering "roti, rice, meat and vegetable curry and dhal" and an island section offering "boiled root crops, beef, pork, [and] tapioca." At first the students ate their own food at separate tables. Eventually, however, they began to experiment. This has worked strongly in favor of the Indian food. When one Indo-Fijian professor travels around the different Pacific countries visiting students, he finds that they often "talk fondly about Indian food. When visiting Suva they eat nothing else."[11]

In the last ten years small bottles of very yellow curry powder have passed from Pacific island to Pacific island, and even on islands where there is no history of Indian immigration the inhabitants can be found cooking curries. These curries are, however, so removed from anything that might be eaten on the subcontinent that they are almost unrecognizable as Indian food. Since the introduction of tinned foods by European missionaries in the nineteenth century, Pacific islanders have developed a preference for tinned foods as markers of high status. In Samoa, they make tinned fish and corned beef curries flavored with curry powder mixed with flour, and curry is a luxury food. Even for a comparatively well-off family earning about 40 Samoan dollars a week, a bottle of curry powder costing three Samoan dollars, which lasts for two meals, is a relatively expensive purchase. Plus the corned beef would also have to be bought from the local store. Curry is rarely eaten with rice and instead is accompanied by boiled taro or breadfruit, which are grown in every Samoan's garden. Surprisingly, curry powder is even beginning to catch on in Tonga, where spices and flavorings, including salt, are very rarely added to food.

The islands of Tonga are home to a small community of immigrant Indo-Fijians and Gujaratis, and the Taste of India restaurant, housed in a tiny white clapboard house in the capital Nuku'alofa, offers a typical Indian restaurant menu. In their homes the Indians continue to cook Indian food: prawns in coconut milk, khicharis of rice and yellow lentils, spiced aubergine, and sweet-and-sour okra. They have not been infected by the islanders' passion for canned goods and retain their preference for fresh ingredients. The one Tongan foodstuff that has been incorporated into their cookery is roro, the leaves of the taro plant. Taro is a root crop like yam and the Pacific islanders boil or roast it in their earth ovens. They also use the leaves once they have carefully removed the main stem because, if eaten, it releases juices that cause an unpleasant sensation like pins and needles in the back of the throat and tongue. Tongans chop up the leaves and fry them with tinned fish and maybe a few onions. The Indians in Tonga rub the leaves with a sweet-and-sour mix of chickpea flour, sugar, treacle, spices, and tamarind. Rolled up and steamed, or cut into pieces and fried, this Indian version of roro is said to be very popular with the King of Tonga when he eats with his Indian friends.

Recipe for roro (taro leaves) Indian style

Taro leaves (remove stalk and slice off center stem)
5 oz. wheat flour
5 oz. gram flour (chickpea flour)
5 oz. rice flour
1 onion, grated
2 tablespoons chilli powder
lemon-sized ball of tamarind pulp
a large ball of jaggery, double the size of the tamarind, grated
2 teaspoons coriander powder
2 teaspoons cumin powder
2 teaspoons salt
coriander leaves, minced

Mix all the flours, onion, chilli powder, tamarind pulp, jaggery, coriander and cumin powders, and salt with enough water to make a thick paste. Spread the mixture on the leaves and make rolls. Steam the rolls for 20 minutes. Cool. Slice the rolls. Serve garnished with coriander leaves or grill in an oven at 200 degrees for 10 to 15 minutes till brown.

Indians living in the Caribbean and South Africa have shown more openness to the foods of their new home countries than the descendants of indentured laborers living on the Pacific islands. In Trinidad, they make a kind of khichari using rice and lentils but flavored with chives, parsley, and thyme, which were themselves introduced to the Caribbean by Europeans.[12] They have also replaced the cayenne chilli peppers commonly used in India with the lantern-shaped Scotch bonnet chillies native to the island. Their sweeter perfume, combined with roasted ground cumin and European herbs, give their food a Caribbean flavor. Here the history of the chilli pepper and Indian food has come full circle. Scotch bonnet chillies were the "Indian peppers" or *aji* that Columbus discovered on his first voyage in 1492.

Similar processes of assimilation have taken place in countries with richer Indian immigrants. In the United States first generation Indians were often thwarted in their attempts to make their dishes taste just as they did at home. In Jhumpa Lahiri's *The Namesake* she describes the frustration of the pregnant Ashima unable, due to a lack of mustard oil, to reproduce the exact flavor of the street snack made from puffed rice that she urgently craves. On the other hand, Ashima is delighted by the fact that in her new country she can buy limitless quantities of high quality rice, flour, sugar, and salt.[13] Indeed, the new-found wealth of many Indian immigrants to America has substantially altered the nature of their cooking. Able to afford lavish amounts of fresh vegetables and lots of butter, their cooking has become much more sumptuous. One American visiting India for the first time was surprised to find that the food "did not taste as good" as in America.[14] One disadvantage has been that many second-generation Indians have failed to acquire the knowledge of how to make many of the elaborate dishes their parents were used to from home. Although Jhumpa Lahiri's mother would spend hours grinding turmeric and chillies on a stone and making fresh chana out of boiled-down milk, manufacturing complicated dishes for her Bengali friends, she failed to teach her daughter how to cook. Even when Lahiri gave her a book in which to write down the recipes she was reluctant to pass on her knowledge in this fashion, having learnt by helping her mother in her kitchen in Calcutta. Jhumpa Lahiri eventually taught herself from Madhur Jafffrey's cookery books. It was only when she began making some of these dishes in her mother's kitchen that she was offered the essential tips, such as adding a little sugar to curries, which gave her mother's food its special flavor.[15]

Surprisingly, one country where curry occupies a position of national importance almost equal to the place of Indian food in Britain is Japan, which has no colonial connection with India and indeed boasts its own sophisticated food culture.

The Japanese love curry. Every train station and shopping mall in Japan has a stand selling *karee raisu* (curry rice). Japanese noodle bars sell *karee udon* (curried wheat noodles), and bread shops offer a bread roll with a blob of curry sauce hidden inside them, called *karee pan*. In 1982, Japanese schoolchildren voted for curry as the favorite meal served to them by the national school-lunch program and pork cutlets, vegetable stir-fry, and curry were the three dishes most often cooked for dinner in Japanese homes. The Curry House Ichibanya chain has 300 stores all serving cheese, banana, frankfurter, fried chicken, and squid curries, which can be ordered at seven levels of spiciness. There are even comic books in which the best ways of cooking a curry are earnestly discussed by the main characters.[16] In January 2003, a curry museum opened in the port town of Yokohama, a fitting place as it was through the port towns that curry arrived in Japan.[17] Until the 1860s Japan had turned its back on the rest of the world, but during the Meiji era (1868–1912) there came into power a new set of rulers who embraced Western culture and technology and raced to modernize Japan. British merchant ships began arriving at the ports and they brought with them a wide range of new foods: bread, ice cream, pork cutlets, potato croquettes, hashed beef, and curry. It became very fashionable among the rising middle classes to eat these Western dishes. They were a luxurious expression of progressiveness and openness to the West. Curry recipes appeared in the new women's magazines and cookery books. The curry that the British introduced to Japan was the Anglo-Indian version of Indian food that was commonplace throughout the Raj and that had found its way on to the menus of merchant ships and P&O steamers.[18] Japanese recipes instructed the novice on how to mix curry powder with flour and then fry it in butter to produce a curry roux to which meat, vegetables, and stock were added. Once the dish had simmered for a while, it was finished off with a dash of cream and a dribble of lemon juice.

Only a few decades later Indian food as eaten by Indians was introduced to Japan. In 1912 Rash Behari Bose, a revolutionary Indian nationalist, fled the British authorities in Bengal. He found refuge with the right-wing militarist Black Dragon Society in Japan. There he married the daughter of a family with Black Dragon connections. While he helped spread anti-British propaganda among Indian students at Japanese universities, he also helped to popularize Indian food. Bose taught his father-in-law, who owned a bakery, how to make curry the Indian way without using either flour or curry powder. Soma Aizo used his new culinary skills to open a restaurant, named after his daughter, Nakamuraya, Rash Behari Bose's wife. The restaurant is still there in Tokyo's Shinjuku district and apparently still serves an R. B. Bose curry.[19] Other Indian restaurants have followed, but the Japanese prefer their own versions of Anglo-Indian curry.

Although Anglo-Indian-style curries were served in the Fegetudo Western-style restaurant as early as 1877, curry found its place in Japan not in elegant restaurants but in canteens. The army adopted curry and rice as an easy meal to cook in large quantities, and curries were also a good way of feeding the troops beef, which the Japanese hoped would strengthen their physique. During the Taisho era (1912–1926), the army even used to advertise that it fed its troops curry, as it drew in new recruits, attracted by the glamorous aura of Westernness that still surrounded the dish.[20] After the Second World War, curry and rice appeared on the school-lunch menu in schools throughout the country. Then, with the production of blocks of pre-prepared curry roux, it became popular in Japanese homes. All the tired cook needed to do was to fry some meat and vegetables, add water and a roux bar (which is a brown, sticky, rather evil-smelling square of flour, spices, and fat) and simmer. The bars come in three strengths, mild, medium, and hot, all of which are mild to Indian or British palates. The resulting brown mess is eaten with fluffy white rice and *fukujinzuke* (pickled vegetables).[21] Part of curry's appeal is that, because it inevitably looks like a sloppy brown mess, it is exempt from *gochiso*, the culinary laws of purity and perfection. Unlike sushi—complex to assemble, served with great care for the aesthetics of the food and eaten delicately—curry is poured over the rice on a Western plate and eaten with a spoon. It has thus become a Japanese comfort food: warm, sustaining, and without need of ceremony.[22]

Over the centuries, new foodstuffs and recipes have transformed Indian food. In modern India, the kitchens of the growing Indian bourgeoisie have joined the imperial kitchens of the Mughal emperors, the bakehouses of the Portuguese settlers at Goa, the Vaisnavite temple kitchens in the south, and the cookhouses of the British in India as the engines of culinary change. Every town and city in India now has a substantial middle class made up of Indians from many different areas. Women living outside their home regions, away from the grandmothers and aunts who are the traditional sources of recipes and culinary advice, have turned to cookery books and recipe columns in newspapers and magazines for inspiration. These new English-language recipe books rarely confine themselves to dishes from one region. Thus, while housewives might look to them to help reproduce traditional food from their own regions, they are increasingly exposed to recipes from all round India. Indeed, it has become quite fashionable for women to widen their repertoire and impress their families and friends with their ability to cook new and unfamiliar dishes from across the subcontinent. Recently, an Indian cable television channel bought Madhur Jaffrey's *Flavours of India* cookery series. In the programs Jaffrey describes how to cook dishes from a variety of areas, thus fueling the process of the interchange of recipes across regions. The series has been dubbed into Gujarati, Marathi, Punjabi, and Bengali, ensuring that the process of exchange has also been encouraged among the non-English–speaking lower-middle classes.[23] These developments have contributed to a process of fusion in Indian food culture and out of the fragmented localized traditions of India, what might be called a national cuisine is beginning to develop.[24]

The new cookbooks promote the mixing and matching of dishes from different regions by dividing Indian food into clearly defined categories. The various recipes are generally grouped together as rice- and lentil-based dishes, breads, vegetable and meat curries, pickles, chutneys, and sweets. These cookbooks even use the British concept of curry to help categorize, and thus unite, the various traditions of Indian cookery. In a culture where all the food is placed on the table simultaneously, this categorizing provides a skeleton upon which a Gujarati lentil dish can be hung alongside a Tamil vegetable curry and a pickle from the Punjab. As a result of this culinary exchange, a core repertoire of dishes common to the whole of India is gradually developing.

Into this national cuisine the high-status Mughlai cuisine has been absorbed alongside dishes from regions in the south and east that were never incorporated into the Mughlai culinary culture. This process has its costs. Along the way the more specialized and complicated recipes tend to be dropped and there is a strong tendency to stereotype different regions so that Bengal curries are associated with mustard oil and Keralan curries with chillies.

Keralans have recently become acquainted with northern Indian samosas and they are just beginning to appear in southern bakeries. No doubt southerners will soon adapt them to their tastes and culinary techniques, perhaps filling them with prawns. This process of exchange and development has already taken place with southern dosas, which are served in Delhi with a filling of northern Indian paneer (cheese).[25] Indeed, cookery books have promoted culinary exchange across the globe as volumes containing recipes from different Indian communities, from the Caribbean to South Africa, arrive on the shelves of bookshops in the subcontinent. This latest injection of foreign influences continues the process of fusion through the introduction of new culinary techniques and new ingredients that has, over many centuries, given Indian food its vibrancy, and made it one of the world's finest cuisines.

Susan's chicken

This recipe was given to me by an Indian lady from Madras who had spent much of her life in Zambia. Indians formed the bulk of the commercial middle classes in countries like Rhodesia (now Zambia and Zimbabwe), Uganda, Kenya, and South Africa, until the 1970s, when Africanization programs in Kenya and Uganda drove many into exile in Britain and America. Serves 4–6.

4 tablespoons vegetable oil
6–8 chicken pieces (breasts and thighs with the skins on)
2 large onions, chopped
¾ in. piece of fresh ginger, finely grated
8 cloves garlic, crushed
1 teaspoon powdered aniseed
1½ teaspoons chilli powder
½ teaspoon freshly ground black pepper
3 teaspoons coriander powder
½ teaspoon turmeric
6 large tomatoes, chopped
salt to taste
fresh coriander, chopped

Heat the oil in a pan, and fry the chicken pieces until they are browned on all sides. Take out of the pan and set aside. In the same oil, fry the onions until browned. Add the ginger and garlic and fry for 6 minutes. Add the aniseed, chilli powder, black pepper, turmeric, and 1½ teaspoons of the coriander powder. Fry, stirring for 1 or 2 minutes. Add the tomatoes and simmer until the sauce thickens. Add the chicken pieces and simmer until the meat has cooked through and is tender. Sprinkle on the last 1½ teaspoons of coriander powder and simmer for 5 minutes. Sprinkle on the fresh coriander and serve.

Glossary

aji	Caribbean word for chilli pepper
aloo	potato
appam	spongy south Indian bread made from a batter of ground rice and lentils
Anglo-Indian	British person living in India; nowadays this term is used to describe people of mixed British and Indian descent but before 1911 it was used to refer to the British in India
areca nut	astringent seed of the areca palm tree
arrack	alcoholic spirit distilled from palm-sap or rice
asafetida	resinous plant gum with a garlicky taste used in Indian cookery (also known as hing)
aub-dar	servant responsible for cooling and serving drinks
Ayurvedic medicine	ancient school of Hindu medicine
Banian	member of a trading caste, merchant, or broker
barfi	fudgy sweet made from milk boiled down until it forms a thick paste
bebinca	Goan dessert made from coconut milk, jaggery, and eggs
betel	leaf of the *Piper betle*, chewed with areca nuts
bhang	Indian hemp
bundobust	Anglo-Indian for contract
burra khana	Anglo-Indian for big dinner
cantonment	Anglo-Indian for a military station
chittack	a measurement equivalent to about 1 ounce

Glossary

choola	stove
chota haziri	early breakfast
chowrie	fan
chuprassee	messenger
dak	post
dak bungalow	rest house for travelers
dariol	medieval sweetmeat of egg custard baked in a pastry shell
dastarkhwan	central tablecloth on which the dishes for a feast are served
deg	cooking pot
dharma	humanitarian conduct
dhye	curds or yogurt
diwan	governorship of a region, granted by the Mughal emperor
dosa	thin pancake made from a batter of ground rice
dum pukht	a technique of cooking where the pot is sealed with dough and then cooked on a bed of ashes with smoldering coals placed on the lid
feni	a potent spirit made from the stem of the cashew plant
firman	Mughal imperial directive (often to regulate trading privileges)
fukujinzuke	Japanese pickled vegetables, eaten with curry
garam masala	mixture of black spices such as black pepper, cinnamon, and cloves
ghee	clarified butter (the favored cooking medium in India)
gobi	cauliflower
gochiso	Japanese culinary laws of purity and perfection
gram	pulses
gulab jaman	sweets made from milk and covered in a rose-water syrup
hookah	Indian hubble-bubble pipe
hookah-*burdar*	hookah servant
hurkarrah	messenger
idli	light doughnutlike bread made from a batter of ground rice and lentils
jaggery	coarse brown sugar made from palm-sap
jeera	cumin
jiyza	a tax imposed by Muslim rulers on non-Muslims

kacca	foods usually prepared fresh each day, using water and susceptible to pollution
kava	intoxicating Polynesian drink made from the root of the kava plant
khansaman	head servant or butler
khichari	dish of boiled rice and lentils
khidmutgar	waiter
khir	sweet milk and rice dish
khud	broken grains of rice
khudkura	huskings and particles of rice, humble or poor food
laddu	sweet made from chickpea flour and sugar
lascar	Indian sailor
maidan	parade ground
masalchi	spice grinder and sometimes in Anglo-Indian households a dishwasher
maval	cockscomb plant, the flower of which is used as a flavoring in Kashmir and gives the food a bright red color
mofussil	remote countryside or the provinces
nanbai	bazaar cook
nautch girls	dancing girls
nimbu	lime
paan	betel leaf and areca nut mixed with lime and chewed as a digestive
pakka	foods usually prepared using ghee or oil and less susceptible to pollution than *kacca* foods
palanquin	an enclosed litter for traveling in, carried by four to six bearers by poles slung across their shoulders
pani	water
prasadum	the leftovers of the gods
pukka	Anglo-Indian for proper
qima	minced meat
rajasic	foods thought to stimulate the passions and induce anger
rakhi	protection charm
rasa	tastes (pungent, acidic, salty, sweet, astringent, and bitter)
rasam	broth

Glossary

ryot	peasant
sadhu	Indian holy man
sattvic	foods thought to promote good health and moderate behavior
seer	a measure of weight equivalent to about 1 kilogram
sepoy	Indian soldier
shikar	hunting and shooting
syce	groom
toddy	alcohol made from the palm-sap
tonjon	open carriage, carried by four to six bearers on long poles
tyre	curds or yogurt
zenana	part of the house reserved for the women of the family

Notes

1 CHICKEN TIKKA MASALA

1 Liza Earle in conversation with the author; Richard J. Scholem, NYC Dining Reviews, www.cityguidemagazine.com.

2 Jonathan Meades, "Goodness gracious!" *Times*, 21 April 2001.

3 Iqbal Wahhab and Emma Brockes, "Spice . . . the final frontier," *Guardian*, 4 November 1999.

4 Babette Crosette, "In New York don't take 'Indian' food too literally," *New York Times* cited at www.himalmag.com/jun2000/content/VOICES.htm.

5 Sharma (ed.), *Rampal*, p. 142.

6 Appadurai, "How to make a national cuisine," p. 18.

7 Conlon, "Dining out," p. 114.

8 Buchanan, *Journey from Madras*, I, pp. 101–2. See also Rao, "Conservatism and change," pp. 127–9; Lewis, *Village Life*, p. 267.

9 Gardener, "Desh-bidesh," p. 6.

10 Phillip Ray in conversation with the author.

11 Jubi and Hafeez Noorani, "A unique culinary culture," *Taj Magazine*, 11, 1 (1982).

12 Cantile, "The moral significance of food," pp. 42–5.

13 Achaya, "Indian food concepts," pp. 221–2.

14 Marriott and Inden, "Toward an ethnosociology," p. 233.

15 Marriott, "Caste ranking and food transactions," p. 134.

16 Ibid., pp. 133–63.

17 Rao, "Introduction and overview," p. 3; Beck, *The Experience of Poverty*, pp. 137–42.

18 Rao (ed.), *Encyclopaedia of Indian Medicine*, IV, pp. 3–8, 45–8.
19 Zimmermann, *The Jungle*, p. 24.
20 Sharma (ed.), *Caraka-samhita*, I, pp. 44–5; Sharma, *Social and Cultural History*, p. 100; Achaya, *Indian Food*, p. 81.
21 Storer, "Hot and cold food beliefs," p. 34.
22 Chattopadhyaya, "Case for a critical analysis," p. 217.
23 Zimmermann, *The Jungle*, p. 126.

2 BIRYANI

1 Manrique, *Travels*, II, pp. 213–20.
2 Ibid., pp. 207–13.
3 Madan, *Non-Renunciation*, p. 143; Sethi, "The creation of religious identities," pp. 16, 202–6; Richards, *The Mughal Empire*, pp. 20, 34.
4 Thackston (ed.), *The Baburnama*, pp. 332, 334, 350–1, 359–60.
5 Ikram, *Muslim Civilization*, p. 136.
6 Thackston (ed.), *The Baburnama*, p. 350.
7 Peterson, "The Arab influence," pp. 321–2.
8 Cunningham Papers, p. 397.
9 Vambery, *Sketches*, pp. 118–19.
10 Schuyler, *Turkistan*, p. 125.
11 Sastri, "The Chalukyas of Kalyani," pp. 370, 453.
12 Zimmermann, *The Jungle*, pp. 30, 55–61, 98, 170, 185; Sharma (ed.), *Caraka-samhita*, I, p. 222.
13 Sastri, "The Chalukyas of Kalyani," p. 453; Arundhati, *Royal Life*, pp. 113–30.
14 Saletore, *Social and Political Life*, pp. 310–11.
15 Arundhati, *Royal Life*, p. 125.
16 Prasad, "Meat-eating," p. 290.
17 Keay, *India*, pp. 96–7.
18 Majumdar, *The Age of Imperial Unity*, pp. 73–4.
19 Murti et al., *Edicts of As'oka*, pp. 3, 9, 11, 105, 107.
20 Wadley, *Struggling with Destiny*, p. 45.
21 Jaffrey, *A Taste of India*, p. 57.
22 Carstairs, *The Twice Born*, p. 109.
23 Tavernier, *Travels*, I, p. 38; Valle, *The Travels*, p. 294.
24 Tavernier, *Travels*, I, pp. 311, 326; Hamilton, *A New Account*, p. 96.

25 Chattopadhyaya, "Case for a critical analysis," pp. 212–13.

26 Jha, *The Myth of the Holy Cow*, pp. 30–7, 95–8; Brockington, *The Sanskrit Epics*, pp. 20–1, 197.

27 Achaya, *Indian Food*, p. 55; Jha, *The Myth of the Holy Cow*, pp. 61–89.

28 Manucci, *Storia do Mogor*, pp. 42–3.

29 Peterson, "The Arab influence," p. 321.

30 Khare, "The Indian Meal," pp. 162–4.

31 Thackston (ed.), *The Baburnama*, pp. 367–8.

32 Eraly, *The Last Spring*, p. 108.

33 Ahsan, *Social Life*, p. 152.

34 Quereshi, *The Muslim Community*, p. 31; Ahsan, *Social Life*, p. 155.

35 Tavernier, *Travels*, I, p. 41.

36 Zubaida, "Rice," pp. 92–4; Fragner, "From the Caucasus," pp. 57–9.

37 Jaffrey, *Madhur Jaffrey's Indian Cookery*, p. 154.

38 Fryer, *A New Account*, III, p. 240.

39 Burton, *Savouring*, p. 197.

40 Richards, *The Mughal Empire*, p. 17; Dalrymple, "That's magic," *Guardian Review*, 1 January 2003, p. 18.

41 Allami, *Ain-i-Akbari*, I, p. 60.

42 Bernier, *Travels*, p. 287; Richards, *The Mughal Empire*, pp. 190–1, 195; Kulshreshtha, *The Development of Trade*, pp. 184–5.

43 www.menumagazine.co.uk/azasfoetida.htm; Fryer, *A New Account* I, p. 286.

44 Singh, *Indian Cooking*, p. 25; Thirty-Five Years' Resident, *The Indian Cookery Book*, p. 16.

45 Allami, *Ain-i-Akbari*, I, p. 61.

46 Ibid., pp. 59, 64.

47 Eraly, *The Last Spring*, pp. 195, 219; Richards, *The Mughal Empire*, p. 47.

48 Eraly, *The Last Spring*, p. 165.

49 Beveridge (ed.), *The Tuzuki-i-Jahangiri*, p. 184; Eraly, *The Last Spring*, p. 239; Srivastava, *Social Life*, p. 2.

50 Eraly, *The Last Spring*, p. 169.

51 Tavernier, *Travels*, I, 95–6.

52 Lal, *Twilight*, pp. 276–7; David, *Harvest*, pp. 246–8.

53 Goody, *Cooking*, p. 98.

54 Manrique, *Travels*, II, pp. 218–19.

55 Terry, *A Voyage to East-India*, pp. 206–11.

56 Eraly, *The Last Spring*, pp. 274, 312.

57 Beveridge (ed.), *The Tuzuki-i-Jahangiri*, p. 215.

58 Manrique, *Travels*, I, pp. 65–6.

59 Manucci, *Storia do Mogor*, p. 68.

60 Chapman, *The New Curry Bible*, p. 111; Jaffrey, *A Taste of India*, pp. 128–9.

61 Thackston (ed.), *The Baburnama*, pp. 423, 445.

62 Foltz, *Mughal India and Central Asia*, p. 7.

63 Beveridge (ed.), *The Tuzuki-i-Jahangiri*, I, pp. 116, 435; II, p. 101.

64 See, for example, ibid., I, p. 116.

65 Bernier, *Travels*, p. 284.

66 Foster (ed.), *The Embassy of Sir Thomas Roe*, p. 152.

67 Manucci, *Storia do Mogor*, pp. 37–8.

68 Thackston (ed.), *The Baburnama*, p. 343; Beveridge (ed.), *The Tuzuki-i-Jahangiri*, p. 116.

69 Eraly, *The Last Spring*, p. 337.

70 Ibid., p. 322.

71 Foster (ed.), *The Embassy of Sir Thomas Roe*, pp. 99, 190, 240, 324–5.

72 Hawkins, *The Hawkins Voyages*, p. 437.

73 Beveridge (ed.), *The Tuzuki-i-Jahangiri*, I, pp. 307–10.

74 Manucci, *Storia do Mogor*, II, p. 5.

75 Eraly, *The Last Spring*, pp. 303, 307.

76 Panjabi, *50 Great Curries*, p. 88.

77 Manrique, *Travels*, II, pp. 186–8. *Reals* were Spanish pieces of eight.

78 Eraly, *The Last Spring*, p. 312.

79 Keay, *The Honourable Company*, pp. 115–16.

80 Manucci, *Storia do Mogor*, II, pp. 5–6.

81 Sen (ed.), *Indian Travels of Thevenot and Careri*, p. 236; Eraly, *The Last Spring*, p. 393; Srivastava, *Social Life*, p. 4.

3 Vindaloo

1 Dalby, *Dangerous Tastes*, p. 89.

2 Tavernier, *Travels*, II, p. 11.

3 Pharmacopoeia, pp. 172, 177.

4 Dalby, *Dangerous Tastes*, p. 91.

5 Peterson, "The Arab influence," pp. 317, 319–20; Scully, *The Art of Cookery*, p. 84; Sass, "The preference," pp. 254–7; Prasad, *Early English Travellers*, p. xxxii; Laurioux, "Spices in the medieval diet," pp. 46–7, 51, 59.

6 Scully, *The Art of Cookery*, p. 30; Laurioux, "Spices in the medieval diet," pp. 56–9.

7 Cohen, *The Four Voyages*, pp. 11–17, 121; Dalby, *Dangerous Tastes*, pp. 148, 150.

8 Dalby, *Dangerous Tastes*, p. 148.

9 Laudan and Pilcher, "Chilies, chocolate and race," p. 65.

10 Andrews, "The peripatetic chilli," p. 92.

11 Subrahmanyam, *The Career and Legend*, pp. 129–38.

12 Silverberg, *The Longest Voyage*, pp. 58–9.

13 Subrahmanyam, *The Portuguese Empire*, p. 63.

14 Pearson, *The Portuguese*, pp. 30–2.

15 Burton, *The Raj at Table*, p. 6.

16 Hyman and Hyman, "Long pepper," pp. 50–2.

17 Watt, *A Dictionary*, II, p. 135.

18 Achaya, *Indian Food*, p. 227; Watt, *A Dictionary*, II, p. 137.

19 Jaffrey, *A Taste of India*, p. 220.

20 Andrews, "The peripatetic chilli," pp. 92–3.

21 Linschoten, *The Voyage*, I, pp. 207–8.

22 Sen (ed.), *Indian Travels of Thevenot and Careri*, p. 162.

23 Fryer, *A New Account*, II, pp. 27–8; Linschoten, *The Voyage*, I, pp. 205, 212–13.

24 Linschoten, *The Voyage*, I, pp. 67–8.

25 Ibid., pp. 222, 228–30; Subrahmanyam, *The Portuguese Empire*, p. 225.

26 Fryer, *A New Account*, I, p. 192.

27 Linschoten, *The Voyage*, I, p. 193.

28 Ibid., pp. 219–22. For the corruption of Portuguese officers of all ranks, see Xavier, *Goa*, pp. 214–15.

29 Fryer, *A New Account*, II, p. 16.

30 Pearson, "The people and politics," p. 10; Subrahmanyam, *The Portuguese Empire*, p. 228.

31 Boxer, *Race Relations*, pp. 60–1.

32 Linschoten, *The Voyage*, I, pp. 212, 207–8.

33 Fryer, *A New Account*, II, pp. 27–8.

34 Laudan and Pilcher, "Chilies, chocolate and race," p. 65.

35 Fitch, in Foster (ed.), *Early Travels*, p. 46.

36 M. Albertina Saldanha, "Goan cuisine. How good is it?," *Goa Today*, XXIII, 12 (July 1989), p. 22; Mundy, *The Travels*, p. 59.

37 Coelho and Sen, "Cooking the Goan way," p. 150.

38 This was Richard Burton, later to become famous as the first white man to enter Mecca, and as the translator of the *Arabian Nights* into English. Burton, *Goa*, p. 104.

39 Laudan and Pilcher, "Chilies, chocolate and race," p. 66.

40 Scully, *The Art of Cookery*, p. 136.

41 Larsen, *Faces*, p. 118.

42 Mandelslo, *The Voyages and Travels*, p. 79.

43 Sen, "The Portuguese influence," p. 290.

44 Bernier, *Travels*, II, p. 182.

45 Burton, *Goa*, p. 98.

46 M. Albertina Saldanha, "Goan cuisine. How good is it?," *Goa Today*, XXIII, 12 (July 1989), p. 22.

47 Coelho and Sen, "Cooking the Goan way," p. 153; Cabral, "Of Goa and gourmets," *Taj Magazine*, 26, 1 (1997); Laudan, *The Food of Paradise*, pp. 88–9.

48 Tavernier, *Travels*, I, p. 150; The Saraswat Brahmans who did not convert to Christianity developed a vegetarian Goan cuisine.

49 Robinson, "The construction of Goan interculturality," pp. 290–1.

50 Manucci, *Storia do Mogor*, pp. 180–1.

51 Hamilton, *A New Account*, p. 143.

52 Richards, *Goa*, p. 25; Priolkar, *The Goa Inquisition*, pp. 116–17.

53 Subrahmanyam, *The Portuguese Empire*, p. 231.

54 Cited by Priolkar, *The Goa Inquisition*, p. 55.

55 Souza, *Goa to Me*, p. 87; Gracias, "The impact," p. 48; Lopes, "Conversion," pp. 69, 72.

56 Scammell, "The pillars of empire," pp. 477–87; Subrahmanyam, *The Portuguese Empire*, p. 231.

57 Priolkar, *The Goa Inquisition*, p. 104; Axelrod and Fuerch, "Flight of the deities," pp. 412–13.

58 Axelrod and Fuerch, "Flight of the deities," pp. 393–4.

59 Ibid., p. 387.

60 Borges, "A lasting cultural legacy," p. 55.

61 Robinson, "The construction of Goan interculturality," p. 309.

62 Burton, *Goa*, pp. 104–5; Axelrod and Fuerch, "Flight of the deities," p. 410.

63 Robinson, "The construction of Goan interculturality," p. 310.

64 Richards, *Goa*, pp. 4–5, 71.

65 Sen, "The Portuguese influence," p. 293.

66 Scully, *The Art of Cookery*, p. 112.

67 Dawe, *The Wife's Help*, p. 62.

68 Coelho and Sen, "Cooking the Goan way," p. 151; M. Albertina Saldanha, "Goan cuisine. How good is it?," *Goa Today*, XXIII, 12 (July 1989), p. 13.

69 Cited by Collins, *The Pineapple*, pp. 9–17.

70 Beveridge (ed.), *The Tuzuki-I-Jahangiri*, I, pp. 215, 350.

71 Nichter, "Modes of food classification," pp. 195–6.

72 Maciel, *Goan Cookery Book*, p. 9.

73 Eraly, *The Last Spring*, pp. 434, 495.

74 Gordon, *Marathas*, p. 35.

75 Fryer, *A New Account*, II, pp. 67–8; Ikram, *Muslim Civilisation*, pp. 196–7, 206.

76 C. Y. Gopinath, "So what's for dinner then?," *Taj Magazine*, 18, 3 (1990).

77 Richards, *Goa*, pp. 33–4.

78 Rao, *Eighteenth Century Deccan*, pp. 227–8.

4 KORMA

1 Ovington, *A Voyage*, pp. 394–8.

2 Farrington, *Trading Places*, pp. 16–20, 39; Richards, *The Mughal Empire*, pp. 196–9.

3 Foster (ed.), *Early Travels*, pp. 60–70.

4 Foster (ed.), *The Embassy of Sir Thomas Roe*, p. xxiv; Terry, *A Voyage to East-India*, pp. 211, 218.

5 Farrington, *Trading Places*, p. 69.

6 Bayly (ed.), *The Raj*, p. 68.

7 Ovington, *A Voyage*, p. 141; Fryer, *A New Account*, I, p. 179; Burnell, *Bombay*, pp. 20–1.

8 Wilson (ed.), *The Early Annals*, p. 208.

9 Richards, *The Mughal Empire*, p. 201; Keay, *The Honourable*, pp. 134–5.

10 Mandelslo, *The Voyages and Travels*, p. 13; Anderson, *The English*, p. 48; Ovington, *A Voyage*, pp. 237–8.

11 *Oxford English Dictionary*.

12 Ramaswami (ed.), *The Chief Secretary*, p. 79.

13 Terry, *A Voyage*, p. 107.

14 Manucci, *Storia do Mogor*, I, pp. 62–3; Major (ed.), *India in the Fifteenth Century*, p. 32.

15 Ovington, *A Voyage*, p. 397.

16 Fryer, *A New Account*, I, p. 177.

17 Terry, *A Voyage*, p. 94.

18 Laudan, "The birth of the modern diet," p. 62.

19 Scully, *The Art of Cookery*, p. 207.

20 Appadurai, "How to make a national cuisine," p. 13.

21 Stein, *Peasant State and Society*, pp. 144–5.

22 Breckenridge, "Food politics and pilgrimage," p. 30.

23 Hultzsch, *South Indian Inscriptions*, p. 189.

24 Breckenridge, "Food Politics and Pilgrimages," pp. 32, 37–40; Jaffrey, *A Taste of India*, pp. 197–8.

25 Richards, *The Mughal Empire*, p. 190.

26 Appadurai, *Worship and Conflict*, p. 37.

27 Hamilton, *A New Account*, p. 211.

28 Achaya, *Indian Food*, p. 68.

29 Jaffrey, *A Taste of India*, p. 220.

30 Aziz, "Glimpses," pp. 170–1; Jaffrey, *A Taste of India*, pp. 170–1.

31 Sharar, *Lucknow*, p. 157.

32 Hasan, *Palace Culture*, pp. 4–5.

33 Fisher, *A Clash of Cultures*, pp. 71–6.

34 Sharar, *Lucknow*, pp. 155–6.

35 "Oude Accounts etc. 1777–1783," Warren Hastings Papers, p. 26.

36 Hasan, *Palace Culture*, pp. 4–5.

37 Panjabi, *50 Great Curries*, p. 25.

38 Tasleem.Lucknow.com.

39 Sharar, *Lucknow*, pp. 157–8.

40 Cited by Allen (ed.), *Food*, p. 239.

41 Sharar, *Lucknow*, pp. 158–62.

42 Praveen Talha, "Nemat-e-Dastarkhwan. Bounty of the table," *Taj Magazine*, 23, 1 (1994).

43 Llewellyn-Jones, *Engaging Scoundrels*, p. 12.

44 Allami, *Ain-i-Akbari*, I, pp. 62–3.

45 Llewellyn-Jones, *Engaging Scoundrels*, p. 44.

46 Ali, *Observations on the Mussulmauns of India*, I, p. 38.

Notes

47 Sharar, *Lucknow*, p. 161; Singh, *Mrs Balbir Singh's Indian Cookery*, p. 132.

48 Ali, *Observations on the Mussulmauns of India*, I, pp. 324–5; II, p. 67.

5 MADRAS CURRY

1 Parks, *Wanderings*, I, pp. 25, 46–7; Williamson, *The East-India Vade-Mecum*, I, pp. 213–14, 238–9; II, p. 180; Campbell, *Excursions*, I, p. 68; Graham, *Journal of a Residence*, p. 30.

2 [Hobbes], *Reminiscences*, p. 14.

3 Richard Burton, cited by Brodie, *The Devil Drives*, p. 51.

4 Young, *Early Victorian England*, pp. 104–108.

5 MacNabb Collection, /4, f. 77; Fenton, *The Journal*, p. 53.

6 Cordiner, *A Voyage to India*, p. 110; Graham, *Journal of a Residence*, p. 30.

7 Cordiner, *A Voyage to India*, p. 110; Roberts, *Scenes and Characteristics*, I, p. 76.

8 Spencer, "The British Isles," pp. 1222–3; Fine et al., *Consumption in the Age of Affluence*, p. 203.

9 Roberts, *Scenes and Characteristics*, I, p. 72; Elizabeth Gwillim, Gwillim Papers /1, f. 48.

10 F. J. Shore, Futtyghur, 23 July 1820, Frederick John Shore Collection /5–8.

11 Elizabeth Gwillim, Gwillim Papers /1, ff. 37–8.

12 Fane, *Five Years*, I, p. 29.

13 Valle, *The Travels*, II, p. 328.

14 Some food writers suggest that the word comes from *kahree*, or *karhi*, the name for a northern Indian dish made with chickpea flour and yogurt. But none of the seventeenth-century writers describe something that sounds like this dish when they use the words caril, carree, or curry. They clearly use them to refer to Indian stews or ragouts in general.

15 Edmunds, *Curries*, p. 10.

16 Tandon, *Punjabi Century*, p. 88.

17 Nichter, "Modes of food classification," p. 200.

18 Thirty-Five Years' Resident, *The Indian Cookery Book*, p. 22.

19 McCosh, *Medical Advice*, p. 83.

20 Dawe, *The Wife's Help*, p. 59.

21 In 1923, C. Lewis recommended for tiffin "a curry with as many concomitants as are available, such as Bombay duck, Popadums, chutney, minced cocoanut, etc. Anyone who has lived on the Madras side or in Ceylon will know how

the additions improve a curry. At the Galle Face in Colombo we have counted as many as 16 different side dishes served with it" (Lewis, *Culinary notes*, p. 59).

22 Williamson, *The East-India Vade-Mecum*, II, p. 128.

23 [Palmer], *Indian Cookery*, p. 184.

24 Burton, *Goa*, p. 296.

25 Campbell, *Excursions*, I, p. 68.

26 *Indian Cookery "Local,"* p. 1.

27 Burton, *The Raj at Table*, p. 105.

28 Jaffrey, *A Taste of India*, p. 87; Panjabi, *50 Great Curries*, pp. 98–9; Behram Contractor, "Eating-out with a difference," *Taj Magazine*, 11, 2 (1982).

29 Roberts, *Scenes and Characteristics*, I, p. 153.

30 Burton, *Goa*, p. 251.

31 Mandelslo, *The Voyages and Travels*, pp. 19–20.

32 Eden, *Up the Country*, p. xiv.

33 Flora Holman, Holman Paper, p. 13.

34 Emily Sandys, 26 August 1854, Stuart Papers.

35 Tayler, *Thirty-Eight Years*, pp. 394–5.

36 Burton, *The Raj at Table*, pp. 113–14.

37 Kaye (ed.), *The Golden Calm*, p. 120.

38 A Thirty-Five Years' Resident, *The Indian Cookery Book*, p. 20.

39 Roberts, *Scenes and Characteristics*, I, p. 51.

40 Burton, *The Raj at Table*, pp. 126–9.

41 Cited by ibid., p. 121.

6 CURRY POWDER

1 Fisher, *The First Indian Author*, pp. 251–66.

2 Hunter, *The Thackerays*, pp. 85–99.

3 Fisher, *The First Indian Author*, p. 260; Holzman, *The Nabobs*, p. 90.

4 Salter, *The Asiatic*, pp. 28–31.

5 Visram, *Ayahs*, p. 15; Salter, *The East*, p. 38; Salter, *The Asiatic*, pp. 25, 69–70, 116.

6 24 October 1813, Spilsbury Collection /1.

7 Shade, *A Narrative*, p. 27.

8 Geddes, *The Laird's Kitchen*, pp. 71–9, 100.

9 Cited by Grove, *Curry, Spice & All Things Nice*.

10 "Indian Cookery," pp. iii–iv.

11 Laudan, "Birth of the modern diet," pp. 62–7; Freeman, *Mutton and Oysters*, pp. 69–71; Goody, *Food and Love*, pp. 130–1.

12 Spencer, *The Heretic's Feast*, p. 280; Twigg, "Vegetarianism," p. 24.

13 C. P. Moritz cited by Palmer, *Moveable Feasts*, pp. 12–13; Laurioux, "Spices in the medieval diet," pp. 48, 66; Peterson, "The Arab influence," p. 333.

14 Cited by Davis, *Fairs*, p. 199.

15 White, *Indian Cookery*, p. 3.

16 Edmunds, *Curries*, p. 9; White, *Indian Cookery*, p. 6.

17 *Punch*, IX (1845).

18 Cited by Chaudhuri, "Shawls," p. 246.

19 Geddes, *The Laird's Kitchen*, p. 100.

20 Freeman, *Mutton and Oysters*, p. 125.

21 See Dawe, *The Wife's Help*, p. 94; [Palmer], *Indian Cookery*, p. 188.

22 Cited by Narayan, "Eating cultures," p. 82.

23 Freeman, *Mutton and Oysters*, p. 137; Cox (ed.), *Mr and Mrs Charles Dickens*, pp. 19, 39.

24 Chaudhuri, "Shawls," p. 239.

25 Haldar, *The English Diary*, p. 85.

26 Terry, *Indian Cookery*, pp. 16–17, 23–4.

27 Panjabi, *50 Great Curries*, p. 32.

28 Terry, *Indian Cookery*, pp. 16–17.

29 Glasse, *The Art of Cookery* (1748 edn.), p. 101.

30 Francatelli, *The Modern Cook*, pp. 12–13, 20, 300; Ketab, *Indian Dishes for English Tables*; Chaudhuri, "Shawls," p. 244.

31 Chaudhuri, "Shawls," p. 244.

32 Ibid., p. 241.

33 Terry, *Indian Cookery*, endpieces; Santiagoe, *The Curry Cook's Assistant*, p. xii (kindly lent to me by Jennifer Donkin).

34 Acton, *Modern Cookery*, p. 345.

35 du Maurier, *Rebecca*, p. 309.

36 White, *Indian Cookery*, p. 9.

37 Jaffrey, *A Taste of India*, pp. 82, 130.

38 Panjabi, *50 Great Curries*, pp. 24, 32.

39 Katona-Apte and Apte, "The role of food," p. 347.

40 Jaffrey, *An Invitation*, p. 18.

41 Petit, *The Home Book*, p. 24; *Good Housekeeping's Casseroles and Curries*, pp. 19–23.

42 Edmunds, *Curries*, p. 52.

43 Allen (ed.), *Food*, p. 29.

44 Acton, *Modern Cookery*, pp. 343–4.

45 Santiagoe, *The Curry Cook's Assistant*, p. ix.

46 Terry, *Indian Cookery*, pp. 5–7; Beeton, *Mrs Beeton's Book*, p. 90; Acton, *Modern Cookery*, pp. 42–3.

47 Terry, *Indian Cookery*, pp. 5–7.

48 Kingston, "The taste of India," p. 45.

49 Valle, *The Travels*, II, p. 383.

50 Fryer, *A New Account*, I, p. 297.

51 David, *Spices*, p. 10.

52 Glasse, *The Art of Cookery* (1983 edn.), p. 168.

53 Glasse, *The Art of Cookery* (1748 edn.), p. 240.

54 Smith, *The Tomato*, pp. 18–20.

55 Cited by Burton, *The Raj at Table*, p. 121; Wright, *The Road from Aston Cross*, p. 31.

56 David, *Spices*, p. 12.

57 MacKenzie, *Propaganda*, p. 97.

58 Erickson, *Her Little Majesty*, pp. 239–47; Glasheen, *The Secret People*, p. 158.

59 Hartley, *Eighty-Eight Not Out*, p. 71.

60 Ibid., pp. 75–8.

61 Gregory, "Staging British India," pp. 152–64.

62 Santiagoe, *The Curry Cook's Assistant*, p. 68.

63 Tollinton Papers.

64 *The Times British Empire Exhibition Special Section*, No. 1, 23 April 1924, pp. 52–4.

65 [Palmer], *Indian Cookery*, pp. 17–18.

7 Cold Meat Cutlets

1 John William Laing, 28 October 1873, Vol. I, Laing Diaries.

2 "*Culinary Jottings for Madras* by Wyvern. 1878," *Calcutta Review*, 68 (1879), p. xiv.

3 Stocqueler, *The Hand-book*, pp. 202–3.

4 Ibid., p. 207.

5 "*Culinary Jottings for Madras* by Wyvern. 1878," *Calcutta Review*, 68 (1879), p. xiii.

6 Kenny-Herbert, *Wyvern's Indian Cookery Book*; Franklin, *The Wife's Cookery Book*.

7 Masters, *Bugles*, p. 157; Annie Winifred Brown.

8 The army officer's son in conversation with the author.

9   *Indian Cookery "Local,"* pp. 41–2.
10 *The Englishwoman in India,* p. 45; Cunningham Papers, p. 515.
11 Lady Minto's Recipe Book, p. 85.
12 *What to Tell the Cook; A Friend in Need,* published by the Ladies' Committee F.I.N.S. Women's Workshop, and kindly lent to me by Maureen Nunn, also printed its recipes in English and Tamil and was much used by the wife of a coffee planter living in the Coorg Hills of southern India in the 1930s.
13 Dench Papers, p. 24.
14 Dutton, *Life in India,* p. 57.
15 Williamson, *The East-India Vade-Mecum,* I, p. 238.
16 Hall Papers.
17 Graham, *Journal of a Residence,* p. 30; W. W. Hooper, "Kitchen servants c.1880," Photo 447/3(56).
18 Lyall Collection, /2, p. 159; 21 March 1926, Maxwell Papers, Box XVII.
19 Bayley Papers, p. 6.
20 Abraham Caldecott, Letter 14, September 1783, Caldecott Collection.
21 Tavernier, *Travels,* I, 109.
22 Parks, *Wanderings,* I, p. 32.
23 Deane, *A Tour,* pp. 15–16, 203.
24 William Dalrymple kindly supplied the information on Kirkpatrick and potatoes; Watt, *A Dictionary,* VI, III, p. 272; Sen, "The Portuguese influence," p. 296. See also: Dalrymple, *White Mughals,* p. 330; Salaman, *The History and Social Influence,* p. 445; Achaya, *Indian Food,* p. 226.
25 Watt, *A Dictionary,* V, p. 100. See also: David, *Spices,* p. 84; Rick, "The tomato," p. 67; Davidson, "Europeans' wary encounter," pp. 7–9; Banerji, *Bengali Cooking,* p. 83.
26 Banerji, *Bengali Cooking,* p. 83.
27 Gandhi, *The Collected Works,* p. 40.
28 Thirty-Five Years' Resident, *The Indian Cookery Book,* pp. 4–8.
29 Mary Symonds, Gwillim Papers /1.
30 Roberts, *Scenes and Characteristics,* pp. 90–102.
31 Parks, *Wanderings,* II, p. 230.
32 A Lady Resident, *The Englishwoman in India,* p. 33.
33 Blanchard, *Yesterday and Today,* p. 45.
34 Campbell-Martin, *Out in the Mid-day Sun,* p. 52; Bourne Papers, pp. 71–2.
35 Hall Papers.

36 Brennan, *Curries and Bugles*, p. 153.
37 Tandon, *Beyond Punjab*, p. 47.
38 A Lady Resident, *The Englishwoman in India*, p. 45.
39 Lawrence, *Indian Embers*, p. 40.
40 Dench Papers, p. 50.
41 Champion Papers, p. 81.
42 *The Art of Ceylon and Indian Cookery*, p. 71.
43 Tandon, *Punjabi Century*, pp. 177–8.
44 Llewellyn-Jones, *Engaging Scoundrels*, pp. 12, 32–3, 44–5, 73.
45 Weeden, *A Year*, pp. 29–30, 58.
46 Rau and Devi, *A Princess Remembers*, p. 20.
47 Ibid., pp. 34, 52, 60.
48 Tandon, *Beyond Punjab*, p. 67.
49 Deane, *A Tour*, pp. 101–2, 107–8.
50 Fitzroy Collection, 8b, pp. 1, 158, 162.
51 Cited by Brown, *Modern India*, p. 75.
52 Misra, *The Indian Middle Classes*, pp. 153–4; Heber, *Narrative*, p. 291.
53 Fryer, *A New Account*, II, p. 113.
54 Deane, *A Tour*, pp. 11–12.
55 Jaffrey, *A Taste of India*, pp. 86–7.
56 Oman, *The Brahmans*, p. 40.
57 Misra, *The Indian Middle Classes*, p. 200.
58 Raychaudhuri, *Europe Reconsidered*, p. 62.
59 Sinha, *Colonial Masculinity*, p. 22.
60 Hay, "Between two worlds," p. 308; Fiddes, *Meat*, p. 67.
61 Cited by Fiddes, *Meat*, p. 67.
62 Hunt, *Gandhi*, pp. 5–6, 18.
63 Ibid., p. 9.
64 Tandon, *Punjabi Century*, p. 202.
65 Gandhi, *The Collected Works*, pp. 80, 93, 96.
66 Twigg, "Vegetarianism," pp. 22–6.
67 Malabari, *The Indian Eye*, pp. 45–7.
68 Lahiri, *Indians in Britain*, p. 156.
69 Tandon, *Punjabi Century*, p. 211.
70 Tandon, *Beyond Punjab*, p. 69.
71 Oman, *The Brahmans*, p. 41.

72 Lawrence, *Indian Embers*, p. 42.

73 Fitzroy Collection, 8b, pp. 46–7, 53.

74 Tandon, *Beyond Punjab*, pp. 97–8.

75 Rasul, *Bengal to Birmingham*, p. 8.

76 These can be seen at the house where he was assassinated in New Delhi, which has a display of his personal possessions at the time of his death.

77 Bayley Papers, p. 3.

78 "Chota Sahib," *Camp Recipes*, p. 53; Maureen Nunn in conversation with the author.

79 Freeman, *Mutton and Oysters*, p. 93.

80 Godden, *A Time to Dance*, p. 98; Margaret Orr Deas, Mrs. Randhawa, and Maureen Nunn in conversation with the author.

81 Rau and Devi, *A Princess Remembers*, p. 16.

82 Fus. H. Simons, "Army Cookery Notebook, 1944"; Eric Warren in correspondence with the author.

83 Mass Observation Winter Directive of 1982; Burton, *The Raj at Table*, pp. 19–20.

84 Margaret Orr Deas in conversation with the author.

85 Panjabi, *50 Great Curries*, pp. 8–9.

86 Sen, "The Portuguese influence," p. 293.

87 Jo Sharma in correspondence with the author.

88 Dalrymple, *City of Djinns*, p. 135; author's own meal at the Fairlawn Hotel, Sudder Street, Calcutta.

89 Menu from Bengal Club dinner, 29 December 2000 (with thanks to Chris Bayly).

90 Suri, "Bombay Dreams," *Observer*, 13 October 2002.

8 Chai

1 Griffiths, *The History*, pp. 626–7.

2 Macfarlane and Macfarlane, *Green Gold*, p. 43.

3 Achaya, *Indian Food*, p. 151.

4 Mandelslo, *The Voyages and Travels*, p. 13; Srivastava, *Social Life*, pp. 11–12; Blake, "Cityscape," p. 159.

5 Jaffrey, *A Taste of India*, p. 199.

6 Hattox, *Coffee*, p. 79; Tavernier, *Travels*, II, p. 20.

7 Terry, *A Voyage to East-India*, pp. 106–7; Mahias, "Milk," p. 280.

8 Scattergood et al., *The Scattergoods*, p. 71. The name Bohea for black tea comes from the European mispronunciation of Wu-i (pronounced "bu-I" in Chinese), the name of the area that produced the tea.

9 Mandelslo, *The Voyages and Travels*, p. 13.

10 Ovington, *A Voyage*, p. 306.

11 Ali, *Observations on the Mussulmauns of India*, p. 331.

12 Tandon, *Punjabi Century*, p. 23.

13 Ovington, *A Voyage*, p. 306.

14 Mandelslo, *The Voyages and Travels*, p. 10.

15 Griffiths, *The History*, p. 16.

16 Banerji, *Bengali Cooking*, p. 93.

17 Kaye (ed.), *The Golden Calm*, p. 120.

18 Cited by Antrobus, *A History*, p. 17.

19 Shineberg, *They Came for Sandalwood*, p. 3.

20 Ibid.; Macfarlane and Macfarlane, *Green Gold*, pp. 101–8.

21 Twining, *The House of Twining*, pp. 12, 16–17, 69.

22 Burnett, *Liquid Pleasures*, pp. 49–52.

23 Mayhew, *London Labour*, pp. 183, 193.

24 Shineberg, *They Came for Sandalwood*, p. 5; Burnett, *Liquid Pleasures*, p. 57.

25 Griffiths, *The History*, p. 38.

26 Antrobus, *A History*, p. 14; Macfarlane and Macfarlane, *Green Gold*, p. 101.

27 Griffiths, *The History*, pp. 31–2.

28 Antrobus, *A History*, pp. 46–7; Griffiths, *The History*, pp. 50, 56; Weatherstone, *The Pioneers*, pp. 32–40.

29 Weatherstone, *The Pioneers*, p. 40.

30 Antrobus, *A History*, p. 65; Macfarlane and Macfarlane, *Green Gold*, pp. 141–8.

31 Griffiths, *The History*, pp. 97, 106.

32 Macfarlane and Macfarlane, *Green Gold*, pp. 160–5; Sanyal, *Record of Criminal Cases*, pp. 25–40.

33 Kingston, "The taste of India," p. 43.

34 Griffiths, *The History*, pp. 579, 582–3, 586–7; Burnett, *Liquid Pleasures*, pp. 61–2; Lahiri, *Indians in Britain*, p. 69.

35 Ali, *Observations on the Mussulmauns of India*, p. 331; Gandhi, *The Collected Works*, p. 22.

36 Jo Sharma in conversation with the author.

37 Watt, *Dictionary*, IV, III, p. 475.

38 Weeden, *A Year*, p. 184.

39 Tea Association Records, /922, p. 21.

40 Griffiths, *The History*, pp. 593, 601.

41 Ibid., pp. 606, 621.

42 Brennan, *Curries and Bugles*, p. 153; Sethi, "The creation of religious identities," p. 78; Griffiths, *The History*, pp. 592–3.

43 Ukers, *All About Tea*, II, p. 324.

44 Griffiths, *The History*, p. 608.

45 Tea Association Records, /924, p. 47.

46 Griffiths, *The History*, pp. 617–19, 626–7.

47 Anil Sethi in conversation with the author.

48 Adams, *Across Seven Seas*, 182.

49 Tea Association Records, /924, pp. 46, 50; Griffiths, *The History*, pp. 608–9.

50 Tea Association Records, /924, report on propoganda operations in India during the period 1 April 1939 to 31 December 1939; report 1 October 1940 to 30 September 1941; report 1 October 1941 to September 1942; October 1942 to September 1943; October 1943 to September 1944; October 1944 to September 1945.

51 Hardyment, *Slice of Life*, p. 5.

52 Preston, *A Yank's Memories*, Photo 934 (54).

53 Tea Association Records, /798, *Notes on the Scheme for Development of Tea Propaganda in India* by the Director of Propaganda (1955), pp. 3–4.

54 Weisberger and Comer, "Tea," p. 716.

55 Banerji, *Bengali Cooking*, p. 93.

56 Beck, *The Experience of Poverty*, p. 140.

57 Weisberger and Comer, "Tea," p. 716.

58 Banerji, *Bengali Cooking*, p. 93.

59 Beck, *The Experience of Poverty*, p. 140.

60 Tea Association Records, /924, p. 47.

61 Pharmacopoeia, p. 181; Mahias, "Milk," pp. 273–6.

62 Oman, *The Brahmans*, p. 35.

63 Tandon, *Punjabi Century*, pp. 16–17, 37, 73, 78.

64 Marriott, "Caste ranking and food transactions," p. 169.

65 Carstairs, *The Twice-Born*, pp. 59, 234.

66 The Constitution of India (1950) made untouchability and its practice an offense. Mendelsohn and Vicziany, *The Untouchables*, pp. 118–27.

67 Sharma, *Rampal*, pp. 36–7.
68 Wadley, *Struggling with Destiny*, p. 224.
69 Forbes, *India of the Princes*, p. 272.
70 Conlon, "Dining out," p. 102.
71 Kanigel, *The Man*, p. 21.
72 Pearson, *Coastal Western India*, p. 137; Wadley, *Struggling with Destiny*, p. 275.
73 Sharma, *Rampal*, pp. 36–7.
74 Mendelsohn and Vicziany, *The Untouchables*, pp. 120–7.
75 Busybee, "Trailing those charming cafés," *Taj Magazine*, 11, 2 (1982); Conlon, "Dining out," p. 99.
76 Conlon, "Dining out," p. 102.
77 Karkaria, Bachi J., "The incredible dabba connection," *Taj Magazine*, 10, 1 (1981).
78 Tandon, *Punjabi Century*, p. 110.

9 Curry and Chips

1 Srivastava, *Social Life*, p. 10; Beveridge (ed.), *The Tuzuki-i-Jahangiri*, p. 150.
2 Banerji, *Bengali Cooking*, p. 7.
3 Sherwood, "Race, nationality and employment," pp. 233–4.
4 Ibid., pp. 239–41; Adams, *Across Seven Seas*, p. 149.
5 Choudhury, *The Roots and Tales*, pp. 41–3.
6 Ibid., pp. 49, 60.
7 Ibid., p. 72; Choudhury (ed.), *Sons of the Empire*, pp. 29–30.
8 Adams, *Across Seven Seas*, p. 152.
9 Choudhury (ed.), *Sons of the Empire*, p. 30.
10 Melendy, *Asians in America*, pp. 185, 206–8, 238–40; Takaki, *Strangers*, pp. 63–5, 295–312.
11 Takaki, *Strangers*, p. 65.
12 Takaki, *Strangers*, pp. 296–7.
13 Ibid., p. 311.
14 Ibid., pp. 309–10.
15 Ibid., p. 311.
16 Ibid., p. 312; LaBrack and Leonard, "Conflict and compatibility," pp. 537, 533.
17 Melendy, *Asians in America*, pp. 238–9; Takaki, *Strangers*, p. 305.
18 Banerji, *Bengali Cooking*, p. 7.

Notes

19 Adams, *Across Seven Seas*, pp. 76–7.

20 Ibid., p. 155.

21 Hosain, "Of memories and meals," p. 141.

22 Choudhury, *The Roots and Tales*, p. 66.

23 Ibid., p. 67.

24 Walton, *Fish and Chips*, p. 2.

25 Adams, *Across Seven Seas*, p. 157.

26 Walton, *Fish and Chips*, pp. 140, 153.

27 Adams, *Across Seven Seas*, pp. 77, 80.

28 Ibid., pp. 80–1.

29 Ibid., pp. 39, 89.

30 Gardner, "Desh and bidesh," pp. 1, 4, 13.

31 Choudhury, *The Roots and Tales*, pp. 197–8.

32 Cotta, *A Heritage*, foreword.

33 Panjabi, *50 Great Curries*, p. 25.

34 Geraldine Bedell, *Observer*, 12 May 2002.

35 Emma Brockes, "Tikka trickery," *Guardian*, 30 July 1999.

36 Liza Earle and Paul White in conversation with the author.

37 Visram, "South Asians," p. 174.

38 Clark et al., *South Asians*, p. 17.

39 Gardner, "Desh and bidesh," p. 7.

40 Basu, *Curry in the Crown*, pp. 27–32.

41 Takaki, *Strangers*, p. 369; Melendy, *Asians in America*, p. 207.

42 Jaffrey, *Madhur Jaffrey's Ultimate Curry Bible*, p. 32.

43 Babette Crosette, "In New York don't take 'Indian' food too literally," *New York Times* cited at www.himalmag.com/jun2000/content/VOICES.htm.

44 Malabari, *The Indian Eye*, p. 45.

45 Blaxter and Paterson, "The goodness," p. 97.

46 Mink, *The Wages of Motherhood*, p. 91; Bentley, *Eating for Victory*, pp. 43, 64.

47 Cotta, *A Heritage*, foreword; Mass Observation Winter Directive of 1982. See also *Good Housekeeping's Casseroles and Curries*, pp. 19–23.

48 Many of the citations from this paragraph are drawn from the Mass Observation Winter Directive of 1982, which asked participants about food and gardening.

49 Kingston, "The taste of India," p. 45.

50 Levenstein, *Paradox of Plenty*, pp. 217–19.

51 Hardyment, *Slice of Life*, pp. 89–95.

52 Ian Jack, "Remembrance of meals past," *Guardian Review*, 24 April 2004, p. 7.

53 Adams, *Across Seven Seas*, pp. 86–9, 105.

54 Margaret Orr Deas in conversation with the author.

55 Hardyment, *A Slice of Life*, p. 124.

56 Adams, *Across Seven Seas*, p. 105.

57 Babette Crosette, "In New York don't take 'Indian' food too literally," *New York Times* cited at www.himalmag.com/jun2000/content/VOICES.htm.

58 Williamson, *East-India Vade-Mecum*, II, p. 122.

59 Postgate (ed.), *The Good Food Guide 1967–8*, p. 500.

60 Petit, *The Home Book*, p. 19; Sethi, "The creation of religious identities," p. 81.

61 Jaffrey, *Madhur Jaffrey's Ultimate Curry Bible*, p. 34.

62 See Chapman, *The New Curry Bible*, p. 59.

63 Lowe and Davidson, *100 Best Balti Curries*.

64 Choudhury, *Roots and Tales*, pp. 101–3; Adams, *Across Seven Seas*, p. 105.

65 Hardyment, *A Slice of Life*, p. 123.

66 Jaffrey, *An Invitation*, pp. 13–14; Jaffrey, *Madhur Jaffrey's Indian Cookery*, p. 7.

67 Jaffrey, *Madhur Jaffrey's Ultimate Curry Bible*, p. 32.

68 Choudhury, *The Roots and Tales*, pp. 108–9.

69 Vickers, *The European Ethnic Foods Market*, p. 11.

70 Mass Observation Winter Directive of 1982.

71 Basu, *Curry in the Crown*, pp. xxvii–xxviii, 48, 88.

72 Vickers, *The European Ethnic Foods Market*, pp. 19, 21.

73 Geraldine Bedell, "It's curry," *Observer*, 12 May 2002.

74 Advert for the *Observer* in the *Guardian*, 7 May 2002.

75 Bell, *Consuming Geographies*, p. 174.

76 Hartley, *Food in England*, p. 1; James, "How British," pp. 83–4; James, "Cooking the books," p. 91.

77 Sonia Kumar, "Why Little India still rules," sonia@indolink.com.

78 The manager of Madras Mahal in conversation with the author; "Dinner in Manhattan," 2 February 2003, *The Hindu*.

79 Kathryn Flett, "Star of India," *Observer*, 11 February 2001.

80 Yasmin Alibhai-Brown, "Why the future may not be orange," *Guardian*, 13 July 2001.

81 Laxman Sharma in conversation with the author.

10 CURRY TRAVELS THE WORLD

1 Gardner, "Desh-Bidesh," p. 11.
2 Jaffrey, *Madhur Jaffrey's Ultimate Curry Bible*, pp. 14, 16–17.
3 Kale, "Projecting identities," p. 74.
4 Clark et al., *South Asians*, p. 8.
5 Jaffrey, *Madhur Jaffrey's Ultimate Curry Bible*, pp. 75, 153.
6 Mohammed Safiq in conversation with the author.
7 Jaffrey, *Madhur Jaffrey's Ultimate Curry Bible*, p. 23.
8 Higman, "Cookbooks," pp. 82–3.
9 Lal, *Mr Tulsi's Store*, p. 108.
10 School menu for the village of Lovoni, Ovalau, Fiji.
11 Lal, *Mr Tulsi's Store*, pp. 92–3.
12 Clark, *West Indian Cookery*, pp. 73–4.
13 Lahiri, *The Namesake*, p. 1.
14 Hellweg and Hellweg, *An Immigrant Success Story*, p. 126.
15 Jhumpa Lahiri, "The long way home. Bengal by way of Julia Child," *New Yorker*, 6 September 2004, pp. 83–4.
16 Kaiya and Hanasaki, *Oishinbo*.
17 Ohnuma, "Curry rice," pp. 8, 12; Travel Day Trip, Spice of Life @ http://metropolis.japantoday.com.
18 Ohnuma, "Curry rice," p. 9.
19 Bayly and Harper, *Forgotten Armies*, pp. 5, 16; Kishi Asako, "Curry on rice," *Nipponia*, 15 September 2001.
20 Ohnuma, "Curry rice," p. 10; Kaiya and Hanasaki, *Oishinbo*.
21 Japanese products @ http://www.house-foods.com.
22 Ohnuma, "Curry rice," pp. 10–11.
23 *Guardian*, 6 March, 2000.
24 This is Arjun Appadurai's argument. See Appadurai, "How to make a national cuisine."
25 Das Sreedharan, "Star of India," *Observer*, 22 July 2001; Anil Sethi in conversation with the author.

Bibliography

Primary Sources

Oriental and India Office Collections

European Manuscripts
Annie Winifred Brown, MSS.Eur.R138
Abraham Caldecott Collection, MSS.Eur.D778
Papers of Sir George Cunningham, MSS.Eur.D670
Fitzroy Collection, MSS.Eur.E312
Gwillim Papers, MSS.Eur.C240
Lyall Collection, MSS.Eur.F132
MacNabb Collection, MSS.Eur.F206
Lady Minto's Recipe Book, MSS.Eur.A79/2
Pharmacopoeia, MSS.Eur.E120
Frederick John Shore Collection, MSS.Eur.E307
Spilsbury Collection, MSS.Eur.D909
Tea Association Records, MSS.Eur.F174
Tollinton Papers, MSS.Eur.D1197

Pictures and Photographs Collection
Bourne and Shepherd, Photo 703
Edward Hilder Colebrook, Photo 469
Robert Arthur Ellis, Photo 304
Higginbothams, Photo 494

Bibliography

W. W. Hooper, Photo 447
M. Charles Preston, Photo 934

Political and Judicial Department Papers
E. B. Ivatts, L/P&J/2/50, File no. 7/345

British Library
Warren Hastings Papers, *Oude Accounts etc. 1777–1783*, British Museum Additional
29,093

Center for South Asian Studies, Cambridge
Mrs. Viola Bayley, Microfilm Box 7, No. 57
Bourne Papers
Champion Papers
Dench Papers
Hall Papers
Holman Paper
Maxwell Papers
Stuart Papers, Microfilm Box 2 No. 17B

Mass Observation Archive, Sussex University Library
Mass Observation Winter Directive of 1982

Royal Commonwealth Society Collection, University Library, Cambridge
Laing, John William, "Diaries in India and Europe 1873–1875"

Newspapers and Magazines
Calcutta Review
Goa Today
Guardian
Hindu
[London] Times
New York Review
New York Times
Observer
Punch or The London Charivari
Taj Magazine

Bibliography

Printed Books

Acton, Eliza, *Modern Cookery, in all its branches: reduced to a system of easy practice, for the use of private families. In a series of practical recipes, which have been strictly tested and are given with the most minute exactness* (Longman, Brown, Green & Longman, London, 1845).

Ali, Mrs. Meer Hassan, *Observations on the Mussulmauns of India: Descriptive of their manners, customs and habits and religious opinions. Made during a twelve years' residence in their immediate society*, 2 vols. (Parbury Allen & Co., London, 1832).

Allami, Abu'l Fazl, *The Ain-i-Akbari*, trans. H. Blochman, 2 vols. (Low Price Publications, Delhi, 1989).

Art of Ceylon and Indian Cookery, The (with Domestic Recipes) (Office of the Times of Colombo, 1918).

Atkinson, George Franklin, *Curry and Rice on Forty Plates; or the Ingredients of Social Life at "Our Station" in India* (2nd edn., London, 1859).

Beeton, Isabella, *Mrs Beeton's Book of Household Management* (S. O. Beeton, London, 1859–1861).

Bernier, Francis, *Travels in the Mogul Empire* (1st pub., in French 1670; William Pickering, London, 1826).

Beveridge, Henry (ed.), *The Tuzuki-i-Jahangiri*, trans. Alexander Rogers (1st pub. 1909–1914; Munshiram Manoharlal, Delhi, 1968).

Blanchard, Sydney, *Yesterday and Today in India* (W. H. Allen, London, 1867).

Brennan, Jennifer, *Curries and Bugles. A Memoir and Cookbook of the British Raj* (Viking, London, 1999).

Buchanan, Francis, *Journey from Madras Through the Countries of Mysore, Canara, and Malabar, Performed under the Orders of the Marquis of Wellesley, Governor General of India, for the express purpose of investigating the state of Agriculture, Arts and Commerce; the Religion, Manners, and Customs; the History Natural and Civil, and Antiquities, in the Dominions of the Rajah of Mysore and the countries acquired by the Honourable East India Company, in the late and former wars, from Tipoo Sultaun*, 3 vols. (T. Cadell & W. Davies, London, 1807).

Burnell, John, *Bombay in the Days of Queen Anne. Being an Account of the Settlement To which is added Burnell's Narrative of His Adventures in Bengal* (Hakluyt Society, London, 1933).

Burton, Richard F., *Goa, and the Blue Mountains; or Six Months of Sick Leave* (1st pub. 1851; University of California Press, Berkeley, 1992).

Bibliography

Campbell, James, *Excursions, Adventures and Field Sports in Ceylon; Its Commercial and Military Importance, and Numerous Advantages to the British Emigrant*, 2 vols., (T. & W. Boone, London, 1843).

Campbell-Martin, Monica, *Out in the Mid-day Sun* (Cassell & Co., London, 1951).

"Chota Sahib," *Camp Recipes for Camp People* (Lawrence Asylum Press, Madras, 1890).

Clark, E. Phyllis, *West Indian Cookery* (1st pub. 1945; published for the Government of Trinidad and Tobago, Thomas Nelson & Son, Edinburgh, 1946).

Cordiner, James, *A Voyage to India* (A. Brown & Co., London, 1820).

Cox, Helen, *Mr and Mrs Charles Dickens Entertain at Home* (Pergamon; General Books, London, 1970).

Dawe, W. H., *The Wife's Help to Indian Cookery: Being a Practical Manual for House-Keepers* (Elliot Stock, London, 1888).

Deane, Mrs. A., *A Tour Through the Upper Provinces of Hindostan; Comprising a Period Between the Years 1804 and 1814: with remarks and authentic anecdotes* (C. & J. Rivington, London, 1823).

D'Oyly, Charles, *The European in India* (London, 1813).

du Maurier, Daphne, *Rebecca* (1st pub. 1938; Pan Books, London, 1975).

Dutton, C., *Life in India* (W. H. Allen, London, 1882).

Eden, Emily, *Up the Country. Letters Written to her Sister from the Upper Provinces of India* (1st pub. 1930; Virago, London, 1983).

Edmunds, Joseph, *Curries and How to Prepare Them. Recipes by Some of the Most Eminent Chefs de Cuisine, Including E. Francatelli ... and C. H. Senn* (Food and Cookery Publishing Agency, London, 1903).

Fane, Henry Edward, *Five Years in India*, 2 vols. (Henry Colburn, London, 1842).

Fenton, Elizabeth Sinclair, *The Journal of Mrs Fenton. A Narrative of Her Life in India, the Isle of France, and Tasmania During the Years 1826–1830*, ed. Henry Lawrence (Edward Arnold, London, 1901).

Foster, William (ed.), *Early Travels in India 1583–1619* (S. Chand, Delhi, 1968).

Foster, William (ed.), *The Embassy of Sir Thomas Roe to India 1615–19. As Narrated in his Journal and Correspondence* (New and revised edn., Oxford University Press, London, 1926).

Francatelli, Charles Elmé, *The Modern Cook; A Practical Guide to the Culinary Art in all its branches, comprising, in addition to English cookery, the most approved and recherché systems of French, Italian, and German cookery; adapted as well for the largest establishments as for the use of private families* (1st pub. 1846; 8th edn. Richard Bentley, London, 1853).

Bibliography

Franklin, E. A. M., *The Wife's Cookery Book, being recipes and hints on Indian cookery* (Wilson's Artistic Press, Madras, 1906).

Friend in Need, A, English-Tamil Cookery Book, compiled by The Ladies' Committee F.I.N.S. Women's Workshop, (2nd edn. Diocesan Press, Vepery, Madras, 1938).

Fryer, John, *A New Account of East India and Persia being Nine Years' Travels 1672–1681*, ed. William Crooke, 3 vols. (Asian Educational Services, New Delhi, 1992).

Gandhi, M. K., *The Collected Works of Mahatma Gandhi*, Vol. I, 1884–June 1896 (Ministry of Information and Broadcasting, Government of India, 1969).

Glasse, H., *The Art of Cookery Made Plain and Easy; which far exceeds any thing of the kind ever yet published* (3rd edn., printed for the author, London, 1748).

Glasse, Hannah, *The Art of Cookery Made Plain and Easy, By a Lady* (Prospect Books, London, 1983).

Godden, Rumer, *A Time to Dance, No Time to Weep* (Macmillan, London, 1987).

Good Housekeeping's Casseroles and Curries. A new book of recipes for savoury and nourishing dishes for family meals, including meat, fish and vegetable casseroles, hot-pots and pot roasts with full instructions for making all kinds of curries and accompaniments for curries from ingredients obtainable in this country (The National Magazine Co., London, 1954).

Graham, Maria, *Journal of a Residence in India* (2nd edn., Longman, Hurst, Rees, Orme & Brown, London, 1813).

Haldar, Rakhal Das, *The English Diary of an Indian Student 1861–62. Being the Scribbling Journal of the late Rakhal Das Haldar of University Hall London, and member of the executive branch of the Provincial Civil Service, Bengal with an Introduction by Harinath De* (The Asutosh Library, Dacca, 1903).

Hamilton, Alexander, *A New Account of the East Indies* (1st pub. 1727), ed. William Foster (The Argonaut Press, London, 1930).

Hartley, Harold, *Eighty-Eight Not Out. A Record of Happy Memories* (Frederick Muller, London, 1939).

Hawkins, William, *The Hawkins Voyages. A Briefe Discourse of the Strength, Wealth, and Government, with some Customs, of the Great Mogul* (Hakluyt Society, London, 1878).

Heber, Reginald, *Narrative of a Journey through the Upper Provinces of India, from Calcutta to Bombay, 1824–1825*, 2 vols. (London, 1828).

[Hobbes, R. G.], A Retired Officer of HM's Civil Service, *Reminiscences of Seventy Years' Life, Travel and Adventure; Military and Civil; Scientific and Literary*, 2 vols. (Elliot Stock, London, 1893).

Bibliography

"Indian Cookery, as practised and described by the Natives of the East," trans. Sandford Arnot, in *Miscellaneous Translations from Oriental Languages*, Vol. I (Oriental Translation Fund, London, 1831).

Indian Cookery "Local" for Young Housekeepers (2nd edn., Imperial Press, Bombay, 1887).

Kaiya, Tetsu, and Akira Hanasaki, *Oishinbo [Men Who Pursue the Exquisite Dish]*, Vol. 24 (Shogakukan, Tokyo, 1990).

Kaye, M. M. (ed.), *The Golden Calm. An English Lady's Life in Moghul Delhi. Reminiscences by Emily, Lady Clive Bayly, and by her father, Sir Thomas Metcalfe* (Webb & Bower, Exeter, 1980).

Kenny-Herbert, Colonel Arthur Robert, *Wyvern's Indian Cookery Book, being a new and revised edition of Culinary Jottings for Madras. A Treatise on Reformed Cookery for Anglo-Indians, both in India and the Colonies, based on Modern English and Continental Principles, with Menus for Little Dinners worked out in Detail.* (7th edn., Higginbotham & Co., Madras, 1904).

Ketab, *Indian Dishes for English Tables* (Chapman & Hall, London, 1902).

Lady Resident, A, *The Englishwoman in India: containing information for the use of ladies proceeding to, or residing in, the East Indies, on the subject of their Outfit, Furniture, Housekeeping and the rearing of children, duties and wages of servants, management of the stables and arrangements for travelling to which are added receipts for Indian Cookery* (Smith, Elder & Co., London, 1864).

Lahiri, Jhumpa, *The Namesake* (Flamingo, London, 2004).

Lawrence, Rosamund, *Indian Embers* (George Ronald, Oxford, n.d.).

Lewis, C. C., *Culinary Notes for Sind* (Daily Gazette Press, Karachi, 1923).

Linschoten, Jan Huyghen van, *The Voyage of John Huyghen van Linschoten to the East Indies*, from the Old English Translation of 1598, ed. Arthur Coke Burnell and P. A. Tiele, 2 vols. (Hakluyt Society, London, 1935).

McCosh, John, *Medical Advice to the Indian Stranger* (W. H. Allen & Co., London, 1841).

Maciel Elsie Antonette, *Goan Cookery Book* (Merlin Books, Braunton, Devon, 1983).

Major, R. H. (ed.), *India in the Fifteenth Century. Being a Collection of Narratives of Voyages to India, in the Century Preceding the Portuguese Discovery of the Cape of Good Hope; from Latin, Persian, Russian and Italian sources, now first translated into English* (Hakluyt Society, London, 1957).

Malabari, Behramji M., *The Indian Eye on English Life or Rambles of a Pilgrim Reformer* (Archibald Constable & Co., London, 1893).

Bibliography

Mandelslo, J. Albert, *The Voyages and Travels of J. Albert de Mandelslo (A gentleman belonging to the Embassy, sent by the Duke of Holstein to the great Duke of Muscovy, and the King of Persia) into the East Indies. Begun in the Year M.DC.XXXVIII. and finished in M.DC.XL. Containing a particular description of the Great Mogul's Empire, the Kingdoms of Decan, Calicuth, Cochim, Zeilon, Coromandel, Pegu, Siam, Cambodia, Malacca, Summatra, Java, Amboina, Banda, the Moluccas, Philipine, and other Islands, Japan, the great Kingdom of China, the Cape of Good Hope, Madagascar, &c.*, In three Books, Rendered into English by John Davies of Kidwelly (2nd edn., J. Starkey & T. Basset, London, 1669).

Manrique, Sebastien, *Travels of Fray Sebastien Manrique, 1629–1643*, 2 vols. (Hakluyt Society, London, 1926).

Manucci, Niccolao, *Storia do Mogor or Mogul India 1635–1708*, trans. and with an introduction by William Irvine (John Murray, London, 1907).

Masters, John, *Bugles and a Tiger. A Personal Adventure* (Michael Joseph, London, 1956).

Mayhew, Henry, *London Labour and the London Poor; A Cyclopedia of the Condition and Earnings of those that will work, those that cannot work and those that will not work*, 2 vols. (Woodfall, London, 1851).

Mundy, Peter, *The Travels of Peter Mundy in Europe and Asia, 1608–1667*, ed. Richard Carnac Temple (Hakluyt Society, London, 1919).

Oman, John Campbell, *The Brahmans, Theists and Muslims of India. Studies of Goddess-worship in Bengal, Caste, Brahmaism and Social Reform, with descriptive Sketches of curious Festivals, Ceremonies, and Faquirs* (2nd edn., T. Fisher Unwin, London, 1897).

Ovington, John, *A Voyage to Suratt, In the Year, 1689. Giving a large Account of that City, and its Inhabitants, and of the English Factory there . . .* (Jacob Tonson, London, 1696).

[Palmer, Edward], Veeraswamy, E. P., *Indian Cookery. For Use in All Countries* (Herbert Joseph, London, 1936).

Parks, Fanny, *Wanderings of a Pilgrim in Search of the Picturesque, during Four-and-Twenty Years in the East; with Revelations of Life in the Zenana*, 2 vols. (Pelham Richardson, London, 1850).

Petit, Leon, *The Home Book of Indian Cookery* (Faber & Faber, London, 1955).

Ramaswami, N. S. (ed.), *The Chief Secretary. Madras Diaries of Alexander Falconar 1790–1809* (New Era Publications, Madras, 1983).

Rasul, Faizur, *Bengal to Birmingham* (André Deutsch, London, 1967).

Roberts, Emma, *Scenes and Characteristics of Hindoostan, with Sketches of Anglo-Indian Society*, 2 vols. (London, 1837).

Salter, Joseph, *The Asiatic in England; Sketches of Sixteen Years' Work Among Orientals* (Seeley, Jackson & Halliday, London, 1823).

Salter, Joseph, *The East in the West or Work Among the Asiatics and Africans in London* (S. W. Partridge & Co., London, n.d.).

Santiagoe, Daniel, *The Curry Cook's Assistant or Curries How to Make them in England in their Original Style* (3rd edn., Kegan Paul, Trench & Co., London, 1889).

Sanyal, Ram Gopal (ed.), *Record of Criminal Cases as Between Europeans and Natives for the Last Sixty Years* (Calcutta, 1893).

Schuyler, Eugene, *Turkistan. Notes of a Journey in Russian Turkistan, Khokand, Bukhara, and Kuldja*, 2 vols. (Sampson Low, Marston, Searle & Rivington, London, 1876).

Sen, Surendranath (ed.), *Indian Travels of Thevenot and Careri. Being the third part of the travels of M. de Thevenot into the Levant and the third part of a voyage round the world by Dr John Francis Gemelli Careri* (National Archives of India, New Delhi, 1949).

Shade, Sarah, *A Narrative of the Life of Sarah Shade, Born at Stoke Edith, in the County of Hereford. Containing many well authenticated and curious Facts, more particularly during her Voyage to the East Indies, in the Devonshire Indiaman, In the Year 1769; and in traversing that country in company with The Army at the sieges of Pondicherry, Vellore, Negapatam, &c, &c, together with some Extraordinary Accounts of the Ferocity of Tigers, Jackals, Piah Dogs, Vultures &c. Taken down by Some Gentlemen, And published for her Benefit* (J. Hatchard, London, 1801).

Shurreef, Jaffur, *Qanoon-e-Islam, or the Customs of the Mussulmans of India; comprising a full account of their various rites and ceremonies, from the moment of birth till the hour of death*, trans. G. A. Herklots (2nd edn., Higginbotham & Co., Madras, 1895).

Singh, Mrs. Balbir, *Mrs Balbir Singh's Indian Cookery* (Mills & Boon Ltd, London, 1961).

Stocqueler, J. H., *The Hand-book of India. A Guide to the Stranger and the Traveller, and a Companion to the Resident* (W. H. Allen, London, 1844).

Tandon, Prakash, *Punjabi Century 1857–1947* (Chatto & Windus, London, 1961).

Tandon, Prakash, *Beyond Punjab 1937–1960* (Chatto & Windus, London, 1971).

Tavernier, Jean-Baptiste, *Travels in India*, 2 vols. (2nd edn., Oxford University Press, Oxford, 1925).

Tayler, William, *Sketches Illustrating the Manners and Customs of the Indians and Anglo-Indians* (T. McLean, London, 1842).

Tayler, William, *Thirty-Eight Years in India. From Juganath to the Himalaya Mountains. With 100 Illustrations by the author*, 2 vols. (W. H. Allen & Co., London, 1881).

Bibliography

Terry, Edward, *A Voyage to East-India wherein some things are taken notice of in our passage thither, but many more in our abode there, within that rich and most spacious Empire Of the Great Mogol. Mix't with some Parallel Observations and inferences upon the storie, to profit as well as delight the Reader* (J. Martin & J. Allsrye, London, 1655).

Terry, Richard, *Indian Cookery* (1st pub. 1861; Southover Press, Lewes, 1998).

Thackston, Wheeler M. (ed.), *The Baburnama. Memoirs of Babur, Prince and Emperor* (Oxford University Press, Oxford, 1996).

Thirty-Five Years' Resident, A, *The Indian Cookery Book: A Practical Handbook to the Kitchen in India, Adapted to the Three Presidencies; Containing Original and Approved Recipes in Every Department of Indian Cookery; Recipes for Summer Beverages and Home-Made Liqueurs; Medicinal and Other Recipes; Together with a Variety of things worth knowing* (Wyman & Co., Calcutta, 1869).

Valle, Pietro della, *The Travels of Pietro della Valle in India*, ed. Edward Grey, 2 vols. (Haklyut Society, London, 1892).

Vambery, Arminius, *Sketches of Central Asia. Additional Chapter on My Travels, Adventures and on the Ethnology of Central Asia* (W. Allen & Co., London, 1868).

Watt, George, *A Dictionary of the Economic Products of India*, 6 vols. (Superintendent of Government Printing, Calcutta, 1889).

Weeden, Edward St. Clair, *A Year with the Gaekwar of Baroda* (Hutchinson & Co., London, 1912).

What to tell the Cook; or the Native Cook's Assistant; being a choice collection of receipts for Indian cookery (2nd edn., Higginbotham & Co., Madras, 1875).

White, Captain W., *Indian Cookery; or Fish Curries; Their Excellent Qualities, Easy and Speedy Preparation; with Selim's Curry Paste* (Sherwood, Gilbert, & Piper, London, 1845).

Williamson, Thomas, *The East-India Vade-Mecum; or Complete Guide to Gentlemen Intended for the Civil, Military or Naval Service of the Honourable East India Company*, 2 vols. (Black, Parry & Kingsbury, London, 1810).

Secondary Sources

Printed Books

Achaya, K. T., *Indian Food. A Historical Companion* (Oxford University Press, Delhi, 1994).

Achaya, K. T., "Indian food concepts," in A. Rahman (ed.), *History of Indian Science, Technology and Culture AD 1000–1800* (Oxford University Press, Oxford, 1999).

Bibliography

Adams, Caroline (ed.), *Across Seven Seas and Thirteen Rivers. Life Stories of Pioneer Sylhetti Settlers in Britain* (THAP Books, London, 1987).

Ahsan, Muhammad Manazir, *Social Life Under the Abbasids 170–289 AH 786–902 AD* (Longman, London, 1979).

Allen, Brigid (ed.), *Food. An Oxford Anthology* (Oxford University Press, Oxford, 1994).

Anderson, Philip, *The English in Western India; being the Early History of the Factory at Surat, of Bombay, and the Subordinate Factories on the Western Coast. From the Earliest Period Until the Commencement of the Eighteenth Century* (Smith, Taylor & Co., London, 1854).

Andrews, Jean, "The peripatetic chilli pepper: diffusion of the domesticated capsicums since Colombus," in Nelson Foster and Linda S. Cordell (eds), *Chilies to Chocolate. Food the Americas Gave the World* (University of Arizona Press, London, 1992).

Antrobus, H. A., *A History of the Assam Company 1839–1953* (T. and A. Constable, Edinburgh, 1957).

Appadurai, Arjun, *Worship and Conflict Under Colonial Rule. A South Indian Case* (Cambridge University Press, Cambridge, 1981).

Appadurai, Arjun, "How to make a national cuisine: cookbooks in contemporary India," *Comparative Studies in Society and History*, 30, 1 (1988), 3–24.

Arundhati, P., *Royal Life in Manasollasa* (Sundeep Prakashan, Delhi, 1994).

Axelrod, Paul, and Michelle A. Fuerch, "Flight of the deities: Hindu resistance in Portuguese Goa," *Modern Asian Studies*, 30, 2 (1996), 387– 421.

Aziz, K. K., "Glimpses of Muslim culture in the Deccan," in Anna Libera Dallapiccola, Stephanie Zingel-Ave Lallemant (eds), *Vijayanagara—City and Empire. New Currents of Research* (Steiner Verlag, Stuttgart, 1985).

Banerji, Chitrita, *Bengali Cooking. Seasons and Festivals* (originally published as *Life and Food in Bengal*, Weidenfeld & Nicolson, London, 1991), (Serif, London, 1997).

Basu, Shrabani, *Curry in the Crown. The Story of Britain's Favourite Dish* (Harper Collins Publishers India, New Delhi, 1999).

Bayly, C. A. (ed.), *The Raj. India and the British 1600–1947* (National Portrait Gallery Publications, London, 1990).

Bayly, C. A., and Tim Harper, *Forgotten Armies* (Allen Lane, London, 2004).

Beck, Tony, *The Experience of Poverty. Fighting for Respect and Resources in Village India* (Intermediate Technical Publications, London, 1994).

Bibliography

Bell, David, and Gill Valentine, *Consuming Geographies. We Are Where We Eat* (Routledge, London, 1997).

Bentley, Amy, *Eating For Victory. Food Rationing and the Politics of Domesticity* (University of Illinois Press, Chicago, 1998).

Blake, Stephen P., "Cityscape of an imperial capital. Shahjahanabad in 1739" in R. E. Frykenberg (ed.), *Delhi Through the Ages. Essays in Urban History, Culture and Society* (Oxford University Press, Delhi, 1986).

Blaxter, Mildred, and Elizabeth Paterson, "The goodness is out of it: the meaning of food to two generations," in Anne Murcott (ed.), *The Sociology of Food and Eating. Essays on the Sociological Significance of Food* (Gower, Aldershot, 1984).

Borges, Charles J., "A lasting cultural legacy. The role of the society of Jesus in reforming Goan society," in Charles J. Borges and Helmut Fieldman (eds), *Goa and Portugal. Their Cultural Links* (Concept Publishing, New Delhi, 1998).

Borges, Charles J., and Helmut Fieldman (eds), *Goa and Portugal. Their Cultural Links* (Concept Publishing, New Delhi, 1998).

Borges, Charles J., Oscar Pereira, and Hannes Stubbe, *Goa and Portugal. History and Development* (Concept Publishing Company, New Delhi, 2000).

Boxer, C. R., *Race Relations in the Portuguese Colonial Empire 1415–1825* (Clarendon Press, Oxford, 1963).

Bratton, J. S., Richard Allen Cave, Breandon Gregory, Heidi J. Holder, and Michael Pickering, *Acts of Supremacy. The British Empire and the Stage, 1790–1930* (Manchester University Press, Manchester, 1991).

Breckenridge, Carol Appadurai, "Food politics and pilgrimage in south India, 1350–1650 A.D.," in R. Khare and M. S. A. Rao (eds), *Food, Society and Culture. Aspects in South Asian Food Systems* (Carolina Academic Press, Durham, NC, 1986).

Breckenridge, Carol Appadurai (ed.), *Consuming Modernity. Public Culture in a South Asian World* (University of Minnesota Press, London, 1995).

Brockington, John, *The Sanskrit Epics* (Brill, Leiden, 1998).

Brodie, Fawn M., *The Devil Drives. A Life of Sir Richard Burton* (Norton, London, 1967).

Brown, Judith, *Modern India. The Origins of an Asian Democracy* (Oxford University Press, Delhi, 1988).

Burnett, John, *Liquid Pleasures. A Social History of Drinks in Modern Britain* (Routledge, London, 1999).

Burton, David, *The Raj at Table* (Faber & Faber, London, 1993).

Bibliography

Burton, David, *Savouring the East. Feasts and Stories from Istanbul to Bali* (Faber & Faber, London, 1996).

Cantile, Audrey, "The moral significance of food among Assamese Hindus," in Adrian C. Mayer (ed.), *Culture and Morality. Essays in Honour of Christoph von Furer-Haimendorf* (Oxford University Press, Delhi, 1981).

Carstairs, G. Morris, *The Twice-Born. A Study of a Community of High-Caste Hindus* (The Hogarth Press, London, 1957).

Chapman, Pat, *The New Curry Bible. The Ultimate Modern Curry House Recipe Book* (Metro, London, 2004).

Chattopadhyaya, Debiprasad, "Case for a critical analysis of the *Caraka-Samhita*," in Debiprasad Chattopadhyaya (ed.), *Studies in the History of Science in India*, 2 vols. (Editorial Enterprises, New Delhi, n.d.).

Chaudhuri, Nupur, "Shawls, jewellery, curry, and rice in Victorian Britain," in Nupur Chaudhuri and Margaret Strobel (eds), *Western Women and Imperialism. Complicity and Resistance* (Indiana University Press, Bloomington, 1992).

Choudhury, Yousuf, *The Roots and Tales of the Bangladeshi Settlers* (Sylheti Social History Group, Birmingham, 1993).

Choudhury, Yousuf (ed.), *Sons of the Empire. Oral History from the Bangladeshi Seamen who Served on British Ships during the 1939–45 War* (Sylheti Social History Group, Birmingham, 1995).

Clark, Colin, Ceri Peach and Steven Vertovec (eds), *South Asians Overseas. Migration and Ethnicity* (Cambridge University Press, Cambridge, 1990).

Coelho, George V., and Promila Coelho Sen, "Cooking the Goan way: Indo-Portuguese culinary arts," in José Pereira and Pratpaditya Pal (eds), *India and Portugal: Cultural Interactions* (Marg Publications, Mumbai, 2001).

Cohen, J. M., *The Four Voyages of Christopher Columbus. Being his own log book, letters and dispatches with connecting narrative drawn from the Life of the Admiral by his own son Hernando Colon and other contemporary historians* (Penguin, London, 1969).

Collins, J. L., *The Pineapple. Botany, Cultivation and Utilisation* (Leonard Hill Books Ltd., London, 1960).

Conlon, Frank F., "Dining out in Bombay," in Carol Appadurai Breckenridge (ed.), *Consuming Modernity. Public Culture in a South Asian World* (University of Minnesota Press, London, 1995).

Cotta, Joseph, *A Heritage of Indian Cooking* (Shalimar Indian Restaurant, Canberra, 1981).

Dalby, Andrew, *Dangerous Tastes. The Story of Spices* (British Museum Press, London, 2000).

Dalrymple, William, *City of Djinns. A Year in Delhi* (Flamingo, London, 1994).

Dalrymple, William, *White Mughals. Love and Betrayal in Eighteenth-Century India* (HarperCollins, London, 2002).

David, Elizabeth, *Spices, Salts and Aromatics in the English Kitchen* (1st pub. 1970; Penguin, London, 1981).

David, Elizabeth, *Harvest of the Cold Months: the Social History of Ice and Ices* (M. Joseph, London, 1994).

Davidson, Alan, with Eulalia Pensado, "The earliest Portuguese cookery book examined," *Petits Propos Culinaires*, 41 (1992), 52–7.

Davidson, Alan, "Europeans' wary encounter with tomatoes, potatoes, and other New World foods," in Nelson Foster and Linda S. Cordell (eds), *Chilies to Chocolate. Food the Americas Gave the World* (University of Arizona Press, London, 1992).

Davis, Dorothy, *Fairs, Shops and Supermarkets. A History of English Shopping* (University of Toronto Press, Toronto, 1966).

Driver, Christopher, *The British at Table 1940–1980* (Chatto & Windus, London, 1983).

Eraly, Abraham, *The Last Spring. The Lives and Times of the Great Mughals* (Viking, London, 1997).

Erickson, Carolly, *Her Little Majesty. The Life of Queen Victoria* (Robson Books, London, 1997).

Farrington, Anthony, *Trading Places. The East India Company and Asia 1600–1834* (British Library, London, 2002).

Fenton, A., and T. M. Owen (eds), *Food and Perspective: Proceedings of the 3rd International Conference on Ethnological Food Research Cardiff, 1977* (Donald, Edinburgh, 1981).

Fiddes, Nick, *Meat. A Natural Symbol* (Routledge, London, 1991).

Fine, Ben, Michael Heasman and Judith Wright, *Consumption in the Age of Affluence. The World of Food* (Routledge, London, 1996).

Fisher, Michael H., *A Clash of Cultures: Awadh, the British, and the Mughals* (Manohar, New Delhi, 1987).

Fisher, Michael H., *The First Indian Author in English. Dean Mahomed (1759–1851) in India, Ireland and England* (Oxford University Press, Delhi, 1996).

Bibliography

Foltz, Richard C., *Mughal India and Central Asia* (Oxford University Press, Delhi, 1998).

Forbes, Rosita, *India of the Princes* (John Gifford Ltd., London, 1939).

Foster, Nelson and Linda S. Cordell (eds), *Chilies to Chocolate. Food the Americas Gave the World* (University of Arizona Press, London, 1992).

Fragner, Bert, "From the Caucasus to the roof of the world: a culinary adventure," in Sami Zubaida and Richard Tapper (eds), *Culinary Cultures of the Middle East* (I. B. Tauris Publishers, London, 1994).

Freeman, Sarah, *Mutton and Oysters. The Victorians and Their Food* (Victor Gollancz, London, 1989).

Frykenberg, R. E. (ed.), *Delhi Through the Ages. Essays in Urban History, Culture and Society* (Oxford University Press, Delhi, 1986).

Gardner, Katy, "Desh-Bidesh: Sylheti images of home and away," *Man (NS)* 228 (1993), 1–16.

Geddes, Olive M., *The Laird's Kitchen. Three Hundred Years of Food in Scotland* (National Library of Scotland, Edinburgh, 1994).

Glasheen, Joan, *The Secret People of the Palaces. The Royal Household from the Plantagenets to Queen Victoria* (B. T. Batsford, London, 1998).

Goody, Jack, *Cooking, Cuisine and Class. A Study in Comparative Sociology* (Cambridge University Press, Cambridge, 1982).

Goody, Jack, *Food and Love. A Cultural History of East and West* (Verso, London, 1998).

Gordon, Stewart, *Marathas, Marauders, and State Formation in Eighteenth-Century India* (Oxford University Press, Delhi, 1994).

Gracias, Fátima, da Silva, "The impact of Portuguese culture on Goa. A myth or reality?" in Charles J. Borges and Helmut Fieldman (eds), *Goa and Portugal. Their Cultural Links* (Concept Publishing, New Delhi, 1998).

Gregory, Breandon, "Staging British India," in J. S. Bratton, Richard Allen Cave, Breandon Gregory, Heidi J. Holder, and Michael Pickering, *Acts of Supremacy. The British Empire and the Stage, 1790–1930* (Manchester University Press, Manchester, 1991).

Griffiths, Percival, *The History of the Indian Tea Industry* (Weidenfeld & Nicolson, London, 1967).

Grove, Peter and Colleen, *Curry, Spice & All Things Nice—the what—where—when* (http://www.menumagazine.co.uk).

Bibliography

Hardyment, Christina, *Slice of Life. The British Way of Eating Since 1945* (Penguin Books/BBC Books, London, 1995).

Hartley, Dorothy, *Food in England* (Macdonald, London, 1954).

Hasan, Amir, *Palace Culture of Lucknow* (B. R. Publishing Corporation, Delhi, 1983).

Hattox, Ralph S., *Coffee and Coffeehouses. The Origins of a Social Beverage in the Medieval Near East* (University of Washington Press, Seattle and London, 1985).

Hay, Stephen, "Between two worlds: Gandhi's first impressions of British culture," *Modern Asian Studies*, 3, 4 (1969), 305–19.

Hellweg, Arthur W., and Usha M. Hellweg, *An Immigrant Success Story. East Indians in America* (University of Pennsylvania Press, Philadelphia, 1990).

Higman, Barry, "Cookbooks and Caribbean cultural identity: an English-language hors d'oeuvre," *New West Indian Guide*, 72, 1 & 2 (1998), 77–95.

Holzman, James M., *The Nabobs in England. A Study of the Returned Anglo-Indian, 1760–1785* (New York, 1926).

Hosain, Attia, "Of memories and meals," in Antonia Till (ed.), *Loaves and Wishes. Writers Writing on Food* (Virago, London, 1992).

Hultzsch, E., *South Indian Inscriptions. Vol. III. Miscellaneous Inscriptions from the Tamil Country. Part II. Inscriptions of Virarajendra I, Kulottinga-chola I, Vikram-Chola and Kulottunga-chola III*, Archaeological Survey of India, New Imperial Series (Superintendent Government Press, Madras, 1903).

Hunt, James D., *Gandhi in London* (Promilla & Co., New Delhi, 1993).

Hunter, Sir William Wilson, *The Thackerays in India and Some Calcutta Graves* (Henry Frowde, London, 1897).

Hyman, Philip and Mary, "Long pepper: a short history," *Petits Propos Culinaires*, 6 (1980), 50–52.

Ikram, S. M., *Muslim Civilization in India*, ed. Ainslie T. Embree (Columbia University Press, London, 1964).

Jaffrey, Madhur, *An Invitation to Indian Cooking* (Jonathan Cape, London, 1976).

Jaffrey, Madhur, *Madhur Jaffrey's Indian Cookery* (BBC Books, London, 1982).

Jaffrey, Madhur, *A Taste of India* (Pavilion, London, 1985).

Jaffrey, Madhur, *Madhur Jaffrey's Ultimate Curry Bible. India Singapore Malaysia Indonesia Thailand South Africa Kenya Great Britain Trinidad Guyana Japan USA* (Ebury Press, London, 2003).

James, Allison, "Cooking the books: global or local identities in contemporary British food cultures?" in David Howes (ed.), *Cross-Cultural Consumption. Global Markets, Local Realities* (Routledge, London, 1996).

Bibliography

James, Allison, "How British is British food?" in Pat Caplan (ed.), *Food, Health and Identity* (Routledge, London, 1997).

Jha, D. N., *The Myth of the Holy Cow* (1st pub. 2001; Verso, London, 2002).

Kale, Madhavi, "Projecting identities: empire and indentured labour migration from India to Trinidad and British Guiana, 1836–1885," in Peter van der Veer (ed.), *Nation and Migration. The Politics of Space in the South Asian Diaspora* (University of Pennsylvania Press, Philadelphia, 1995).

Katona-Apte, Judit, and Mahadev L. Apte, "The role of food and food habits in the acculturation of Indians in the United States," in Parmatma Saran and Edwin Eames (eds), *The New Ethnics. Asian Indians in the United States* (Praeger, New York, 1980).

Keay, John, *The Honourable Company. A History of the English East India Company* (HarperCollins, London, 1991).

Keay, John, *India. A History* (HarperCollins, London, 2000).

Khare, R. S., "The Indian Meal: Aspects of Cultural Economy and Food Use," in R. S. Khare, and M. S. A. Rao (eds), *Food, Society and Culture. Aspects In South Asian Food Systems* (Carolina Academic Press, Durham, NC, 1986).

Khare, R. S., and M. S. A. Rao (eds), *Food, Society and Culture. Aspects in South Asian Food Systems* (Carolina Academic Press, Durham, NC, 1986).

Kingston, Beverley, "The taste of India," *Australian Cultural History*, 9 (1990), 36–48.

Kiple, Kenneth F., and Kriemhild Coneè Ornelas (eds), *The Cambridge World History of Food*, 2 vols. (Cambridge University Press, Cambridge, 2000).

Kulshreshtha, S. S., *The Development of Trade and Industry Under the Mughals (1526–1707 A.D.)* (Kitab Mahal, Allahabad, 1964).

LaBrack, Bruce, and Karen Leonard, "Conflict and compatibility in Punjabi-Mexican immigrant families in rural California, 1915–1965," *Journal of Marriage and the Family*, 46 (1984), 527–37.

Lahiri, Shompa, *Indians in Britain. Anglo-Indian Encounters, Race and Identity 1880–1930* (Frank Cass, London, 2000).

Lal, Brij V., *Mr Tulsi's Store. A Fijian Journey* (Pandanus Books, Canberra, 2001).

Lal, Saran Kishori, *Twilight of the Sultanate. A Political, Social and Cultural History of the Sultanate of Delhi from the Invasion of Timur to the Conquest of Babur 1398–1526* (Asia Publishing House, London, 1963).

Larsen, Karin, *Faces of Goa. A Journey Through the History and Cultural Evolution of Goa and Other Communities Influenced by the Portuguese* (Gyan Publishing House, New Delhi, 1998).

Bibliography

Laudan, Rachel, *The Food of Paradise. Exploring Hawaii's Culinary Heritage* (University of Hawaii Press, Honolulu, 1996).

Laudan, Rachel and Jeffrey M. Pilcher, "Chilies, chocolate, and race in New Spain: Glancing backward to Spain or looking forward to Mexico?" *Eighteenth-Century Life*, 23 (1999), 59–70.

Laudan, Rachel, "The birth of the modern diet," *Scientific American* (August 2000), 62–7.

Laurioux, Bruno, "Spices in the medieval diet: a new approach," *Food and Foodways*, 1, 1 (1985), 43–75.

Levenstein, Harvey, *Paradox of Plenty. A Social History of Eating in Modern America* (Oxford University Press, Oxford, 1993).

Lewis, Oscar, *Village Life in Northern India. Studies in a Delhi Village* (University of Illinois Press, Urbana, 1958).

Llewellyn-Jones, Rosie, *Engaging Scoundrels. True Tales of Old Lucknow* (Oxford University Press, New Delhi, 2000).

Lopes, Maria de Jesus dos Martires, "Conversion as a means to cultural adaptation. The catechumens of Betim in the eighteenth century," in Charles J. Borges and Helmut Fieldman (eds), *Goa and Portugal. Their Cultural Links* (Concept Publishing, New Delhi, 1998).

Lowe, Diane, and Mike Davidson, *100 Best Balti Curries. Authentic Dishes from the Baltihouses* (Pavilion, London, 1994).

Macfarlane, Alan, and Iris Macfarlane, *Green Gold: The Empire of Tea* (Ebury Press, London, 2003).

MacKenzie, John, *Propaganda and Empire. The Manipulation of British Public Opinion, 1880–1960* (Manchester University Press, Manchester, 1984).

Madan, T. N., *Non-renunciation. Themes and Interpretations of Hindu Culture* (Oxford University Press, Delhi, 1987).

Madan, T. N., *Pathways. Approaches to the Study of Society in India* (Oxford University Press, Delhi, 1994).

Mahias, Marie-Claude, "Milk and its transmutations in Indian society," *Food and Foodways*, 2 (1988), 265–88.

Majumdar, R. C. (ed.), *The Age of Imperial Unity. The History and Culture of the Indian People* (1st pub. 1951; Bharatiya Vidya Bhavan, Bombay, 1960).

Marriott, McKim, "Caste ranking and food transactions: a matrix analysis," in Milton Singer and Bernard S. Cohn (eds), *Structure and Change in Indian Society* (Aldine Publishing Company, Chicago, 1968).

Bibliography

Marriott, McKim, and Ronald B. Inden, "Toward an ethnosociology of South Asian caste systems," in Kenneth David (ed.), *The New Wind* (Mouton, The Hague, 1977).

Melendy, H. Brett, *Asians in America: Filipinos, Koreans, and East Indians* (Twayne Publishers, Boston, 1977).

Mendelsohn, Oliver, and Marika Vicziany, *The Untouchables. Subordination, Poverty and the State in Modern India* (Cambridge University Press, Cambridge, 1998).

Mink, Gwendolyn, *The Wages of Motherhood. Inequality in the Welfare State, 1917–42* (Cornell University Press, Ithaca and London, 1995).

Misra, B. B., *The Indian Middle Classes. Their Growth in Modern Times* (Oxford University Press, London, 1961).

Murti, G. Srinivasi, A. N. Krishna Aiyangar, and K. V. Rangaswami Aiyangear, *Edicts of As'oka* (Priyadars'in) (Adyar Library, Madras, 1951).

Narayan, Uma, "Eating cultures: incorporation, identity and Indian food," *Social Identities*, 1, 1 (1995), 63–86.

Nichter, Mark, "Modes of food classification and the diet-health contingency: A South Indian case study," in R. S. Khare, and M. S. A. Rao (eds), *Food, Society and Culture. Aspects in South Asian Food Systems* (Carolina Academic Press, Durham, NC, 1986).

Ohnuma, Keiko, "Curry rice: Gaijin gold. How the British version of an Indian dish turned Japanese," *Petits Propos Culinaires*, 52 (1996), 8–15.

Palmer, Arnold, *Moveable Feasts. A Reconnaissance of the Origins and Consequences of Fluctuations in Meal-Times with Special Attention to the Introduction of Luncheon and Afternoon Tea* (Oxford University Press, London, 1952).

Panjabi, Camellia, *50 Great Curries of India* (Kyle Cathie Ltd., London, 1994).

Pearson, M. N., *The Portuguese in India* (Cambridge University Press, Cambridge, 1987).

Pearson, M. N., "The people and politics of Portuguese India during the sixteenth and early seventeenth centuries," in Dauril Alden, and Warren Dean (eds), *Essays concerning the Socioeconomic History of Brazil and Portuguese India* (University Presses of Florida, Gainesville, 1977).

Peterson, Toby, "The Arab influence on western European cooking," *Journal of Medieval History*, 6 (1980), 317–40.

Postgate, Raymond (ed.), *The Good Food Guide 1967–8* (Hodder & Stoughton, London, 1968).

Bibliography

Prasad, Chandra Shekar, "Meat-eating and the Rule of—Tikotiparisuddha," in A. K. Narain (ed.), *Studies in Pali and Buddhism. A Memorial Volume in Honor of Bhikkhu Jagdish Kashyap* (B. R. Publishing Corporation, Delhi, 1979).

Prasad, Ram Chandra, *Early English Travellers in India. A Study in the Travel Literature of the Elizabethan and Jacobean Periods with Particular Reference to India* (2nd edn., Motilal Banarsidass, Delhi, 1980).

Priolkar, Anant Kakba, *The Goa Inquisition* (A. K. Priolkar, Bombay, 1961).

Quereshi, Ishtiaq Husain, *The Muslim Community of the Indo-Pakistan Subcontinent (610–1947) A Brief Historical Analysis* (Ma'aref Ltd., Karachi, 1977).

Rahman, A. (ed.), *History of Indian Science, Technology and Culture A.D. 1000–1800* (Oxford University Press, Oxford, 1999).

Rao, M. S. A., "Conservatism and change in food habits among the migrants in India: a study in gastrodynamics," in R. S. Khare and M. S. A. Rao (eds), *Food, Society and Culture. Aspects in South Asian Food Systems* (Carolina Academic Press, Durham, NC, 1986).

Rao, P. Setu Madhava, *Eighteenth Century Deccan* (Popular Prakashan, Bombay, 1963).

Rao, S. K. Ramachandra (ed.), *Encyclopaedia of Indian Medicine Vol I Historical Perspective* (Popular Prakashan, Bombay, 1985). Rao, V. M., "Introduction and overview," in V. M. Rao (ed.), *The Poor in a Hostile Society. Glimpses of Changing Poverty Scenario in India* (Vikas Publishing House, New Delhi, 1998).

Rau, Santha Rama, and Gayatri Devi of Jaipur, *A Princess Remembers. The Memoirs of the Maharani of Jaipur* (Weidenfeld & Nicolson, London, 1976).

Raychaudhuri, Tapan, *Europe Reconsidered. Perceptions of the West in Nineteenth-Century Bengal* (Oxford University Press, Oxford, 2000).

Richards, John F., *The Mughal Empire*, The New Cambridge History of India I.5 (Cambridge University Press, Cambridge, 1993).

Richards, J. M., *Goa* (Vikas Publishing House, New Delhi, 1982).

Rick, Charles M., "The tomato," *Scientific American*, 239, 2 (1978), 66–77.

Robinson, Rowena, "The construction of Goan interculturality. A historical analysis of the Inquisitorial edict of 1736 prohibiting (and permitting) syncretic practices," in Charles J. Borges, Oscar Pereira, and Hannes Stubbe, *Goa and Portugal. History and Development* (Concept Publishing Company, New Delhi, 2000).

Salaman, Redcliffe N., *The History and Social Influence of the Potato* (1st pub. 1949; ed. J. G. Hawkes, Cambridge, University Press, Cambridge, 1985).

Bibliography

Saletore, B. A., *Social and Political Life in the Vijayanagara Empire (A.D. 1346–A.D. 1646)* (B. G. Paul & Co., Madras, 1934).

Saran, Parmatma, and Edwin Eames (eds), *The New Ethnics. Asian Indians in the United States* (Praeger, New York, 1980).

Sass, Lorna, "The preference for sweets, spices and almond milk in late medieval English cuisine," in A. Fenton and T. M. Owen (eds), *Food and Perspective: Proceedings of the 3rd International Conference on Ethnological Food Research Cardiff, 1977* (Donald, Edinburgh, 1981).

Sastri, A. K. Nilakanta, "The Chalukyas of Kalyani and the Kalachuris of Kalyani," in G. Yazdani (ed.), *The Early History of the Deccan*, 2 vols. (Oxford University Press, Oxford, 1960).

Scammell, G. V., "The pillars of empire: indigenous assistance and the survival of the *Estada da India* c.1600–1700," *Modern Asian Studies*, 22, 3 (1988), 473–89.

Scattergood, Bernard P., Lavinia M. Anstey, and Richard Carnac Temple (eds), *The Scattergoods and the East India Company: Being a Selection From the Private Letters and Business Correspondence of John Scattergood, East India Merchant 1681–1723* (The British India Press/J. Jeffrey, Bombay/Harpenden, 1921–33/1935).

Scully, Terence, *The Art of Cookery in the Middle Ages* (The Boydell Press, Woodbridge, 1995).

Sen, Coleen Taylor, "The Portuguese influence on Bengali cuisine," in Harlan Walker (ed.), *Food on the Move. Proceedings of the Oxford Symposium on Food and Cookery 1996* (Prospect Books, Devon, 1997).

Sharar, Abdul Halim, *Lucknow: The Last Phase of an Oriental Culture*, trans. and ed. E. S. Harcourt, and Fakhir Hussain (Oxford University Press, Delhi, 1989).

Sharma, Brijendra Nath, *Social and Cultural History of Northern India c. 1000–1200 A.D.* (Abhinav Publications, New Delhi, 1972).

Sharma, Priyavrat, *Caraka-samhita. Agnivesa's Treatise Refined and Annotated by Caraka and redacted by Drdhabala* (Chaukhambha Orientalia, Delhi, 1981).

Sharma, Ursula, *Rampal and His Family* (Collins, London, 1971).

Sherwood, Marika, "Race, nationality and employment among lascar seamen 1660–1945," *New Community*, 2, 17 (1991), 229–44.

Shineberg, Dorothy, *They Came for Sandalwood. A Study of the Sandalwood Trade in the South-West Pacific 1830–1865* (Melbourne University Press, London, 1967).

Silverberg, Robert, *The Longest Voyage. Circumnavigators in the Age of Discovery* (Ohio University Press, Athens, 1972).

Singh, Dharamjit, *Indian Cooking* (Penguin, London, 1970).

Bibliography

Sinha, M., *Colonial Masculinity. The "Manly Englishman" and the "Effeminate Bengali" in the Late Nineteenth Century* (Manchester University Press, Manchester, 1995).

Smith, Andrew F., *The Tomato in America. Early History, Culture and Cookery* (University of South Carolina Press, Columbia, SC, 1994).

Souza, Teotonio de, *Goa to Me* (Concept Publishing, New Delhi, 1994).

Spencer, Colin, "The British Isles," in Kenneth F. Kiple, and Kriemhild Coneè Ornelas (eds), *The Cambridge World History of Food*, 2 vols. (Cambridge University Press, Cambridge, 2000).

Spencer, Colin, *The Heretic's Feast. A History of Vegetarianism* (Fourth Estate, London, 1993).

Srivastava, M. P., *Social Life Under the Great Mughals [1526–1700 A.D.]* (Chugh Publications, Allahabad, 1978).

Stein, Burton, *Peasant State and Society in Medieval South India* (Oxford University Press, Delhi, 1980).

Storer, Jenny, " 'Hot' and 'cold' food beliefs in an Indian community and their significance," *Journal of Human Nutrition*, 31 (1977), 33–40.

Subrahmanyam, Sanjay, *The Portuguese Empire in Asia, 1500–1700: A Political and Economic History* (Longman, London, 1999).

Subrahmanyam, Sanjay, *The Career and Legend of Vasco da Gama* (Cambridge University Press, Cambridge, 1997).

Takaki, Ronald, *Strangers from a Different Shore. A History of Asian Americans.* (2nd edn., Backbay Books, London, 1989).

Till, Antonia (ed.), *Loaves and Wishes. Writers Writing on Food* (Virago, London, 1992).

Twigg, Julia, "Vegetarianism and the meanings of meat," in Anne Murcott (ed.), *The Sociology of Food and Eating. Essays on the Sociological Significance of Food* (Gower, Aldershot, 1984).

Twining, Stephen H., *The House of Twining 1706–1956 Being a Short History of the Firm of R. Twining and Co. Ltd. Tea and Coffee Merchants 216 Strand London W.C.2* (R. Twining, and Co. Ltd., London, 1956).

Ukers, William H., *All About Tea*, 2 vols. (The Tea and Coffee Trade Journal Company, New York, 1935).

Veer, Peter van der (ed.), *Nation and Migration. The Politics of Space in the South Asian Diaspora* (University of Pennsylvania Press, Philadelphia, 1995).

Vickers, Rachel, *The European Ethnic Foods Market Market Intelligence Section Special Report* (Leatherhead Food Research Association, Market Intelligence Section, Leatherhead, 1998).

Bibliography

Visram, Rozina, *Ayahs, Lascars and Princes. The Story of Indians in Britain 1700–1947* (Pluto Press, London, 1986).

Visram, Rozina, "South Asians in London," in Nick Merriman (ed.), *The Peopling of London. Fifteen Thousand Years of Settlement from Overseas* (Museum of London, London, 1994).

Wadley, Susan S., *Struggling with Destiny in Karimpur, 1925–1984* (University of California Press, Berkeley, 1994).

Walton, John K., *Fish and Chips and the British Working Class, 1870–1940* (Leicester University Press, Leicester, 1992).

Weatherstone, John, *The Pioneers 1825–1900. The Early British Tea and Coffee Planters and Their Way of Life* (Quiller Press, London, 1986).

Weisberger, John H., and James Comer, "Tea," in Kenneth F. Kiple, and Kriemhild Coneè Ornelas (eds), *The Cambridge World History of Food* (Cambridge, University Press, Cambridge, 2000).

Wilson, C. R., *The Early Annals of the English in Bengal. Being the Bengal Public Consultations for the first Half of the Eighteenth century, Summarised, Extracted, and Edited . . .* (1st pub. 1895), 3 vols. (Bimla Publishing House, New Delhi, 1983).

Wright, Louise, *The Road from Aston Cross. An Industrial History 1875–1975* (Smedley-HP Foods Ltd., Leamington Spa, 1975).

Xavier, P. D., *Goa: A Social History (1510–1640)* (Rajhauns Vitram, Panaji, Goa, 1993).

Young, G. M., *Early Victorian England 1830–1865* (1st pub. 1934), 2 vols., (Oxford University Press, Oxford, 1988).

Zimmermann, Francis, *The Jungle and the Aroma of Meats. An Ecological Theme in Hindu Medicine* (1st pub. 1982; University of California Press, Berkeley, 1987).

Zubaida, Sami, "Rice in the culinary cultures of the Middle East," in Sami Zubaida, and Richard Tapper (eds), *Culinary Cultures of the Middle East* (I. B. Tauris Publishers, London, 1994).

Zubaida, Sami, and Richard Tapper (eds), *Culinary Cultures of the Middle East* (I. B. Tauris Publishers, London, 1994).

PhD Thesis

Sethi, Anil, "The creation of religious identities in the Punjab, c. 1850–1920," PhD, Cambridge University, 1998.

Index

Note: Page numbers in *italics* refer to illustrations.

Index

Index

chicken (*cont'd*)
  chicken, 148; smoky roast chicken tikka, 236;
    Susan's chicken recipe, 256
chickpeas, 22
chilli peppers, 47–48; and Europeans, 50, 134;
  and Marathas, 71–73; and Portuguese, 51, 53;
  prejudice against, 230; and vindaloos, 68–70
China: Chinese cuisine, 232; and soy sauce, 148;
  and tea, 136, 188, 190, 192; trade with, 191
chinaware, 202
chips, 231
Choudhury, Yousuf, 237–38
Chowdhury, Akbar, 229
Christians, 4, 48, 64, 89, 92
chutneys, 147, 240
cinnamon, 48, 135
Clive, Robert, 98
clothing, 55
cloves, 135
Clutterbuck, Lady Maria, 139
Cockerell, Charles, 136
cockscomb plant (maval), 34
coconut and coconut milk, 60, 62, 143–44,
  248
coffee houses, 129, 188–89, 196
"cold meat Cutlets" recipe, 161
colors of food, 227
Columbus, Christopher, 49–50, 70, 250
communalism, 201
confections, 61
containers, 167–68
Cooch Behar family, 172
Cook, Robin, 2
cookbooks, 134, 159–60, 254
Cordiner, James, 111, 113
coriander, 135, 142
Counter Reformation, 63
country captain, 124
cows, 23, 30, 31, 66, 91
creamy chicken kormas, 226
creolization of ethnic foods, 240
Crystal Palace, 150
cucumbers, 144, 166
cumin, 37, 135, 143
Cunningham, George, 161–62
curried veal recipe, 144
currie powder recipe, 142
Curries and How to Make Them in England, 152

Curries and How to Prepare Them (Edmunds), 115,
  144
curry (term), 115, 118
The Curry Cook's Assistant (Santiagoe), 152
Curry House, 152
Curry House Ichibanya, 252
curry paste, 225–26
curry powder, 140–43, 182
"Curry Row," 1

dabba (tiffin boxes), 207
dak bungalows, 123
dariols, 61
Daudi Bohras, 4–5
David, Elizabeth, 232
Dawe, W. H., 69
Deas, Margaret Orr, 234
Delhi, Agra, 99
desserts, 169–70
dhal, 121
dhansak, 121, 126–27, 205, 227
dinners, 168, 169, 182
Diwani Bhelpuri House (restaurant), 228–29
dopiazas, 29, 226
dosas, 240
Drummond Street, 229
duck, 125, 154
dum pukht dishes, 96, 148, 163, 226
Dutch, 82, 85, 165, 189

Earle, Cliff, 227, 233
East India Company: abolition of, 150, 159; and
  burra khanas, 112–13; and China, 148, 191–92;
  establishment of, 85–86; imports, 147;
  lunches, 81; and nabobs, 130–32, 136, 141, 150,
  159; and Parsees, 121; power of, 98–99, 108–9
"Economical Curry Paste" recipe, 152
Edmunds, Joseph, 115–16, 118, 144
education, Western, 171, 174, 176–79
elite, Indian, 176
Elizabeth II, 231
Empire of India Exhibition, 151–52
"Empress" Currie Powder, 128
England. *See* Britain
environment, equilibrium with, 7, 24
Epicure's Almanack, 130
E. P. Veeraswamy & Co., Indian Food
  Specialists, 153

Index

Index

Hindustan, 15–18, 22, 26, 32
homespun cotton, 180
hookahs, 107–8, 158, 159
Hosain, Atia, 222
Howrah, 199
Humuyan, 24–25
hunger, 199
hunting, 21
Husain, Shehzad, 239
Hyderabad, 92–93, 99
hygiene, 6, 55, 66, 163–64, 206

idlis, 240
immigrants and immigration: to Britain, 228;
    and British restaurants, 233; Immigration Act
    of 1965, 229; influence on cuisine, 8–9; and
    "Londonis", 224; and restaurant ownership,
    242; to Untied States, 218, 219–21
indentured laborers, 245–46, 248
India. *See also* caste system: Indian Civil Service,
    177; Indian independence, 180, 183, 224;
    Indian National Congress, 245; map,
    xviii–xix; pan-Indian cuisine, 125; Western
    attitudes toward, 241
Indian Cookery, 139
"Indian Cookery" (Oriental Translation
    Committee), 141
Indian Cookery (Palmer), 118
Indian Cookery (Terry), 140, 145–46
The Indian Cookery Book, 117, 124
Indian Cookery "Local" for Young Housekeepers, 120, 161
"Indian Cookery" pamphlet, 134
Indian Cooking, 237
"Indian risotto", 242
Indian Tea Association, 187–88, 190, 194–200
Indo-Fijians, 246–47
Indo-Pakistan war, 224–25
industrialization of India, 195–96
Inglis, James, 194
ingredients for Indian food, 237–38, 246–47,
    248
Inquisition, 63–67
interdining, 175, 176, 179–80, 246
Iranians, 205–6, 208
Ireland, 137
Islam. *See* Muslims and Islam
Islam, Haji Shirajul, 233, 234, 236
Italian restaurants, 232, 233

Italy, 135
Itinerario (Linschoten), 56

Jaffrey, Madhur, 229, 237, 254
jaggery, 62
Jaggerynatt temple, 91
Jagirdar, Razaur Rahman, 218
Jahan, Nur, 33
Jahangir: drinking, 36–37, 87; eating practices, 31,
    33–35; on Syhleti eunuchs, 215; and trade, 83;
    and turkeys, 70
Jainism, 4, 20, 72, 166
jam, 231
Jamaica, 246
Japan, 199, 251–53
Jerusalem Coffee House, 130, 136
Jesuits, 63
The Jewel in the Crown, 239
jhol, 228

kacca foods, 5
kaffir leaves, 245
kaju katli, 71
Kandola, Nav, 241
kangaroo tail, 146
Kannadan, 115
Karachi (restaurant), 233
Karaikudi (Tamil Nadu), 187
karee pan (bread rolls), 252
karee raisu (curry rice), 252
karee udon (curried wheat noodles), 252
karil (spices), 115
Karim, Abdul (the Munshi), 151
Kashmir, 34, 142, 233
kata panis (sour waters), 246
kava, 248
kebabs: of Afridis cook, 18; in Britain, 233;
    development of, 96; and Mughlai cuisine,
    92–93; by *nambais*, 97–98; recipes, 40, 103
kedgeree, 119, 145
ketchup, 149
Khan, Asaf, 13–15, 31, 32
Khan, Ghengis, 18
Khan, Nawab Sadaat Ali, 170–71
Khan, Sadaat Ali, 173
Khayam (restaurant), 224
khicharis: and Anglo-Indians, 119, 145; and
    Humuyan, 25; and "Indian risotto", 242; and

Index

Jahangir, 33; recipe, 41; special preparations of, 95; as staple food, 22; in Tonga, 249; in Trinidad, 250

khidmutgars, 193

Kirkpatrick, James, 165

Kismet, 242

"Kitchen Calendar", 166

kitchens, 163

korma, 81–100, 227

kosher Indian food, 240–41

kurma, 116, 117

Lady Minto's Soufflé de Volaille Indiénne, 231

Lahiri, Jhumpa, 251

Laing, John William, 157–58

Lal, Shri Shankar, 202–3

lamb, 23, 62, 101–2

language, 110

lascars (Indian sailors), 131

lassis, 208, 211, 212

Lawrence, Henry, 179

leeks, 135

leftovers (*prasadum*), 23, 138

Leicester Square Oriental Depot, 141

lemon juice, 144

lentils, 22

lettuces, 166

lime water, 208, 213

Linschoten, Jan Huyghen van, 54–55, 56, 58, 82

Lipton, Thomas, 194

Little Conjeeveram temple, 90

"Little Indias," 229, 240

London Health Exhibition of 1888, 193

London Labour and the London Poor (Mayhew), 191

Lucknow, 93–94, 95, 97–98

lunches, 169, 206–7

Macaulay, Thomas, 174

Macnabb, James Munro, 111–12

Madras, India, 118; Boddy on, 225; and British, 86; and East India Company, 108; and Mulligatawny soup, 120; recipe, 118; tea in, 199; at Veeraswamy's, 154, 226

Madras Mahal (restaurant), 241

Mahabharata, 19, 23

Maharajas, 174

Mahomed, Sake Dean, 129, 130–31, 237

Mahumdu, 97

Malabar Hill, 157

Malabari, Behramji, 179, 230

Malayalam, 115

Malcolm, Wilhelmina and Stephana, 133

Manasollasa, 19–20

Mandelslo, Albert, 61, 86–87, 122–23, 188, 190

Mangee Real ("Food for a King"), 89

Mango buttermilk recipe, 212

mangoes, 35–36, 118, 144, 146, 147, 167

Manoekjee Poojajee's of Bombay, 141

Manrique, Sebastien, 14–15, 33

Manucci, Niccolao, 22

Marathas, 71–73, 85, 99

marjoram, 145

Marks & Spencer's, 239

Marriott, McKim, 6

marrows, 144

masala chai recipe, 209, 210

masalas, 142

masalchi, 140, 147

Masulipatnam, 82

Mauritius, 246

Mayhew, Henry, 191

meat. *See also specific meats, including* chicken: and Ayurvedic medicine, 20, 22; Brahmans on, 21; and British, 89, 112, 135, 146, 163, 176–79; and curry, 112–13, 138; and food taboos, 4; and masculinity, 19; minced meats, 29, 96–97; and Portuguese cuisine, 62; and purity rituals, 5; wild meat, 21

Meer, Meer Taqi, 93–94

Melay curries, 115, 140

memsahibs, 159, 160, 161, 163

merchant navy, 182

merchants, 165. *See also* East India Company

mestiços, 58

"Mexican Hindu" cuisine, 220

Mexican women, 219–20

middle class, 137–38, 158–59, 176, 230

military, 182

milk, 198

milk punch recipe, 88

Miller, Philip, 149

millet, 4, 22, 33

mistresses, Indian, 110–11

Modern Cookery (Acton), 142, 145

Modern Domestic Cookery, 138

Moghs, 61–62

Index

molo tunny, 120
Monsoon Wedding, 241
Moti Mahal (restaurant), 233
Mughal India: breakup of, 92; and British, 88; cuisine, 24–39, 89, 92–93, 94, 118, 226; eating practices in, 23, 33, 175; Great Mughal dynasty, 18; map, *16*; and peppers, 71–73; and regional variations, 255; Surat (port), 81
Mughlai pilaus, 144
Mukhopadhyay, Bhudev, 176
mulligatawny soup, 120–21, 133, 145–46, 159, 182
murrabba, 93
mushroom curries, 226
mushrooms, 135
Muslims and Islam: and Aurangzeb, 38; and bread, 97; and communalism, 201; cooks, 160, 179; cuisine, 89; eating practices, 13–14, 23, 204; and food restrictions, 4, 62, 68; in Hindustan, 15, 17; influence on cuisine, 29; and interdining, 175; and tea demonstrations, 197
mutton, 23
Mysore, 99

nabobs (retired East India Company officials), 130–32, 136, 141, 150, 159
Nagarathars, 187–88, 198
nanbais (bazaar cooks), 96, 97–98
national Indian cuisine, 125
Natural History of the Indies (Oviedo), 70
nawabs, 94, 96
The Newcomes, 130
nimbu pani (lime water), 208, 213
Nirvana (restaurant), 234–35
Nizam-ul-Mulk, 92
Noon, G. K., 238–39
Norris Street Coffee House, 130
nutmeg, 135

Observer, 239
okra, 165
olive oil, 230
onions, 29, 135, 226
orientalization of food, 161
Oriental Translation Committee, 141
Osborne House, 150
Ottomans, 49

Oudh region, 94, 95, 99
Ovington, John, 81, 85, 88, 96, 148
oysters, 135

paan, 88
Pacific islands, 248–49
Padshahnama, 37
paella, 26
Pakistan, *xviii*, 2, 224, 228, 236, 242–43
Palepuntz, 87–88
Palmer, Edward, 153, 182, 236
Palmer, William, 153
pan-Indian cuisine, 125
Panjabi, Camellia, 183
papads, 121
papayas, 70
paprika, 54
parathas, 97
Parks, Fanny, 107–8, 109, 158, 167
Parsee dhansaks, 226
Parsees, 121, 175, 205–6
patra fish, 205
Payne's Oriental Warehouse, 141
pears, 165
peas, 166
peasantry, 38, 165
Pernambucco peppers, 51
Persia, *16*
Persian cuisine, 25, 92–93, 188–89
Petit, Leon, 144
pickles, 133, 147, 148, 167, 172, 235
pilau rice, 226
pilaus, 18–19, 25–27, 94–95, 137, 144, 148
pilav, 26
pineapples, 70–71
Piper longum, 48
Piper nigrum, 48
piquant shikari sauces, 149
pistachios, 28
plantations for tea, 193
"A poem to curry" (Thackeray), 133–34
Polish restaurants, 233
poppadoms, 121, 235
porcelain, 136
pork, 62, 66, 67
Portugal and Portuguese: *casados* in India, 58; and chilli peppers, 47–48; cuisine, 59; cultural assimilation, 54–55; and "curry" term, 115;

Index

and Indians, 50–51; and Marathas, 71; and
  potatoes, 165
potatoes, 71, 165–66
poverty, 6–7, 113, 199, 227–28, 241, 245
prawns, 249
prejudice against curry, 230
preparation of food, 5
presidency towns, 109
princes of India, 171
pulao, 95
pumpkins, 166
puncheon, 88
Punch magazine, 137
Punja & Sons, 248
Punjabis, 3, 116, 218–21, 228, 235
punkahs, 108
purdah, 55
puris, 97
purity rituals, 5, 6, 58, 175

Qadar, Mirza Asman, 93
Qaurama, 94
qima (minced meat), 29, 96–97
quail, 125
quaramas, 116
Queen magazine, 137, 139
quorema, 116, 117

rabbit, 125
railway curry, 182
railways, 169, 182, 195–96
raisins, 28
rajasic foods, 72
Rajasthan, 5–6
rasa (six tastes), 7–8
rasam (broth), 120
Rash Behari Bose, 252–53
Rasul, Syed, 198
rat, roast black recipe, 20
rat recipe, 20
Ray, Phillip, 4
Rebecca's masala chai recipe, 210
regional variations. *See* variations in Indian food
religion. *See also specific religions, including* Hinduism:
  and Akbar, 30; and bread, 60; conversions,
  64–65; and cultural assimilation, 58; and food
  taboos, 4–5; historical background, 17; and
  Inquisition, 63–67; and vegetarianism, 21

restaurants. *See also specific restaurants, including*
  Veeraswamy's: in Britain, 221–27, 233–35;
  critics, 232; decor, 206, 236–37, 241–42; and
  home cooking, 233–35; and immigration, 233;
  owners, 2; and seaman's cafés, 218; and
  Syhletis, 215–18, 221–26, 229, 233–35, 242;
  trends, 1–2
restrictions on food: and caste system, 6, 67, 196,
  201–2; and religion, 4, 62, 68
Rhemon, Abdool, 131–32
rice: and Bangladeshis, 221; and British dishes,
  139; and curry, 158; and Mughlai cuisine, 28;
  of Oudh, 94; and regional variations, 3, 22, 25,
  248; speciality dishes, 95; as staple food, 4, 60;
  status of, 231
risotto, 26, 242
roast black rat recipe, 20
Roberts, Emma, 112, 113, 122, 125, 149
Robinson, Matty, 144–45
Roe, Sir Thomas, 32, 35, 36, 83
rogan joshes, 34, 226
Roman Catholic Church, 63
Rome, 134–35
rotis, 247
Russian/Indian creoles, 240

sadhus (holy men), 199
saffron, 28, 135
Sahib, Tipoo, 139
sahibs, 159
Sainsbury's (restaurant), 238
Salter, Joseph, 131–32, 217
Samad, Abus, 27
Samarkand, 15
Samoa, 248
Sandys, Marcus, 149
Santiagoe, Daniel, 152
sauces, 60, 149, 226
Sauvou, Salote, 247–48
Savoy (restaurant), 221
Schuyler, Eugene, 19
seamen, 217–18, 222–23
Sedley, Jos, 130
Select Committee (1832), 174–75
Selim's Curry products, 136
servants, 164, 167
Shade, Sarah, 132
Shafi's (restaurant), 222, 226

313

Index

Index

trading ports, 57, 84
travels, 33–34, 232, 245
trickery, food, 93, 181–82
Trinidad, 246, 250
turkeys, 70
Turkish cuisine, 54
turmeric, 141, 142–43
Twining, Tom, 191

Udipi temple, 90
United Kingdom. *See* Britain
United States, 218–21, 229, 233
University of the South Pacific, 248
untouchables, 203
Utsav (restaurant), 1

Vaisnavite Hindu temples, 89–90
Valle, Pietro della, 21, 22, 147
Vambery, Arminius, 18–19
Vanity Fair (Thackeray), 130, 133, 134
variations in Indian food, 3–4, 115–16, 118
veal recipe, 144
Veeraswamy's (restaurant), 2, 153–54, 221, 226, 235, 236
vegetables, 135, 165–66
vegetarianism: and Akbar, 30, 31; and Buddhism, 20; of Gandhi, 177–79; in Hindu temples, 90; and *hing*, 28; and Indian marketplace, 122; of Jains, 4; perceptions of, 176–79; prevenance of, 20–21, 62
Venice, 48
ver, 142
Verenigde Oostindische Compagnie, 82
vesta packet foods, 238
Victoria, 150–51

vindaloos, 67–68; in Britain, 68, 224; duck vindaloo, 154; and Goan cooks, 169; recipes, 69, 74–75; term, 227; at Veeraswamy's, 226
vinegar, 147
virility in men, 48
vitamin C, 53

Wadud, Shamsher, 234–35
Waitrose (restaurant), 238
Warren, Eric, 182
water, 189
Watt, George, 165, 166, 194
wattlebird, 146
Weeden, Edward St. Clair, 171–72, 195
Wellesley, Arthur, 99–100
What Shall We Have for Dinner? (Clutterbuck), 139
What to Tell the Cook, or the Native Cook's Assistant, 162–63
wheat, 4, 25, 28, 60, 143
White, Edmund, 136, 142
The Wife's Cookery Book being Recipes and Hints on Indian Cookery, 160
The Wife's Help to Indian Cooking (Dawe), 69, 118
Williamson, Thomas, 107, 108, 163, 235
women, 158–59, 202
Worcestershire sauce, 149, 162
worms, 163–64
Wyvern's Indian Cookery Book, 160

Yash Muthanna's appam, 78–79

Zaika (restaurant), 2, 242
zard birinj, 29
Zoffany, Johann, 153
Zoroastrians, 121